THE HUMAN-DIMENSIONS OF HUMAN-COMPUTER INTERACTION

The Future of Learning

Learning is becoming more and more important as one of the indispensable tools to ensure future prosperity and well-being. This is the case not only for the individual, alone or as a member of a group, but also for organisational structures of all kinds. New learning paradigms and pedagogic principles, new learning environments and conditions, and new learning technologies are being tested in order to find the right combination of parameters that can optimise the outcome of the learning process in a given situation.

This book series presents to all stakeholders the latest advances in this important area, based on a sound foundation. Schools, higher education, industrial companies, public administrations and other organisational structures, including providers of learning and training services, including life-long learning, plus all the individuals involved, researchers, students, pupils, citizens, teachers, professors, instructors, politicians, decision makers etc., contribute to and benefit from this series. Pedagogic, economic, structural and organisational aspects, the latest technologies, and the influence from changing attitudes and globalisation are treated in this series, providing sound and updated information, which can be used to further improve the learning process in both formal and informal contexts.

Series Editors:

N. Balacheff, J. Breuker, P. Brna, K.-E. Chang, J.C. Cherniavsky, J.P. Christensen, M. Gattis, M. Gutiérrez-Díaz, P. Kommers, C.-K. Looi, C.J. Oliveira, M. Schlager, M. Selinger, L. Steels and G. White

Volume 3

Recently published in this series

Related publications by IOS Press:

ISSN 1572-4794

The Human-Dimensions of Human-Computer Interaction

Balancing the HCI Equation

Elspeth McKay

School of Business IT, RMIT University, Melbourne, Australia

IOS
Press

Amsterdam • Berlin • Oxford • Tokyo • Washington, DC

ISBN 978-1-58603-869-4
Library of Congress Control Number: 2008928729
doi:10.3233/978-1-58603-869-4

Publisher
IOS Press
Nieuwe Hemweg 6B
1013 BG Amsterdam
Netherlands
fax: +31 20 687 0019
e-mail: order@iospress.nl

Distributor in the UK and Ireland
Gazelle Books Services Ltd.
White Cross Mills
Hightown
Lancaster LA1 4XS
United Kingdom
fax: +44 1524 63232
e-mail: sales@gazellebooks.co.uk

Distributor in the USA and Canada
IOS Press, Inc.
4502 Rachael Manor Drive
Fairfax, VA 22032
USA
fax: +1 703 323 3668
e-mail: iosbooks@iospress.com

LEGAL NOTICE

The publisher is not responsible for the use which might be made of the following information.

PRINTED IN THE NETHERLANDS

Dedicated to Sandy and Tanj

Foreword

"The qualitative aspects of communication and personal relationships take into account such items as the opportunities for problem solving, creativity, confidence, security, interest, listening, emotional involvement. Even before we became concerned about the impact of computers on 'man-machine' communication, too little attention was directed towards qualitative aspects of communication 'man to man' (Bradley 1989:17).

Dr. Gunilla Bradley, Professor Informatics, Royal Institute of Technology (KTH), Department of Electronic. Computer and Software Systems (ECS), IT-university campus, Sweden

Learning is an integrated part of our life; in one's professional role, in one's private role and in our role as citizens. The deep and widespread use of ICT is entering into these life-roles, and so has become a considerable part of our daily lives. This book deals with the human side of learning and Human Computer Interaction (HCI) in a broad sense.

I happened to meet Dr McKay at the HCI International conference in Beijing in 2007. Among the 4,000 delegates and after talking about my own writings, I was asked to read the book manuscript and contribute with a foreword. I am most happy that I accepted. It is a fantastic and unique book!

As university professors we understand the importance of using a variety of different lenses to guide our students. This guidance often involves interactive cycles of learning when students and their facilitators exchange experiential moments to enhance each other's vision of the world. It is truly a wonderful time to be involved in the education and research sector. We have a simply dramatic set of information and communications technology (ICT) tools that have a great potential for successful instruction in the modern society.

However, for many of us, efficient ICT tools in the education sector are just a means to an end. It is well and truly time that educational technology provides us with effective HCI that is sensitive both to individual and group differences across the globe. Indeed it is vital that the online learning environments are designed to be useful, usable and available to everyone. Without the effective integration of the richness of the *human-dimensions of human-computer interaction*, these wonderful technological tools will remain hidden from those who need them the most.

The book tells a story to encourage us to understand that computing technology could and should serve to enhance the quality of life. This book embraces the social nature of computer usage by emphasizing the wealth of the *human-dimensions of HCI*. We must remember that technology is meant for human beings; not the reverse.

In many cases of professional IT practice the *human-dimensions of HCI* still needs to be recognized and addressed: more so when continuously new ICT applications are being developed and used.

One strategy for doing this is compartmentalization and specialization. However, creativity often arises at the boundaries of traditional disciplines. Research involving the social context of HCI, has to bring together skills and knowledge from multiple disciplines. This is crucial to the solution of important problems involving HCI. This book exposes the need for bringing together otherwise disparate disciplines by involving the principles of computer science and educational technologists, with the knowledge and skills from HCI grounded practitioners, within a social science context. The book provides an awareness of how to design and implement efficient and effective *human-dimensions of HCI*. By taking this multi-disciplinary approach Dr. McKay's book stimulates discussion on computer usage that gives an insightful view both for academics and for ordinary non-technical users.

The Human-Dimensions of HCI speaks to everyone involved in online teaching and learning because it is a book that is written through the eyes of ordinary people. The readers are taken on a journey. Each chapter may not speak directly to every reader, but as the reader progresses through this story, they can adapt and apply their insights to their own situations. The ten chapters are organized into four substantive themes that relate to HCI: *the historical perspective of computing development, the human-dimension, the machine-dimension*, and *the interactive effect of human-machine activities*. One chapter addresses important gender aspects using an impressionistic approach. A useful prelude guides readers through the book and provides valuable contextual information.

The strength of *The Human-Dimensions of HCI* is that it deals with social and psychological aspects with great insight. (Psychosocial aspects are an established concept in the Nordic countries.) The book further addresses the area of collaboration in distributed environments: learning and working at a distance. This is more and more a part of the lifestyle in both professional life and privately in the globalized world. In addition to presenting important HCI issues, the book also deals with ICT tools and explains how they can be designed with an awareness of basic human needs and requirements. The author recognizes the advantages and challenges of using ICTs to transform education. This by supporting social interaction within ordinary communities, non-technical neighborhoods, organisations and individuals around the world.

To conclude *The Human-Dimensions of HCI* is a "*must read book*" for all those who set out to improve the world through enhanced educational and learning tools, through effective HCI.

With Dr. McKay's book in hand, people hopefully will get together virtually; and through such personal meetings work for common visions to shape a better world.

Stockholm, New Year 2008
Gunilla Bradley

Prelude

One of the primary reasons for writing this book is to commence a non-technical discussion about everyday computer usage. In the process, I aim to fill a gap in the literature that only sparsely deals with the human-dimension or social context of *effective HCI*. To get the message across to the general community, this book uses a narrative writing style, and so endeavours to appeal to a wide cross section of non-technical people. In the telling of this book, the reader is taken on a long journey which indeed commenced a long time ago: when human beings began their adoration for all things electro-mechanical.

In bringing forward many of the hidden complexities of the *human-dimensions of HCI*, and owing to the educative nature of the techno-saga; it was entirely fitting to launch this book within *The Future of Learning* series with IOS Press. Hence, the target audience for this book includes IT professionals, postgraduate information systems' students, corporate trainers, general computer users, educational technology researchers, academics at universities and other types of community-based learning Institutions.

This techno-tale begins with a brief peek at the past. It is important to look back and understand the way people perceived the emerging computerized machinery. Certain linguistic decisions, taken up by the back-room boffins or early computer scientists, still survive today. Perhaps a primary techno-leftover from those early computer laboratories is that some people still believe that technology can completely replicate human cognition.

The *human-dimensions of HCI* are but one piece of the complicated usability or techno-puzzle; that could be shown after all to have two distinct and quite separate contexts. One relates to the human dimension or social context of computing; while the other relates to the machine-side, with people's perspectives molded around the performance of the technical components. The literature deals more often with the latter, while it is really only in more recent times that a voice has risen for usability issues that involve the human-dimension.

Because of this duality of people and computer machinery our techno-saga travels through carefully devised chapters. We therefore separate the human-side from the machine-side of the HCI equation to explain why there is an imbalance of sensible solutions for *effective HCI*. The first three chapters are designed to set the background for the duality of the human/machine dimensions of HCI. Chapter-2 is very much about the techno-usability that places human beings as the primary focus. Chapter-3 is where the reader can see more technical aspects of HCI; it's more about the nuts and bolts that combine to provide the technical solutions.

Chapter-4 leaves the machine-side of the techno-saga to re-enter the usability context. Consequently, in this chapter people's techno-interactions are combined with the machine-side of the HCI equation to evaluate effective solutions that try to achieve techno-satisfying outcomes. Still maintaining the human-side, Chapter-5 covers cognitive performance. It also brings forward the intellectual content or ad hoc digital information that is often captured in haphazard and mindless repetitions.

At this point, Chapter-6 becomes quite demonstrative, drawing away from the more usual linguistics to speak to the reader through a series of metaphorical human-dimensioned HCI models. To this end, a metaphoric framework suggests that an individual's techno-humanoid landscape is affected by two layers of techno-influence: an external techno-humanoid contributor, and the more personal digital-awareness characteristics of each individual that uses a computer. Chapter-7 brings the reader back to earth to concentrate again on the human-side of the HCI equation; this time to speak about expectations that people have in seeking techno-solutions to everyday issues. Chapter-8 returns the focus to the machine-side; emphasizing that a balanced approach is necessary for achieving *effective HCI*. This commentary would not be complete without a section for dealing with gender and how it relates, if at all, to HCI.

Acknowledgements

I am grateful to the School of Business IT for allowing me to take the time away from departmental chores to publish this monograph. I wish also to thank Keven Asquith for his tireless support while I wrote this book at home. Without his endless patience my ideas would have remained hidden. Finally, I would like to thank Michael J. Mullany PhD, lecturer/researcher in Computer and Information Systems, North Tec Polytechnic, Whangarei, New Zealand http://www.northtec.ac.nz, for reviewing the initial manuscript and assisting me in generating the comprehensive index.

CONTENTS

List of Figures

List of Tables

The Human-Dimensions of Human-Computer Interaction
E. McKay
IOS Press, 2008

Chapter-1

Looking Back to See the Way Forward

In bringing forward many of the hidden complexities of the *human-dimensions of HCI*, and due to the educative nature of the techno-saga-this book was launched within *The Future of Learning* series with IOS Press. The target audience for this book is: IT professionals, postgraduate information systems' students, corporate trainers, general computer users, educational technology researchers, academics at universities and other types of community-based learning Institutions.

> There is a way that nature speaks, that land speaks. Most of the time we are simply not patient enough, quiet enough, to pay attention to the story.

> **LINDA HOGAN**: http://www.wisdomquotes.com/cat_awareness.html

Introduction

The techno-landscape has become festooned with electronic gadgetry for all sorts of human-computer interaction. It seems that our fascination for understanding our environment has taken off at lightening speed with the advent of exceedingly powerful computing grunt that is readily available these days. It is relatively easy, even for the most entrenched techno-phoebes or techno-Luddites, to buy a machine from a department store, plug it in, and take off into the Internet. However, keeping up the pace is much easier for those of us who know how to describe the various pieces of the information and communications technology (commonly referred to as ICT); while others are left wondering why new computers don't come with a 3" floppy disk drive any more. For those particular Luddites every thing could be a whole lot easier if we had a common linguistic framework in which they could understand this endless bevy of electronic gadgetry. Let's first take a look at what's happening with the way we use technology to communicate with each other.

This book is about the inseparable relationship between people and their unquenched (perhaps, continued, radical) reliance on information technology. To begin this saga, it is useful to examine the history of electronic data processing. No time at all has passed since the 101-type introductory computing programmes were explaining to us about how the input/output processing cycle works in diminutive detail. These days we don't need such prescriptive advice. Rather like the days when car-drivers were expected to know how to fix a troublesome engine themselves, today the average computer-user gets on quite well without any knowledge of what a central processing unit is.

A look back at where we've come from, highlights how quickly our technological vista has altered our environment. The ICT developmental timeline reveals that even in the early days there were a number of people who were worried about the Big Brother effect of the emerging computing technologies. This growing suspicion was long before people were serious about describing a phenomenon we now call human-computer interaction, or HCI for short. There were real fears among the generally non-technophobe population, that an eventual dehumanizing-dimension of this relatively new-found electronic computing technology would tear families apart [1].

In the beginning, large and expensive mainframe computers were being developed in secretive computer laboratories; while these days, at the top end of techno-sophistication, mainframes and supercomputers still fall under the auspices of the computer scientists. Over time, micro-chips and more sophisticated operating systems' development enhanced the accessibility to personalized computing unlike anything that had been achieved previously. Suddenly the general population's acceptance of a more graphical user interface (commonly called the GUI) and Microsoft's WINDOWS environments turned our attention to subsequent ICT tools that enabled easier access to our electronic files. No longer did we require the same level of computer-literacy as with the earlier machines running on the cumbersome disk operating systems commonly called DOS.

At first the number of people involved with computing technology was limited to the computer scientists. No one really paid any attention to the social context of computer-use. In fact, the human-dimension remained so small due to a more mechanistic approach towards this embryonic ICT discipline. At this early point, the communications experts were aware of the potential for ICT to provide useful services, however most of the work was about using the machinery to deal exclusively with data-processing.

At one point it was easy to articulate the techno-development in terms of generational profiles. The initial machines in 1942 to 1959, were thought of as the First Generation of computers; there was little thought given to the social organization of information. From 1959 to 1965, this lack of HCI consideration continued through the Second Generation, with the arrival of the transistor technologies to replace the vacuum tubes of the original computers. Then, in the period 1965 to 1970, the Third Generation of computers became the forerunner of HCI with the micro-chip development that enabled bulk-storage of data. However it took the Fourth Generation, from the 1970s and onwards to promote HCI with a common input/ output/ storage/processing metaphor. This meant that a renewed socio-linguistic context broadened the types of users interested in talking about computer usage, leaving the computer scientists to concentrate on their bits and bytes.

Once again HCI was viewed on a strictly mechanistic level; yet application's software development at this point took a more prominent position than it did previously. There was still no practical solution to the usability issues surrounding the socio/human-dimension. The talk of generational profiling has all but disappeared from the literature, with the identification of the Fifth Generation. Some machines are believed to have the potential to take on human qualities such as: reasoning, learning, inferential thought, etc. In this way, systems' developers seem to still be trying to emulate the human-dimension.

Can we see an elasticity effect of HCI and ICT when we consider this historical picture? Is there a consistent relationship that reflects the *human-dimensions* of computing and ICT uptake? Is there a worrying global trend already surfacing?

Figure 1 : Acting Out the Dreyfus & Dreyfus Prediction

Consider the pace at which mobile technologies are entering the HCI arena. All around the world, people who are wealthy enough and have interests in these tools appear to be adopting them at a rapid rate. This is where the whole techno-vista becomes problematic! Over two decades ago, [2] sounded the warning bells that still reverberate today. They worried that the next generation would defer many of their usual life-skills to this type of computational machinery *(see Figure 1)*. For instance, the ability humans have to recall memories of past behaviour as experiential learning tools.

There has not been much progress towards dealing with this vision, when we see from [3]: it is only natural that as the production of faster, more efficient means for global connectivity continues; the race to innovate new ICTs has already highlighted the negative effects of distributed cognition.

As time moves on, is this worrying trend to dehumanize our HCI really playing out before our very eyes? As we get brighter, smarter machinery, does it follow that the digital divide becomes even greater? If this is the case, then the predicted Big Brother phenomenon has already won. One only needs to look at the wireless technologies poised on the current techno-horizon. No doubt, the connectivity that is possible today seems endless. However, at the present moment, people still need to be in a position to purchase these devices to join in this electro-knowledge revolution. What is to happen with the people who cannot afford to join in? This is where an effective model of HCI has an important role to play to avoid or lessen the inevitable widening digital divide whereby the access to information through ICT remains inequable.

The rate at which we are adapting to the techno-landscape is astonishing. We have invited ICTs to take their place alongside all the other non-finite global resources. Because of this, our reliance on techno-solutions plays out the Dreyfus & Dreyfus prediction that humans may one day reach the position in which our ability to make the distinction between the naturally occurring and techno-landscape becomes saturated by our blindness to knowing whether there is any difference. Look at how we take for granted the habit of placing the "e" to signify electronic in front of whatever takes our fancy or the proposal to accept text message short forms in exam papers and assignments.

Nature's Way of Speaking

It is really difficult to dislocate ourselves from the techno-jungle; our thirst for knowledge has taken us down an ePathway with no easy way for us to back out. Not unlike the ways in which people engage with nature to draw strength for their inner being; we are now turning towards our gadgetry and the Internet in a similar fashion. In this sense, the techno-nature of the Internet is now speaking to many of us. Look around when you are out and about. See how many people have various eDevices clamped upon various parts of their bodies. The mobility of these ICTs is creating its own sub-culture. Worshipers communicate only with other like techno-clamped individuals. People of all ages readily adapt their life-styles to receive their unlimited communications, anywhere, anytime. Instead of being at one with nature, like watching the coming of Spring in our gardens, with the adoration onset for these mobile communications technologies, we may well question whether people in the next decade will still recognise the rewards offered to us by Mother Nature.

Rather than knocking our propensity to engage with ICTs, we should recognize the rewards that could be forthcoming by engaging with an appropriate techno-nature environment, and take the opportunity. Consider the rewards afforded through the newest ICT Internet tools called podcasting; both audio and video distribution falls within this type of digital broadcasting through the Internet. The term podcasting is derived from a combination of two words (iPod and broadcasting). Although we knew it would be possible to send/receive multi-media files in this fashion by the end of the last millennium (this ended with the year 2000); it was not until 2001 that the technical components were readily available in the stores. By 2003, it was realized that people did not need to engage in regular airwave radio reception to receive their music files, and so podcasting quickly took off through the Internet. These days there are literally millions of happy podcasting customers.

It is not necessary to have a biology or physics degree to appreciate the beauty of Mother Nature; we participate, happily taking in whatever she lays out for us, like watching the regrowth following a devastating bush fire, or human beings defying gravity while they travel to outer space. So too, will the plethora of ICTs that support podcasting remain hidden to most users? Only a select few will get to know first hand about making MP3 audio files that are suitable for Internet broadcasting. Most of us will be happy enough just turning on our eDevices and tuning in to enjoy our digital listening. At this point only those of us who wish to involve ourselves in serious podcasting will need to become digitally savvy enough to comprehend the significance of machine-readable feed-files. Unlike our encounters with Mother Nature, we operate comfortably within the full spectrum of our techno-nature environment: something that will continue to be perceived as more hazardous by the techno-Luddites. This is the way our techno-nature environment speaks to us. On the one hand it is all encompassing. Multi-media provides a visual/audio digital feast, with full television capacity and movie making wonderment, all within reach of your handy laptop computer. The flip side of this techno-panacea is not so rosy. People awaiting universal access to information technologies for those of us without the full range of human abilities (sight, mobility and intellectual faculties) still have many hurdles to overcome.

Examples of techno-nature are all around us, increasing exponentially at a rate not seen before. This is the way of things. Even the most entrenched techno-Luddite cannot escape. Whether we like it or not, the techno-landscape is here to stay. Take the print media, for instance. On opening any volume of National Geographic these days we can see how entrenched is this search for knowing about our land and its natural habitats; we can experience the full gambit of civilization. In living colour we can tread the lush Alaskan ecosystem, where it soon becomes apparent that Mother-Nature is crying out for protection from the ravages of oil exploration. In the same edition Vol: 209, No. 5 (May 2006), we can read about how the Judas Gospel has been uncovered after 1,700 years.

Our Techno-Landscape is Speaking

From our earliest days on this planet we have been fascinated by the various ways in which the land speaks to us. Archaeology digs have provided evidence from which we learn about the changing nature of civilization. These treasured items often include: stone, bone and ancient metals. As these ancient artefacts are unearthed they are carefully cleaned, restored and preserved for all to share in their wonderment. Before they are stored away, these new found artefacts are usually placed in bags, and marked with identification. Comparisons are made with archaeological material found at other locations, to investigate whether there are any common characteristics. Detailed topographical maps are drawn to locate each archaeological site. Over time, we can make sense of these ancient materials, which help us to test out theoretical assumptions and make predictions for the future. Much can be learned. Important knowledge is shared during this process of group behaviours, social impact of trends and influences.

It may be useful for us to apply this type of archaeological listening to our sprouting techno-landscape. In some respects the Internet is already doing this in a somewhat fragmented and ad hoc basis. The trouble is, we are continually adding to this vast collection of Internet data in such fragmented increments, that over time, it will be impossible to locate repositories that make any sense. Already the techno-landscape is crying out for standardization; however, the very open nature of the Internet that we value most, prevents any such control. Always looming nearby are the notions that abuse and criminal intent sits alongside every individual Internet heart-beat. Because of this, thousands of dollars are spent in designing spy-ware to guard against unwanted callers.

Figure 2 : Seizing Back Control

This book is about recognizing the untapped power of *effective HCI (Figure 2)*. Now is the time for us to take a jolly good look at the many different ways people use their eTools for work and play.

Thus we have commenced our journey. We have set the scene for what lies ahead. The techno-metaphor is introduced to convey the tendency people have towards converting almost anything related to our daily lives into an electronic or computerised context. This is why referring to Mother Nature and all things computerised, seems timely.

Chapter Reference List

[1] Fuori, W.M. and W.V. Gioia, *Computers and Information Processing*. (3rd Edition). Vol. 1. 1986, NY: Prentice-Hall. 610.

[2] Dreyfus, H.L. and S.E. Dreyfus, *Mind Over Machine: The power of human intuition and expertise in the era of the computer*. 1986, NY: Free Press. 231.

[3] Salomon, G., Editor. *Distributed Cognitions: Psychological and educational considerations*. 1993, University Press Syndicate: Cambridge.

Chapter-2

The Human-Side of HCI: Enhanced Corporate Training

Our journey will first pass through the *'human-side'* of the HCI equation. This chapter places humans at the centre of the techno-universe. We will peel back the techno-veneer to uncover some of the more irritating issues that relate to computer use. Apart from the usability of the equipment per se, we may have already lost site of the need to slow down and have patience when accessing a computer. Many of us have become button pressing experts looking for instant gratification. The techno-vista includes many different devices, these days. The techno-lines have become quite blurred. Multi-media's changed things forever. The plethora of media is complicating our sensory management. No longer are we content to think black and white. Instead there is eMovement, eSound and eColour to capture our imaginations.

Is Using a Computer Easy for Everyone?

These days, many people simply rely on intuition to make a computer work; they sail through their computerised tasks with ease. For others, however, it can be an uncomfortable ride; with unseen difficulties lurking everywhere. For those of us who are more familiar with computers, all we really need to do is switch it on and get going. One way to explain this is to look at how WYSIWYG orchestrate the way we approach our computing activities. The WYSIWYG has become a commonly used acronym (pronounced wizziwig), an acronym for *What You See Is What You Get*; they are supposed to melt away all the worry about what our avid key-rattlings will look like. While we type, clever software imitates printer resolution, allowing people to rely on these intuitive visual displays. Through the popular onset of WYSIWYGs, reading manuals has become a thing of the past. Unfortunately, this joyful approach towards the digital environment is not universal. Aversion to computers is still felt by a large number of people who remain troubled when faced with the opportunity to use a computer. Computer phobia was first spotted in the early 90's when personal computers were on the rise; when the general population were invited to try and buy. Off we went to the department stores, following the latest marketing promise to fulfill our dreams and own a digital-gadget.

For some, using a computer remains a difficult aspiration. There are other things that come into play here. Firstly there is the issue related to the awareness of the many ways people will expect machines to react; like why computers can't find a file to open without requiring human intervention to browse the computer's file tree. Reluctance towards technology is understandable. One explanation for why using a computer becomes problematic for adults, may be to suggest there has been an event to associate computer-use with an emotional trauma. These unpleasant memories can also be triggered by a number of seemingly unrelated events; like seeing something on television that brings back such memories, or even just simply watching another person having difficulty using a computer. These days, people may be treated for their computer phobia by expert psychologists in much the same manner as they would be treated for other anxieties.

For the young, techno-phobia is not such an issue. Instead there is added pressure elsewhere, in wanting to be like everyone else during their formative years. Advanced telecommunications are elevating a type of techno-empowering as an essential modern day human trait through the stimulating nature of multi-media. Moreover, Web hosting companies make it really easy for the young to dive straight into the Internet without any specialised technical knowledge. Despite the claims for limiting the access to children under the age of 13-years, young people well under this age are joining in at an alarming rate: often without the knowledge and/or consent of parental influence. Once in, these embryonic-technophiles take off. Web-site building tools that are relatively easy to use, entice novice Web developers into places unknown, rather like the story of the young Lion King. According to this legend, the young lion would not listen to his father and adventured way off into the forbidden and dangerous waste land, eventually causing untold damage and grief for everyone. Herein lies much of the danger for the unwary. The Internet technologies support ordinary people, many of whom have no previous computer experience; talking to each other, and sharing knowledge in ways that were unimaginable previously.

However, let us not ignore the fact that using a computer is very complex. It involves an interactive combination of our senses. Consequently we need to watch a screen and react appropriately to what we see; either through voice-input, or touch-sensitive screens, or by using a keyboard, often using all our fingers on our two hands. Herein is the dilemma: try patting your head with one hand, while you rub your tummy using a circular motion with the other; do all this while you hum a favourite tune, and read a poem in a book! When using a computer, not only do you need to have excellent eye-hand coordination, you will need a better than average ability to concentrate and respond appropriately to what you see on the screen in a timely manner.

Touch technologies are springing up to give us a whole new dimension to our computer use. In reaching out to share knowledge with another human being, just imagine how good it would be to share a common touch sensation through a computer screen. Crazy as it may sound, researchers at the State University of Buffalo, New York, USA, have been working away at this very aspect of the *human-dimensions of HCI*; they have invented a special glove which captures the sense of touch over the Internet. On the far techno-horizon, there is yet another reward for humanity in *effective HCI*; Web-mediated medical procedures. The surgeon will be in one location directing the procedure through a virtual interface; while the patient lies in a distant operating theatre undergoing the surgical procedure orchestrated by the sophisticated software.

At a less sophisticated level, touch screen technologies that have been in use for many years already have broadened the number of people who use computers. Business applications have led the way in this field, without us really noticing that the replacement of the keyboard as the sole input device has been evolving. Fast food chain stores are a good example of touch screen usage. Imagine how tacky a keyboard would become in these environments.

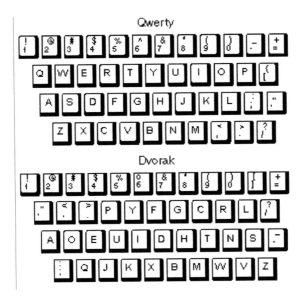

Figure 3 : Common Keyboards

How good is the keyboard these days? Along with the other computing gadgetry we have certainly come a long way since the old QWERTY *(pronounced kwer-tee)* keyboard became the de facto standard keyboard. (The name reflects the first row of keys on the top alphabetic row on the left hand side of the keyboard.) Christopher Sholes invented a typewriter in 1868 that arranged the keys in such an order that prevented frequently used key-mechanisms from colliding when struck, according to popular myth. Since then, this style of keyboard arrangement has been challenged from time to time. Because colliding keys are no longer an issue; other keyboard configurations have emerged. Increasing the speed of typing saw the advent of a DVORK keyboard (named after the inventors, Dvork and Dealy, in the 1930's). It was designed so that the middle row of keys had the most common letters used. Other common letter combinations were then placed for quick access *(Figure 3)*.

Although the newer designs make more sense for easy use, they have not been widely accepted and we continue to use a QWERTY design.

The sophisticated keyboard technology these days is differentiated by the switching gear that activates when the key is pressed. There are 80 to 110 switches needed to take care of each key press and the actual distance of that press. Most often, hybrid designs employ a combination of the mechanical keyboard and a membrane. Known as dome-switch (or direct-switch) keyboards, they utilize a rubber dome or bubble coated in a conductive substance to convey two circuit board traces. Often the pattern on the PC board is gold-plated. Pressing a key collapses the dome, which in turn connects the two circuit traces to register the pressed character.

Capacitative keyboards are another interesting technology which permits the sensing of a pulse. This technology is less expensive due to the thin insulating film employed. Capacitative keyboards are a very popular technology because they resist wear, and are impervious to water and foreign matter. Then there are membrane keyboards, which are mostly found on appliances in and around the home and office on anything from a washing machine, or microwave oven to a photocopier. Due to the unusual flatness of these keyboards, they do not necessarily have a particular feel. Because of this, they will be designed to emit a beep or flash a light when the key is pressed. Modern keyboards offer more than just a switching platform. They include control processors and indicator lights that provide the user with feedback about current functionality levels.

What about voice activated access? It would seem a reasonable assumption to make that people can talk to a computer, and have it capture the speech in a digital format. After all we have been doing this quite nicely with our tape-recorders for many years. Of course, filing such recordings away to a digital storage device may have been a little more challenging in yesteryear. We know that CD technologies have replaced the cumbersome serial nature of the filing arrangements of the older audio tapes, so we know the technology is with us to stay. Wouldn't it be great to be able to say there are alternative devices for people who may have difficulty using a keyboard or screen display to carry out their computing activities? Looking around for practical solutions for people who do not have the full range of senses, or body functioning, opens a huge gap that widens with each new eGizmo that enters the market place. Have we arrived at the pointy-end of computer-use?

Interest in voice-over-the-Internet (now commonly referred to as VoIP) is perhaps bringing the urgency of this untapped potential forward. It is interesting to watch how those who know how to play in this audio-broadband sandpit are now leading the way forward. We are forcing the back-room boffins to respond to our desire to broaden our capacity to reach out to each other using sound related technologies and the Internet. Unfortunately there won't be any real progress for the everyday Jo Blow, until the business or corporate giants see the benefits to their profit margins. Gains are definitely to be made with the increasing propensity people are showing for preference towards decentralized working environments, inviting the go anywhere, anytime, any how-ness of *effective HCI*. Flexibility of working arrangements is already here to stay. There can be no doubt that VoIP plays an important role in this new style of techno-sandpit. The corporate sector is seeing the gains for reducing absenteeism in terms of increasing productivity.

What about poor eyesight? How does the current computing environment measure up for the visually impaired population? Here's where the story on listening to the techno-environment becomes a little more interesting than what is currently available for aiding those with sight or hearing loss. There are a number of products that cater for visual impairment and computer usage. Here is where the digital/electronic technologies can excel. In the 1980s the Braille computer was devised, involving; voice recognition, special keyboards and optical scanners. These computers can input, output and translate a range of documents into a Braille coding system. People who do not have access to a computer can still participate by having digital material transcribed for them by certified transcribers; providing translations both to and from documents into the Braille format. Among the products currently available there are:
- Braille computer keyboards
- Electric frying pans with Braille controls

- Alarm pill boxes – that remind people to take their medicine
- Watches – involving specially hinged clock-faces to respond to tactile time reading

It is interesting to note that a number of the talking products developed involve health issues.

These include:

- Blood pressure/pulse meters
- Calculators
- Computer bar scanners
- Currency scanners
- Heart rate monitoring
- Organizers – with the full range of functionality expected for sighted use

- Scales
- Portable cassette book recorders
- Tape measuring devices
- Thermometers – equipped to compare previous readings

People Want Information in Quick Snap Shots

These days, our busy lifestyles dictate how we find out what's happening in the world. So much of our information gathering has become a push-button mentality as we plonk ourselves in front of the telly at the end of an exhausting day. All we need to do is hook up to a broadband network, giving us finger-tip access to look and listen to the news from every corner of the earth. Watch though, how the stories are usually presented in small bite sized chunks. Television news channels offer up 15-minutes of news on short stories that are constantly repeated. In no time at all we are able to recite the commentary. The flip side to this, of course, is to take time-out and read a newspaper. Even then we tend to skim the headlines and pick out the stories that can be read quickly.

This is where *effective HCI* is taking off. The Internet technologies have given rise to a plethora of new broadcasting possibilities. Satellite or cable TV beams out of one's PC if one is prepared to pay the cost. Once a subscription is paid, there are literally thousands of stations whose programmes can be downloaded to your PC. Here's another dilemma: managing the mountain of information we gather into our homes at the press of a button. Many hours can be spent in fiddling around in the Internet-news. Take the accessibility of the WSJ.com site in the screen-grab in *Figure 4*. Once the subscription is paid, one is treated to the rich array of global knowledge.

The way we have absorbed ourselves in constant activity is interesting when thinking about the *human-dimensions of HCI*. On the one hand we super-absorb ourselves to the point where it may cause harm to our sense of well-being; while on the others, it is really difficult to cognitively sit still and not click on another link.

Our ability to remain engaged among all this information and seemingly endless bevy of encounters with new knowledge, saps our perceptive senses. When using the Internet, there are so many ways in which our attention is kept under constant fire. In the past, as we experienced new concepts, we would have gone and checked our understandings of new experiences with another person. In this manner, we were able to develop our own interpretation of our place in the world. These days, this push-button mentality limits our chance to reach the same type of inherent communication validation; or does it?

Figure 4 : A Busy Information Rich Web-site

Reaching the same level of cooperative knowledge sharing through the Internet means that we commit ourselves to even more computing. There are endless forums where knowledge sharing happens; but it's more of a one way process while one waits for a response. Without a Web-enabled camera and sound-card, one doesn't have the same instant recognition of how one's opinion is really being perceived.

All sorts of difficulties arise for people who spend more and more of their waking moments tapping away on a computer in communication with others on the Internet. Nonetheless in terms of our capacity to stay fully engaged, and maintain quality attention as we get tired, our diminishing attention may bring out an inappropriate response. Prior to current technology, we communicated not only through speech and writing, but also through the use of forms of unspoken agreement, such as body language. It is twice as hard to verify meaning in an online discussion without our trusted eyeballing techniques or sensing of our regular forms of unspoken agreement. While constant Internet activity may have short term gains with the feelings of instant gratification, the downside may prove too costly, long-term. Putting aside the negative issue of isolating us from those more immediately around us, there are many reasons why people should not sit for hours on end-using a computer. Long-haul air travellers are now encouraged to take care of themselves: to increase circulation and decrease the nasty onset of deep-vein-thrombosis. The same cannot be said for spreading the word for preventing the same injury while spending many unbroken hours in front of a computer.

Choice is everywhere; the Internet is a marketing panacea. At the click of our mice we can get into just about anything our hearts desire. Where will these endless possibilities take us? Because there's been a convergence of technologies that goes way beyond the bits and bytes of yesterday, we no longer think in terms of what makes a computer tick. Instead we adopt a more intuitive approach to using our techno-gadgetry. Our trust in manufacturers' promises to deliver an ever increasing range of computerized products is well entrenched. One reason for this can be seen in the rate at which audio devices have moved seamlessly into the computing arena, they surely take first place. It is truly wonderful to have access to digital sound. It seems as though anything is possible these days, from enhanced radio broadcasting through one's PC, to speaking with friends on the other side of the world for a fraction of the cost of an international call.

There's a whole new meaning to our creative spirit. Digital video means we can receive high quality imagery on our computer screens. In watching a video it provides us with information in such a form that we find relatively easy to understand. According to Pettersson (1993), this is because of the many combinations of linguistic expressions that are possible through video media. When watching a video we apply a personal linguistic framework to the combination of the spoken words we hear, with the audial language of the video (both sound effects and music) and the symbols and pictorial content that may be present in the video [1]. Perhaps this is the most exciting phase of the *human-dimensions of HCI*. Is this where we tap right into our personal dream-land to ignite our techno-imagination in exciting and new ways?

In our quest to unlock memories of previous events we are now able to understand how to assist people who may be having some difficulty with some part of their learning processes. Although the scientists don't fully understand how our memories work, we have come a long way in understanding. We know, for example, that human beings have two distinctive types of memory: short-term memory that stores only something we saw on the last Web-page we've looked at, and long-term memory that for instance depicts experiential events, like how to ride a bike. For more information on this topic see the following NASA Cognition Web-site http://human-factors.arc.nasa.gov/cognition/tutorials/ModelOf/index.html .

Effective HCI is all about capturing imagination in productive and enjoyable environments. One of the aims for writing this book is to explore how we can do this. Capturing imagination can take on various characteristics; in a business sense – it can mean motivating employees to adopt a new approach rather than a traditional administrative process. In a learning environment it can mean empowering individuals to try something new by showing an imaginative metaphor. The trick is to adopt appropriate strategies that draw on the principles of instructional design to deliver the expected result. Designing the interface and content in such a way has a better chance of maintaining concentration especially if we understand why we now expect our information to be given to us in quick snap-shots.

Internet Opens Many Extra Opportunities

Podcasting is one of the most dramatic changes in our techno-landscape. Some think about it as the newest method for distributing multi-media files over the Internet; often with playback capability through mobile phones and PCs. The concept is not really all that new. Although it was known about at the beginning of the 21st century, the technology was not available for people to use for several years. It took until 2003 for the first podcasts to emerge. Now there are literally thousands that have sprung up all over the Internet. Some find the term puzzling. It is formed from two well known computing terms (iPod and broadcasting). Although the synthesis of this term does not necessarily mean that you need to engage an iPod, nor does it mean that you will be involved in air-wave broadcasting, mostly associated with radio frequencies. Once the corporate training sector catches on to the popular nature of podcasting there will be no stopping. Exploitation of that fact that many people these days have mobile devices that receive voice, text and video, will follow. This potential for building virtual consumerism is not lost on the marketing industry. They have been quick with the uptake of the instant gratification opportunities associated with podcasting. Additionally, they have recognized the power of this catchy multi-media transmission medium to promote the word-of-mouth culture for selling anything they set their minds to. It may take a little longer for the education sector to become as enthusiastic and adopt podcasting into their teaching and learning strategies. Generally much of the professional practice of teaching takes a conservative view of techno-education. This reluctance may be attributed to lack of sufficient funding for professional development of the teachers and their lack access to reliable/powerful computing equipment.

Even with a small slice of imagination we can have an individualized virtual gateway to understanding our world. The trick is to know how to work through the various search engines to find what you want. Google is an easy and excellent place to commence. Google even caters for the techno-Luddites among us, by taking care of their poor typing or spelling ability. Not to forget there are people who spell well, but are still resistant to technology. Examine the following screen-grab to see how the Google engine has reacted to a typographical/spelling mistake *"soomwhere"*. It is interesting also to note how this type of cultural interpretation reveals some rather surprising results *(Figure 5)*.

Ask any parent of 10 year olds these days whether they know if their kids have played on the Internet. Currently, many schools are encouraging this type of interactive learning in their classrooms. There are literally millions of ways children (and adults) can pass away the time playing computerized games. Through many imaginative Web-sites they can participate in (often with other people to investigate and discover things that catch their interest.

For some, it's the irresistible attractiveness of sharing their thoughts with another human being on the Internet that draws them into many hours of online interactivity, and yet feeling their anonymity is protected *(Figure 6)*. Actually many of these Web-sites are very suspicious. It is only in a closed environment where strict controls on membership can be verified that a degree of safety can be guaranteed. There are, of course happy tales of people meeting through these safer environments, striking up a closer relationship in real life, marrying and living happily ever after. Unfortunately there probably are more people who report the exact opposite. This identifies one unfavourable aspect of online misbehaviour, well described by Patricia Wallace in her book *The Psychology of the Internet* [2].

Figure 5 : Spelling Errors

It seems that some people just can't help themselves. According to Patricia, too many of us use the faceless nature of the Internet to vent our frustrations on other individuals. She believes there is a real psychology of aggression to be found on the Internet. Moreover, we do need to watch how we use language; for instance in our email communications. Without thinking, we can cause considerable harm by using unfamiliar linguistics. For instance: an eMail recipient may read unintended connotation into a message sent in haste. It is far too easy with eMails to press the *[SEND]* button. This means we often send messages without really checking our linguistics. Before eMailling taking over our lives, one would write out a message, address an envelope, lick a stamp and post the letter. These bygone communication activities would allow a more suitable reflection upon the written message.

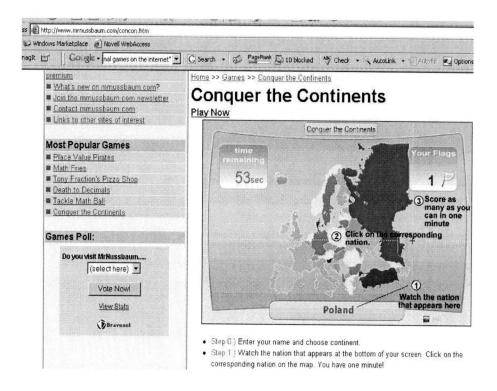

Figure 6 : Protecting Anonymity

Herein is another difficulty of the *human-dimension* of our HCI; in some circles the cross-cultural nature of online sharing is bringing forward a new awareness for improving our techno-communication skills.

Is Watching eInformation Really Relaxing?

Some of us use the Internet as an entry point for our thinking space. The ways we enter these private spaces surely vary. In the working environment, some turn to flip-charts to jot down their thoughts before they melt away. In less formal places, some may choose a comfortable chair to sit listening to music while gathering their thoughts. In using a flip-chart we try to capture our creative thoughts using lists of words or quickly written sentences. When the words are not enough to express our ideas, we may draw squiggles and shapes, often with lines pointing to represent relationships between concepts. These various methods of visual notation take practice. Researchers know that away from a computer, our mode of thinking about the information we receive, will vary according to the task at hand [3]. People will choose to think of the information they are receiving in terms of verbal (text-driven) or mental images (visualizing concepts).

Cognitive style preference: Researchers in general, have been aware of learners' cognitive (learning style) differences - and the implications for instructional design. Richard Riding at Birmingham University, describes a model for assessing the position of an individual on two basic dimensions of cognitive style *(Figure 7)*.

Understanding Cognitive Style

Drawing on Pavio's Dual Coding Theory, Riding shows us that *some people think in terms of mental pictures* (let's call them the visualisers): *while others think in terms of words* (these we will call the verbalisers). Riding points out that people are capable of utilizing either cognitive mode. He says that some people have a tendency to use only one mode - visual or verbal. Preferred cognitive style affects performance in both the perceptual and conceptual domains of the learning process. The more effective learning strategy would facilitate active integration of both these cognitive modes.

The horizontal line represents the first dimension (Verbal/Imagery) depicts the way people prefer to represent information during thinking. This is the way many people refer to cognitive style. It is that part of cognition that can change, according to the personal choice and the task at hand. People will naturally revert to the easiest thinking mode according to what they are doing at the time. Past experience may also play an important role in this dimension.

However it is the second dimension (Analytic/Wholist) that identifies people's mode of processing information, that is not changeable. Riding believes this cognitive dimension is inherent and may remain constant over time.

Our cognitive style is therefore made up by the combinations of these two basic dimensions, which Riding believes are independent. *There is a common belief that imagers will learn better if offered visual material and that verbalisers will do best with text.* However, my doctoral research into the acquisition of introductory programming concepts, shows how common beliefs can lead researchers and courseware designers down the wrong path [4].

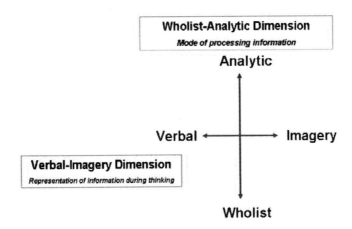

Figure 7 : Integrating 2-Basic Dimensions of Cognitive Style

Figure 8 : Fitting Square Pegs into Round Holes

We Know Perfectly Well that One Size Does Not Fit All

According to Dr. Cyndi Rowland, director of the *'Accessibility In Mind'* project, the rationale for developing accessible Internet-based materials is founded on really simple principles:

First, providing equal access to educational opportunities is simply *"the right thing to do"*. Vast amounts of valuable educational material are being gleaned from the Internet every day by students and professors alike. Just as physical accessibility is routine across campuses, virtual accommodations are just as necessary across the Internet. From this ethical perspective most individuals agree that education should be made accessible to everyone.

Second, creating accessibility formats for education is smart from an economic standpoint. When Internet courses are accessible to individuals with disabilities (or in remote areas), the institution will see an increase in the number of learners registering and paying for, tuition.

However Realize That You May Also be Breaking the Law!

Even though much work has progressed with the folk at the Universal Access to HCI forum, in dealing with the issues of accessibility to the Internet, common sense is slow to catch on. The UK Disability Discrimination Act uses a wider definition of the term, *'disabled person'*. It can include people with:

- physical or mobility impairments
- visual impairments

- hearing impairments
- dyslexia

- other medical conditions, and
- mental health difficulties

The Disability Rights Commission in the UK says [5]:

"Institutions are only expected to do what is "reasonable". What is reasonable will depend on all the individual circumstances of the case, including the importance of the service, the financial or other resources of the institution and the practicality of the adjustment. Other issues, such as the need to maintain academic standards, health and safety and the relevant interests of other people including other students are also important."

Does this will mean you don't have to put everything in Braille? It may be sufficient just to know that there is a Brailler in your organization.

The Dualistic Nature of the HCI Thinking Space

Deciding which technology to implement adds to our dilemma. While hardware and software standards are still evolving [6], the standards developments emanating from the *'Institute of Electrical and Electronics Engineers Inc.'* (IEEE) and the *'International Organization for Standardization'*(ISO) are largely mechanistic and concentrate on interoperability and integration. However the human dimension is taken up by the *'World Wide Web Consortium'* (W3C) and *'Web Access Initiative'* (WAI) accessibility standards (W3C 2005). The W3C makes recommendations for Web-technologies; while the WAI deals with the issues of increasing accessibility for people with disabilities. The WAI Web-content accessibility guidelines are making progress to clarify the distinctions between technology and content. Unfortunately Web-technologies can only be viewed as inert mechanisms that initiate nothing more than a means for online communication. Instead, our expectations of the social interface that implements *information and communications technology* (ICT) tools in a global context should involve two levels [7]: secure ideological exchange between individuals, and clear representation of cultural perspectives. Therefore Web-mediated knowledge sharing in this multi-dimensional environment will always be problematic.

Tension Between Some ICTs and HCI

What is to happen then with the people who cannot join in? This is where the *human-dimensions of HCI* has an important role to play, to avoid or lessen the widening of the digital divide. Sadly this role is not currently being fulfilled. Inequable access to information through ICT tools remains the status quo. The digital divide emphasizes the weaknesses of the *human-dimensions* of current HCI ideology. Moreover, there is a wrongly focused assumption that all people can access information through a normal range of perceptual senses. To this end, we can see that the literature reveals there is a growing awareness of the belief that one-size-fits-all. This is more poignant through the business/government sectors where access to information affects the bottom line. An example of where ICT is not serving the wider community is to recall our recent graphic witnessing of naturally occurring disasters that affect whole nations. For example the tsunami which devastated parts of Indonesia in 2005. Much of this global information sharing was only made possible through ICT tools. These types of macro-events test out our ability to provide accessible information to all. Although the initial tsunami struck Indonesia 3½ hours before landing in Sri Lanka and India, our ICT tools failed to convey any effective warnings! While it may be reasonable to think that equitable access to information is on the rise, the reverse may be true.

How Does This Apply to the Workforce?

A highly skilled workforce is widely viewed as essential for prosperity in economies characterised by rapid technological change. The implication is that high and growing incomes can only be sustained by high and growing levels of worker productivity, which in turn demand ever-increasing levels of worker skills [8]. However, the development of high level skills across the workforce is expensive and requires major investment from individuals, governments and employers. These days, the cost to employers of vocational education and structured training has been estimated by the Australian National Training Authority in 1996 as $6.186 billion, which is only 57% of the total training cost of $10.845 billion [8].

Traditionally, employers view training as an expensive solution that is implemented to fix problems. In a climate of changing work practices, every time a new technology enters the work-environment, employers seem to pour endless amounts of money into upgrading their employees' skill base. What then is the impact on institutional effectiveness of this continual investment in work-place learning? Furthermore, with people remaining in the workforce beyond the traditional retirement age, what are the consequences of their need for retraining in a continually changing work environment?

Navigating a way around online training is proving cumbersome. Research is underway to overcome this problem, with computerized tools to facilitate this. The *'Collaborative Learning Environment with Virtual reality'* (CLEV-R) is one example [9]. Interest in work-place reform is growing among the HCI community with virtual reality promising to bring about optimal learning outcomes, for the new workers entering the workforce (novice learners) as well as longer-term (experienced) workers who need to increase their knowledge and skill profiles. It is important to differentiate what an individual knows, from what they do not [4]; [10]. However, accurate measurement of employees' knowledge and skill is adding to the training dilemmas facing employers, made worse through some inappropriate implementations of ICT tools. Often problems arise following training sessions, when employees are expected to carry what they have learned during their training sessions into their work-place. Consequently, we say there is a real need for a learning strategy that provides dynamic change management to accommodate changing information requirements.

Important new Web-based learning management tools have emerged recently such as the *'Learning Activity Management System'* (LAMS). The LAMS foundation, based at Macquarie University, is a non-profit organisation researching the concepts of learning design. However, while this type of learning management tool may engage an active participation in learning activities per se, it cannot take account of individual skill development.

Are We Blurring the Differences Between Web-Based Training/Education?

In days gone by, interpretive misunderstandings occurred between *Education* and *Training* nomenclature, when the term *Learning* was incorrectly applied to a *Corporate Training* environment. Some people thought that *Training* should always involve predictable, Skinner-like behaviours to invoke trainees' memories of conceptualized facts and conditioned responses. *Learning* in *Education* on the other hand, should always seek to promote a student's ability to understand why certain actions may or may not occur. The Web-mediated learning/training environments have changed all this – hopefully for ever.

When considering the online learning environment, there's absolutely no way we can put the lid on how people are going to learn. The age of Web-based constructivist knowledge development has well and truly arrived. It is important to provide a safe and comfortable environment in which people can relax enough to construct the concepts comprising their knowledge within the social context of the Internet. It is equally important that people are given their own (intellectual) space while they engage in Web-mediated instruction, so as to attend to their own perceptions and interpretations of what they see and sometimes hear. Otherwise only a collective identity will be achieved [11].

This individualised thinking space should also include a social context of the work-place examples made available for use to support the construction of new or refreshed knowledge [12]. What should happen in these types of Web-mediated knowledge exchanges, and especially when there is a wide range of non-conventional learners among the participants, is that the focus for any type of eLearning or educational information system should be on the active processing among the learners. In this manner they may personalize their active cognitive processing space to construct their new knowledge. Moreover, this knowledge thinking/construction space requires an integration of new, incoming information from the environment with existing knowledge in memory. In the cognitive view, learning is about active construction of new knowledge by interacting with new information received and instruction is about promoting the psychological processes that mediates that construction.

Off With the Birds – Nobody Home

Some people really like listening to digital music all day. They would say it's clean, crisp and inviting. That's the upside, when surely the concept of, drowning in a digital music pool could be the downside. Imagine for one moment here that you are standing in a lift travelling up a building on your way to work. The doors slide open, in step a number of people all wearing hearing devices of various configurations, some with head clamps, others with things just poked into their ears. The type of device does not matter. Now examine closer their expressions as the lift doors close and you all continue on your way. Instead of making eye-contact around the lift you notice some of them have a similar distinct cloudy quality about their facial expression. You get the feeling that you could wave your hand in front of their eyes, without shifting their introspective gaze. It's quite a frightening prospect that, once again, with us not really paying too much attention, there's already been a sizeable shift in how some of us respond to worldly events. This of course is not to say that all head-sets are dangerous nor should we criticize an individual's preferences of using these digital listening devices. But when people on mass choose to lock themselves away from social interaction, we perhaps should consider where this is all heading to.

Surfing the White Noise

Perhaps this plethora of digital media has formed a crescendo of disturbance to our well-being that we should become more aware of. The notion of *white noise* is known in the music industry as a type of noise which emanates from the combination of many different frequencies that are heard all together. The concept of *white* stems from the manner in which a type of white light is produced by the range of beautiful rainbow-like colours. If we extrapolate this understanding from the music industry and apply it to the *human-dimensions of HCI*, could we not use this definition to demonstrate how we are now being bombarded by excessive Web-noise that may have become quite intolerable for some of us? The trick is going to be managing to stay on top of the wave to merge all the signals into a consolidated view or understanding. Of course, we won't necessarily be able to correctly discern the type of noise that is affecting us the most.

For some it's far too late. They are already well entrenched within the uncharted waters of the techno-environment. In fact, iPod experiential programmes are now much used at many universities around the world. Captured by the opportunistic marketing push to spread the word among the young, some universities have been reasonably quick to respond. In some cases, these devices were given out freely to higher-degree students. Moreover funding incentives were offered as research grants for education faculty staff to experiment with their products. What a wonderful opportunity to corner the market. Since early 2005 the range of digital music players has increased and spread to include PC compatible software products. It's nothing short of an iPod revolution.

Is There No Such Thing as Quiet Space Any More?

Trouble is, as we have said before in this book; the advent of this technology has caused a terrible dichotomy, in that it isolates the people who don't have one, while it puts others into a kind of digitally induced stupor. Either way, people who use these digital devices without remembering to interact with those who don't, are playing out the most terrible aspects of the distributed cognition that was identified many years ago. Meaning those people may not really understand the importance of blindly following the techno-pack. The end result could be a dulling of their sense of individuality, because they have become so accustomed to taking in excessive amounts of digital stimulation.

Groovy ICTs

Perhaps the largest techno-revolution in the *human-dimensions of HCI* can be witnessed in the amount of change brought about by the entry of wireless capability into our home environment. For some, it has changed everything. No longer are we satisfied to do our computing on one PC at home that has to be anchored to an electric socket, with its only access to the Internet enabled through an ordinary telephone line. Boring! Provided their home is located in a techno-savvy community, even the techno-Luddites can easily organize to get an account with a broadband *'Internet service provider'* (ISP), go to their nearest department store, purchase a wireless router and join the techno-cultural revolution. Without even the slightest clue about computer systems' networking technologies, ordinary people can plug in their multiple devices (laptops and PCs) into line sharing routers. That's the upside. The downside is not so rosy. When their ISP strikes trouble – a well-known Sunday phenomenon in this community - this dilemma throws all those wonderful digital-moments out the window. Ordinary people are then forced to join the queue of frustrated callers seeking help from equally frustrated ISP technicians, once they get through to them by telephone. These are rather early, home networking, days for all of us. Even the most experienced computer scientist will have some gory-story to tell about their techno-time out. The trick is going to be in having enough expert communications systems in place to manage the people component when things go wrong with the digital signaling. Most times, it's the passage of time and much patience by everyone in the techno-provider loop to remain calm, and wait for the (emotional) storm to pass.

Already we are used to computerized household appliances. No longer do we marvel at the range of things that are controlled by a digital device. The age of the smart house is here. Intelligent rooms can sense when someone enters, tracking movement, even in some cases recognizing commands given through gestures or spoken words. Some of the better of these systems make James Bond look ordinary. One of the worrying issues relating to our aging population is the rate at which we are all staying at home longer [13]. The dilemma of this pressing issue is to drain the caring professions, in terms of how to keep people functioning safely on their own. There are all sorts of techno-gadgetry in the pipe-line to support our home-stay. There are talking washing machines that speak perfect middle-class Hindi and English. Outside it's pretty common to find anything from computerized watering systems for our prized flower-beds, or even lawn-mowers to manicure our lawns. When you think of it, there's simply no end to the *human dimension of HCI*.

Moving away from the wonders of the techno-house, and back into the corporate sector, already we are able to change our working location with seamless comfort: surely a boon to people who wish to remain foot loose and fancy free. All we need is a smart phone, a wireless laptop, and we are away. Because of this, we are seeing a surge of interest for corporate training programmes that cater for people on the move. The trick here will be to capture the existing knowledge of older/more experienced workers, and storing their valuable expertise for others to learn from. Employees haven't been exactly sitting in isolation from the booming multi-media offerings. They are quite techno-ready, demanding high quality information processing capability in their work settings. Moreover there have been some interesting research studies carried out to investigate whether older and longer serving employees are too techno-phobic to warm to technological work practice. It would appear that in simulated management decisions concerning employee retirement, controlling for job status produced no significant effects [14]. Consequently, our earlier notions of the wonders of the GUI seem rather old-hat. It's hardly ever a topic of conversation around the departmental tea-trolley these days. Instead people are embracing their professional development with gusto. There's an expectation that corporate training is taken for granted. Updating skills is no longer the bad-boggy training officer waiting around the corner to trap us. This means there's also been a type of corporate knowledge revolution that recognizes the corporate knowledge base as a valuable company asset. *'Learning management systems'* (commonly known as LMSs) have been popping up all over the place. Many of these educational management systems are designed as generic repositories (database systems) that ordinary people are finding very difficult to use. It will only be the ones that can demonstrate adaptability to the changing local environment that will survive.

Meanwhile, whole departments (or expensive outsourcing contracts) are now dedicated to managing the corporate IT resources, when less than a decade ago, this job would have been handled by one or two people.

Why Are Young People Attracted To ICTS?

Unlike the people born before the computer age, many of whom may still be in awe of the techno-environment, the generation of people born between 1982 and 1995 *(commonly referred to as echo boomers or generation-X and even millennials)*; have a very different perspective. These techno-savvy millennials have grown up absorbing digital gadgetry as if they were silent ingredients in a techno-osmosis. Because of this, our younger users enjoyed the full range of digital computing toys without giving a second thought to what life would be like without them. Any wonder the younger generation-Ys now expect to have unlimited access to things like: multiple television channeling, mobile phones, and instant Internet messaging? In other words they are well plugged into the digital world; often their baby-boomer grandparents fork out the money to pay for these digital gadgets without fully understanding what they are or how they work.

The Internet has instantly transported younger people into a global community of providers. They have grown to expect to meet each other in virtual media cafés that offer HCI restricted only through the limitations of their imaginations. They have come to know there is a clickable someone there for them around the clock. In this sense they have bypassed the steeper techno-learning curve that some of the older generations of computer users have to endure. Instead most of the generation-Ys dive head first into the technology. There is no gradient on their skills acquisition, because of their plug and play attitude. When something doesn't work properly they have absorbed enough confidence while growing up around all this gadgetry that their techno-problem solving skills are now an inherent part of the psyche.

Being part of the echo boomer generation means they have also acquired a tacitly inherent sense of having to continually broaden their experiential horizons. It has been said that they are a generation less interested in rebellion, where recognition for rules has brought forward their aspirations to please. Perhaps this is due to the increased opportunities their parents took to enrich their experiential vista; providing a never ending supply of extra curricular events. It's quite common, these days, to hear of exhausted (generation-X) parents transporting their offspring to ballet, tennis, music lessons, etc, etc. So maybe it's not so surprising to know these echo boomers show evidence of being entrenched in the more traditional aspects of life. They believe it is better to please their doting parents, rather than pursuing individualistic recognition where rebellion may lead to alienation. It is quite possible these techno-savvy generations will continue to rocket themselves around the planet once they mature and reach adulthood. The Internet may then become the de facto parent, offering the full range of digital experiential awareness opportunities.

This propensity for techno-connectedness has not gone unnoticed by the next generation referred to as the youthful generation-Ys. Regardless of whether they are school aged and may be attending college or have passed their 21st birthday, these young people may also live independently of their parents or remain at home.

Irrespective of their personal circumstances, the drop in techno-cafés also fits perfectly into their daily routines. Here is where they extend personal channels through their global networking [13]. All on their own, they can develop new friends in chat rooms, play games, build new skills, seek career advice, look for part-time work and find out about the latest trends in leisure activities.

There seems to be a natural attraction towards using ICT tools that act much like a honey pot. It does not matter whether the user knows how to use the technology, for the technology is the seductive side of the *human-dimensions of HCI* that is quite palpable. Those who wish to be drawn in can find themselves captured by the attractiveness of going anywhere, at any time, without leaving much of a footprint. For some it is quite easy to blot out the peripheral issues of daily drudgery by immersing themselves in a nothing-to-lose approach to their key-rattling sessions. For others it is the sheer inventiveness of the Internet technologies, where there are no apparent rules to inhibit their HCI.

Multi-Media Invites Experimentation

We have before us a technicolour wonderland. If we thought about the *human-dimension of our HCI*, as a spectacular rainbow of digital opportunities; we would only come half way to describing the enabling effect that multi-media technologies can provide for the ordinary *"you(s)-&-me(s)"* in the computer users' techno-landscape. These days, as we move across the spectrum of techno-colours we have so many ways to feed our creativity. Perhaps it may also be useful to consider the physical process that must be in place for us to see the delights of a rainbow. Putting it simply, the rain particles in the air refract the sun's light splitting white light into its colour components and outlining the sun to give the circular shape of the rainbow. Instead of the sun causing the curve, let's say it's the human-dimension around which bands of technological wonder form.

Keeping the sense of the techno-rainbow, let's think about the ways in which humans receive information. Just as we absorb information in variations of light, colour, and contrasting textures, our ears can sense a spectrum of sound, through distinctive tones, loudness levels, and pitch. Sound information is mostly received by us through speech and music. For some of us, sound can remind us of events with amazing precision, allowing us to think of abstract concepts, and visualize concrete objects. In one sense, the Internet acts as the conduit for this array of information. These days we've grown used to associating safety for crossing the road with the high pitched sound when we push a traffic-light button. In business, people wear pagers to keep them informed. We have only just commenced our techno-journey using sound on the Internet. Our sound association extends our informational recall combining the relationship of the physical interaction with a subsequent reaction. Over time a user becomes very familiar with the auditory feedback that immediately tells them what they've done. Like the sound that a computer can make when you click-on your back-up hard drive. Research is underway to evaluate how the use of sound can help people navigate the Internet, such as which audio cues fit best with which task. The trick will be in finding ways to limit the stretch of the digital sounds so that people can apply digital noise filters much like the way we wear sunglasses to limit the harmful effects of the sun's rays. It would be useful to monitor the total amount of informational noise we are receiving before we place ourselves in harm's way; like taking account of how a particular digitally produced noise is mixing in with the background noise.

Movement is another *human-dimensions of HCI* that we can add to the techno-spectrum, with the arrival of easy-to-use multi-media technologies that non-technical people can use. Yet our sense of world is incomplete without the sense of movement. Imagine the difference between looking at a still image of your favourite tree in your garden with all the wonderful natural colour of the leaves, against a sun drenched blue sky then imagine that same tree with a strong northerly wind tossing the branches to and fro. It would be difficult to replicate the intensity of the movement of the branches and leaves as they react to the various wind currents. Imagine how much more interesting it becomes when you can capture on a video to show how birds protect their young during a howling gale by sitting in their lofty tree-top nests.

Multi-media can provide a virtual techno-lolly shop of delicious media to convey information. With skilful artistry the full techno-rainbow of ICT tools step forward, presenting us with never ending ways to enhance the *human-dimensions* of our HCI. It has never been easier to say the same thing in many different ways. As we have seen earlier in this chapter, people process the information they receive in many different ways. Therefore it is incumbent upon Web-designers to ensure that digital information draws on the techno-rainbow of text/pictorial modes. Also that it includes appropriate colour patterns, and textual/graphical exemplars that are enriched, only when necessary, with sound and movement.

It has also never been easier to keep in touch with each other, nor has it been more of a trap to fall into the Pandora's box of marketing hype. For marketing firms, gaining the knowledge of how their products and territories are responding to service can be instantly rewarding. Customers can be made to feel appreciated with very little effort, compared with business operations prior to the advent of the Internet. It's almost effortless for companies to thank their customers by eMail for their online purchases. The Internet lends itself to the competitive nature of staying one step ahead of the competition. In seamless slickness the digital technologies capture minute detail for storing in bottomless information repositories.

Do Visuals Really Improve Our Recall of Events?

Have you ever noticed how looking at a particular picture arouses a long forgotten memory? For some this ability may be more powerful than for others. Recalling events involves a fascinating sequence of complex information processing that scientists are still trying to understand. It would appear there are thousands of ways to invoke our long-term memory. The variety of triggers seems endless and not restricted to things like: hearing a song, seeing a familiar face, cooking smells, or reading a piece of text. According to the cognitive scientists we have two types of memory; procedural *(often referred to as implicit memory)* and declarative *(known as semantic, episodic)*. Retrieving our life experiences involves the combination of both procedural and declarative. Procedural memory stores routine actions commonly known as *the how* of doing something automatically, without explaining the why. These things can be very simple, like walking along a path, brushing your hair; or immensely complex things like flying a plane, or understanding the meaning or words. The more we perform these tasks the less we think about what we are doing, so that at some point the only way to recall how to do something is to simply go and do it.

Look for instance at how a ballet company learns to perform a new ballet. A choreographer will need to demonstrate the sequence of steps set to music, while the watching dancers commit to memory what they have seen. Later, the music is used by the dancers to trigger their procedural memories to recall the dance steps to perform. At first, the dancers will need to practice the sequence of these new steps many times before they are committed to their long-term memory. Not all our skills involve such physical activity. Reading for instance requires a different type of practice and recall. In learning to read we practice looking at single words then watch a sequence of words using our eyes to travel from one word to another across a page. At first this is a slow process as we digest the meaning of each word and its relationship with the accompanying words in the same sentence. After much practice we know how to construct meaning from the collection of these words, sentences and paragraphs. People generally don't need to be aware of the mental activity involved in this type of recall.

In contrast, when we need to recall information for the purpose of speaking or writing, it involves a set of very different processes. Unlike our procedural memory where automation eventually takes over from our cognitive processing, the declarative memory requires conscious effort. In discussing past events we draw on our intellectual skills to consciously remember things in minute detail. Instead of the automated responsiveness of the procedural memory, our declarative memory allows us to consciously remember and talk about what a particular something is, as well as to describe past events. This represents a dualistic *human-dimensions of HCI* that now becomes really interesting to explore. It seems that our declarative memory is divided into two distinctly different categories: the episodic (the remembering of where and when information was received) and semantic (symbolic representations of things, including words and their meanings, the rules for structuring sentences, chemical formulae and one's general world knowledge). This propensity for our minds to play tricks on us can be seen in the way randomising letters in the middle of words has little or no effect on the ability of skilled readers to understand the text.

See what you think when you read the following paragraph as retrieved from the Internet from http://www.mrc-cbu.cam.ac.uk/~mattd/Cmabrigde/index.html .

"Aoccdrnig to a rscheearch at Cmabrigde Uinervtisy, it deosn't mttaer in waht oredr the ltteers in a wrod are, the olny iprmoetnt tihng is taht the frist and lsat ltteer be at the rghit pclae. The rset can be a toatl mses and you can sitll raed it wouthit porbelm. Tihs is bcuseae the huamn mnid deos not raed ervey lteter by istlef, but the wrod as a wlohe."

Graham Rawlinson reports in the New Scientist (Vol:162, Issue 2188, 29 May, 1999, page 55) that one rapid reader noticed only four or five errors in an A4 page of muddled text.

Haven't we all experienced a time when we suddenly remembered how to do something we've not thought about for years? Digital technologies can potentially tap into this *human-dimensions of HCI* to enhance experiential recall. Much of Web-based information is presented in a verbal manner. As we saw earlier, researchers have discovered ways to describe the differences in the way people like to receive their information. Therefore if people cannot communicate in the most comfortable manner when they are using the Internet, they become frustrated. If the intention is to make people read copious screens of text; those of us who prefer to use pictures to enhance our comprehension may not read through enough of the material to make any sense. Considering that we are told that our memories do not store the information we receive in neat little compartments, how then do we retrieve isolated memories? Apparently it is through a cognitive reconstruction process. Some scientists believe our brain discriminates between information that comes in various modes such as visual, auditory and others. During the recall process we apparently can draw material from various parts of our brain to provide an integrated, holistic understanding.

Many tricks can come into play when triggering experiential learning, using words like: *picture this*, or *I think I saw* may guide people's recall, particularly if they like responding in a visual manner. Here are some more strategies, which people adopt when receiving information and how they may wish to communicate with others *(Table 1)*:

Table 1 : Strategies People Adopt to Communicate With Others

STRATEGY	GENERAL CHACTERISTICS
Visual	Communicates using colours, drawings, and maps.
Aural	Works with sound and music – discriminates pitch and rhythm really well.
Verbal	Uses written and spoken words – plays on the meaning and sound of the word.
Physical	Uses hand gestures to communicate – learns from the sense of touch – sensitive to physical world.
Logical	Likes mathematical reasoning, recognizes patterns easily – often makes sense of connections between seemingly disparate materials.
Social	Communicates well with people (both verbally and non-verbally), is sensitive to others motivations and feelings – likes to listen to others, may like to bounce ideas off other people.
Solitary	More private, introspective and independent – concentrates well – stays focused and likes to continually analyse the way they think and feel.

Cool Ways of Using Text - Long Live Story Telling!

Before talking about ways of using text; it may be useful for this discussion on the *human-dimensions of HCI*, to first think how computerized information is presented to people through many different guises. Let's take a step back to consider that the Latin noun *informatio* (meaning *conception* or *idea*) provides a clue to why our current expectations for information are based on receiving either raw data, details or factual material. These days we rely upon the newer discipline of information science or informatics to show us how to store and classify the growing mass of collectable information spinning around the world through the Internet. As with most things there are many ways of defining information. For some of us, information has a *soft* or human-linguistic dimension; whereas others may hold a *hard* or more technical dimension. Depending upon one's orientation there are so many ways to think about information. In Rune Pettersson's book Visual Information, he describes the following ways that different professional paradigms view information [15] *(Table 2)*.

Apart from the social/political information we receive, most people don't really stop to discern the information genre. Instead, more often than not they may admit to feeling constantly hounded by the media overloading them with tonnes and tonnes of mindless information. There are three types of interface styles in which this occurs: 2-dimensional, 2½ dimensional, or 3-dimensional. 2-dimensional interfaces are static and not intended to encourage knowledge exploration. The most common of these are road maps, books, magazines, and advertisements. Information presented in a 2D information framework focuses on the issues with no real detractions from other informational objects *(or eye-candy)* in the message. Users explore their own volition with no help from this type of information interface. In a 2½-dimensional interface the designer can use multi-media tricks to embellish the message: anything from shading and beveling the edges of buttons to mouse-over colouration with an associated sound. While 2½D environments encourage (knowledge) navigation and interactive digital-pages, it's largely for local travel within the actual information device (or object). It does not necessarily provide the means for ordinary people to journey off and away from the source informational media. Commonly used 2½D information frameworks are seen in many Web-pages, Internet cafés, and in fact anything that involves a digital video disk (DVD) where they provide the perfect medium for movie marketing. There is no universally agreed-on interpretation for DVD. These days, it's the 3-dimensional information frameworks, which epitomizes the full range of ICT tools that tap into the very core of *human-dimensions of HCI*. The 3D interface is designed to immerse the user within the context of the device. It taps all our senses. The ICT tools employed by the 3D designer enables us to understand information through our perception, sight, sound and touch. These days the excitement of this emerging information discipline is the capacity for us to personally experience and understand spatial relationships.

Another embellishment for customizing the style of our information interface can be found in the placement of textual marquee design. Perhaps this is where the techno-sheep are sorted out from the techno-goats; meaning these informational devices should be applied with extreme caution. Thankfully they cannot be applied in a 2D environment. The trouble with using them is that our brains are too busy taking in the meaning of words and sentences while they hurtle across the screen in front of our eyes. The Microsoft PowerPoint presentation software application provides users with customizing text tools that are simply amazing. Text can be made to blink, move in either horizontal or vertical directions, and all at varying speeds. For some, the process of choosing which information interfacing technique can prove troublesome.

Table 2 : Paradigmatic Information Views

INFORMATION GENRE	SPECIFIC ORIENTATION TOWARDS INFORMATION
Information processing	Using the notion of data as the raw facts, information processing is often used as a synonym for data processing relating to the systematic series of operations that are performed on data.
Information theory	The scientific discipline of the information theorist will comprise measurement of transmitted information and comparison of various communications systems, especially telecommunications.
Psychological information theory	A main branch of cognitive psychology that describes the brain's work as a process in which the flow of information between different types of memory functions that determines whether or not we are able to solve different intellectual problems, like the ability to learn something.
Semantic information theory	Grounded in philosophy, referring to information as supplied by a proposition's probability, specifying the principles for measuring information.
Information technology Information society	In the past, IT grew from the science that deals with technical nature of systems, production, distribution, storage and other efficiency issues. Similarly, and still residing within IT, the term information society reflects an industrial society's view supported by information processing and telecommunications techniques, where information replaces energy, raw materials, labour and capital.
Social information	The whole aim is to make it easier for ordinary people to know their rights, privileges, and obligations. A central focus is to ensure information is readily accessible, tailored to individual needs, and creates a sense of preparedness for the receiver. Closely integrated with authorities, professional bodies, and disseminated efficiently.
Information economy	The application of IT in the work-place, comprising the use of computers and networks. An increasing number of employees are working with information. Due to the business sector interests much research has been conducted that involves the impact of information and communication.
Information ergonomics	Sometimes referred to as human-factors and based on studies of the information user's aims, knowledge, experience, and way of working that include: lighting, design of instrument panels, video display units, characters, symbols, signals etc.
Infology	An interdisciplinary term encompassing many aspects from established fields such as: aesthetics, art, audio-visual media, cinema, computer science, IT, information theory, journalism, linguistics, mass communications, media, pedagogics, photography, physiology, psychological information theory semantic information theory, semiology, sociology, speech communication, television, trade language, visual arts, visual thinking, etc

To ease the way for people who may be creating their materials perhaps for the first time, there are a number of tricks of the trade that may make their life a little easier.

There are various ways we can capture our ideas for later recall. Some people may simply write out a list of their ideas, or scribble a rough outline, or represent diagrammatically the relationships among their fledgling concepts. For this purpose, it is sometimes useful to borrow from the moviemakers and compile a schematic representation of these rough concepts indicating sequencing, and logic flow. Early sketches can also provide rough notes for additional media such as narration, video, music, audience interactivity, etc. The presentation story can then be organized into pages, much like a PowerPoint presentation. These pages are placed on a type of time-line. Notations are then applied to the drawings or presentation pages. This method is more commonly known in IT circles as taking a top-down approach, whereby the diagram creates an overall impression of the main focus of the information/message to be conveyed. These diagrammatic pages and special effects can be moved around so that the relationships can be more easily seen by everyone concerned in the design of the information.

For some, this type of exploratory drawing takes considerable practice and may not be your way of achieving the best result. Sometimes people become so immersed with the drawing of the boxes and arrows and to such an extent, they forget they may be dealing with a top-level diagram and put far too much fine detail into the storyboard. When this happens, one should make a number of storyboards, taking care to install a coding system by numbering each level and sub-level to keep track of the relationships among the objects that are drawn *(Figure 9)*.

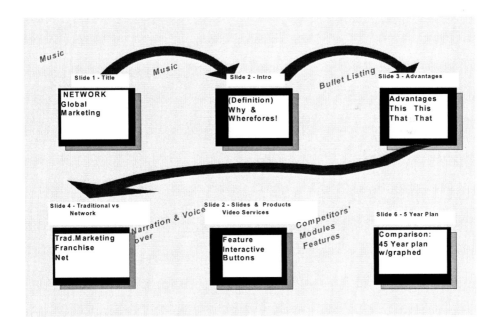

Figure 9 : Top Level Storyboard Diagram

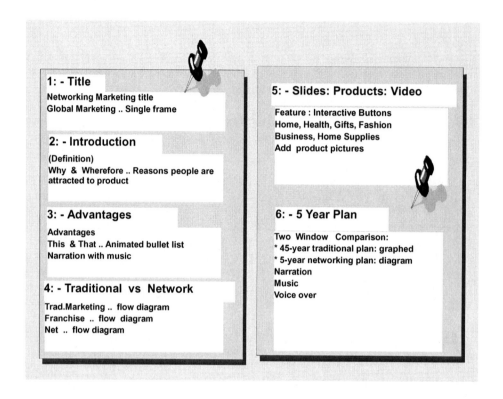

1: - Title

Networking Marketing title
Global Marketing .. Single frame

2: - Introduction

(Definition)
Why & Wherefore .. Reasons people are
attracted to product

3: - Advantages

Advantages
This & That .. Animated bullet list
Narration with music

4: - Traditional vs Network

Trad.Marketing .. flow diagram
Franchise .. flow diagram
Net .. flow diagram

5: - Slides: Products: Video

Feature : Interactive Buttons
Home, Health, Gifts, Fashion
Business, Home Supplies
Add product pictures

6: - 5 Year Plan

Two Window Comparison:
* 45-year traditional plan: graphed
* 5-year networking plan: diagram
Narration
Music
Voice over

Figure 10 : Bottom-up Tabular Approach to Record Specific Details

Another way people capture their information is to use a tabular approach. This type of information capture is commonly known in IT circles as taking a bottom-up approach. A bottom-up approach looks at the details at the coal-face and groups upwards to determine the structure needed to support the coal-face requirements *(Figure 10)*. Each notation method has merit. Some people will prefer one of these storyboarding techniques over the other. For instance, the top-down approach may require taking a holistic view some individuals will find difficult [4].

One purpose of this type of textual diagram is to capture each abstract thought as a type of modular presentation concept before it is forgotten, while another is to provide a physical means to tease out possible conceptual relationships that may remain hidden between particular concept modules. These documentation techniques can often help a novice-presenter get started. Knowing these few tricks on how to start, can reduce what otherwise may be a painful process.

Customizing an Online Personality

Armed with these few presentation development specifications your emphasis can shift from the cryptic nature of the storyboard towards making a complete technological replica. This is the time for considering the cultural aspects of your ePresentation. Templates are available in most presentation applications that have an amazing array of graphical page themes. The novice-presenter has only to choose from the standard templates to alter the cultural theme according to the desired presentation message and audience profile.

What is Behind the Message

Due to our almost natural tendency towards imaging, and the highly visual nature of e-Presentations, attention to choosing the imagery suitable to enhance the underlying goal should be the first decision made *(Figure 11)*.

Choose a suitable theme to set the cultural context according to the presentation goal identified during the writing of the storyboard. See the example above that shows how two themes can be created to provide very different contexts. For instance, on the left, the screen could engender a more formal flavour than the one on the right.

Extend the cultural aspects of the ePresentation theme into the required artwork, sound, animation, and template pages. This is where attention to the detail shown on the storyboard will begin to make sense. If necessary take time to create any of the clipart, special sound effects, narration files, and video clips, etc.

A word of warning should be issued at this stage for the novice-presenter. It is wise to know basic housekeeping routines. Handling the diverse multi-media file formats means that soon working with graphics will strain even the most prudent computer user. Novice-presenters therefore should learn how to perform basic computer system back-ups in general, and in particular know how to back-up strategic files to secondary storage devices (zip disks etc) and perform disaster recovery (run the Disk Defragmenter application to free up the contiguous memory registers and protect the pc hard-disk).

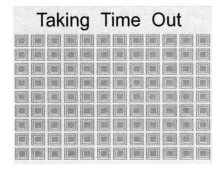 

Figure 11 : Guard Against Ambiguity

Beyond Desk-Top Publishing

Architecture of Type, or Traps for the Unwary

Designing the look and feel of your first publication can be quite a challenge. These days the richness of the multi-media tools found in many of the desktop publishing *(commonly known as DTP)* can trap the novice graphic designer. In 2000 Computer Education published a series of three lectures on the advantages of developing graphical presentation skills [16]; [17] [18]. Typography is the term that describes the design of the characters that make up text and display type (headlines, subheadings, captions, etc), and the way they are configured on the page. Consequently typography influences the appearance of our print communications more than any other single visual element.

The first task for the budding desktop publisher is the choice of text style (commonly known in the desktop publishing arena as, *'the typeface')*. There are many different typefaces available today. They grow in number constantly, increasing in complexity with each new version of software application. There are literally thousands. Herein is the first obstacle to a professional or quality publishing outcome. It relates to the temptation to include special effects, especially in relation to the type style chosen for the regular passages of text.

Typography is definitely a learnt behaviour and does not occur naturally. Creating a good impression with textual displays requires an expert's touch. Too often a new desktop publishing user is blown off track with the range of exciting looking text enhancements. It is so easy to fall for the trap of selecting multiple textual enhancements simply because they are presented in a font option listing. Actually the novice-desktop publishing-author straying in this manner is quite understandable, when one considers the cheapness of home grown publishing compared to the cost of professional printing. Not surprisingly, this decision process is somewhat similar to what happens when people need to pick out their preferred chocolates from the rest of the box. Similarly, in desktop publishing you really do not know the quality of the outcome until the printed result is evaluated. Even then a second opinion should be sought!

Typeface

In days gone by textual characteristics of type were fashioned in metal. Each letter was usually struck in relief on a three-dimensional plate, inked and then printed. If the printer were using a California Job Case to store their fonts of type, to print the name *'McKay'* would mean there would be several trips back and forth to collect the letters from a wooden font type case. It was likely in getting the capital *'M'* from the right side of the printer's font type case where the capital letters were stored in alphabetical order. The lower case *'c'* would have to be retrieved from the left or middle of the printer's front type case. Then back to the right side to select the upper case *'K'*; with another trip back to pick up the following lower case *'ay'*. It may have also been possible that the printer would have stored the vowels separately in a larger compartment, as they are used more often. The printer would memorize the layout of the case and increase in speed and accuracy as he learned his trade.

Today however, most type is produced electronically. In many instances only the terms have remained, providing a useful common understanding across many different media domains. The most powerful aspect of typeface is the ability for speaking to the reader. Consider how carefully speech is chosen for small children compared with someone much older. It remains the same conceptual issue with printed media. For instance, if your Internet publication contains heavy application of textual displays, it is useful to keep the reading level of the audience in mind.

One of the most misunderstood of desktop publishing terms is the meaning of the word *font*. A font is the collection of all of the characters of one size and style of typeface. This error may be due in part to the advent of font option listings found in a computer menu. For instance, *Times* is a typeface, four fonts are needed to complete the typeface: *roman*, *italic*, *bold*, and *bold italic*. The complete set of a typographical font in any given face, size and style will comprise: capitals, lower case, old style figures, modern figures, small caps, ligatures, diphthongs, Swash characters, accented and international characters, punctuation, monetary symbols, math signs, fractions, reference marks, superscript and subscript.

There are also common terms for describing text in detail. Much care and thought has been given to the design of each typeface brushstroke. For instance Figures 12 (a, b & c) show the terminology for describing the characteristics of typographic elements (text). Knowing these terms can assist when dealing with a digital copy in a print shop. Within many typefaces, there may be a range of options. Therefore it may be necessary for the font to be saved as a separate file. Among the numerous typefaces available today, there are two major categories from which to make an informed selection. Firstly the Roman letterforms have thick and thin strokes, secondly there are letterforms which have vertical upright strokes, used to distinguish them from oblique or italic designs, which slant to the right.

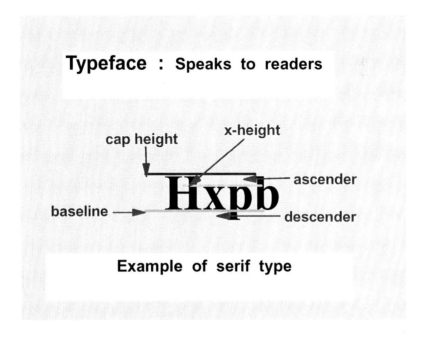

Figure 12(a) : Height and Baseline

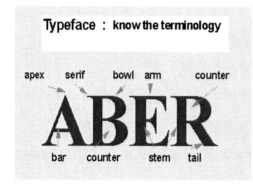

Figure12(b): Upper Case Letter Components   **Figure 12(c):** Lower Case Letter Components

Actually, the desktop publishing novice needs to only concentrate on knowing the difference between the older letterforms that involve a special ending to each stroke, called Serif (see Figures:12 a,b,&c), while the newer ones are called sans serif.

See how the text for this paragraph is an example of bolded Arial (sans serif). Notice this letterform design does not include serifs (curly bits), and usually involves mono-line stroke weighting (no variation of stroke thickness).

Some desktop publishing authors also refer to this as the stroke stress factor, which describes the variations of the thickness of the letterform stroke. For instance, the serif typeface tends to have more stress than sans serif. This means it usually contains vertical and horizontal strokes of varying thickness.

Style, Weight and Size

Modifications in style can also occur in letterform design variety while retaining the essential visual character of the typeface. To lend contrast and conceptual emphasis use, bolding, underline, shadow, italic, embossing, and small caps. To provide emphasis through letter width and stroke thickness, review the following san serif typeface fonts:

Abdi MT Condensed Light, AGaramond Bold, Arial Black, Arial Condensed Bold

The measurement of typeface also stems from the construction of those metal letters of days gone by. The point size of each letter was measured by the height of its metal block. This is the explanation of why fonts that have the same point size sometimes print at different sizes relative to each other. One point (pt) is nearly equal to 1/72 inch or 0.35 of a millimetre.

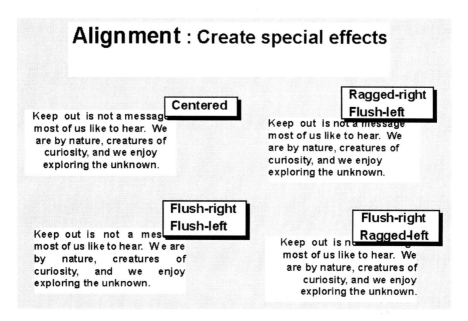

Figure 13 : Text Alignment

Alignment

The style or arrangement of setting textual displays is called alignment. Consider the special effects that movie credits are sometimes viewed. An example of these techniques is shown in the Figure 13.

One final word on alignment is to warn the novice desktop publisher to be careful with hyphens. This would be a common problem when first working with desktop publishing packages. It is better to turn hyphenation off, when learning basic desktop publishing skills. If not carefully monitored, the system can create hyphens for many consecutive lines, rendering comprehension almost impossible. In fact, some desktop publishing applications allow the user to set the number of hyphens that may occur in a row.

Kerning and Tracking

Some text management packages allow the user to change the spacing between characters. Each font has built-in spacing for pairs of characters. However, certain pairs, such as:

'WA' and *'Yo'*, often appear too far apart with traditional spacing.

The process of adjusting spacing between pairs of characters is called kerning, while the process of governing the amount of space between each character is called tracking. The track or letter spacing is the average space between characters in a block of text.

Here is an example of text without kerning (normal line position):

Tms Rmn 20 point. Notice there is no adjustment of space between selected pairs of letters.

Here is an example of the same paragraph with kerning, notice the adjustment of space between selected pairs of letters:

Tms Rmn 20 point. Notice the adjustment of space between selected pairs of letters.

Here is an example of raised text (positioned above line) with adjustment made between each character.

Tms Rmn 20 point. Line is raised by 8pt.

Remember, when all else fails, the novice desktop publisher can resort to the more traditional use of tabulation (tabs), indents or inserting extra space between paragraphs to enhance readability. Moreover, these textual display features are best altered and saved for reuse in most text style formatting options. Line spacing in fact affects overall readability. Try using tighter leading (vertical line space) for integrating words into a distinct visual unit. After all, people often prefer to only partly read each sentence. They do not necessarily concentrate on single words when extracting the overall sense of a paragraph.

Special Type Effects

There are limitless means to alter textual characteristics. Depending upon the package, typical effects are:

- reversing and screening
- stretching and compressing
- rotating
- setting type along a path

- filling
- 3-d
- shading

Other Typographic Refinements

If all of this is too confusing, remember the more traditional methods to refine punctuation, very handy with email formatting, dashes, and quotation marks '...', "—" or "-:)".

Visual Design

History reveals that humans were using symbolic representations some 45,000 years ago. These days visual communication is taken for granted. Symbols are the foundation for all significant communication [19]. Take a trip around a foreign airport and observe how effective the signage is for things like leading people to the appropriate floor, safety procedures, finding the food halls, etc. Information technology has played a major role in recent years, with the advent of the internet sharpening our opportunities to engage in visual communication like never before.

Moreover, the GUI has opened the way for the use of text and graphics in practically everything we produce on a computer. The rush to embrace the latest computerized visual tools to enhance even the more simple publication means to be effective. Desktop publishing authors require well developed visual thinking skills. To this end there are many good books written on visual communication. However, visual literacy is complex. In fact, due to inadequate training in the interpretation of pictorial material, many individuals have a preference for textual communication [20]; [4]. Be that as it may, desktop publishing is here to stay.

Many desktop publishing books concentrate on the end product rather than the conceptual processes involved in a reader translating the textual/graphical messages. However, it is the conceptualisation of the combination of text and graphics that makes an effective desktop publishing product. Producing good desktop published products take time and effort. There are two quite separate issues involved here. The first relates to the actual making of the desktop published product, while the second relates to the conceptual nature of the desktop published context. Conceptualisation is an intellectual process used when visualizing messages [21].

Keeping this in mind for the next section we turn now to concentrate on ways a novice desktop publishing can improve the visual nature of their publications. This means the conceptual aspects of visual design. Good desktop publishers should know all about clarity and unity, white space, cognitive style, and coding images.

Clarity and Unity

Visuals must be clear, and easy to interpret. On the one hand, the intended audience must understand what they see on the screen or printed page. While on the other, although the information displayed may be clear, it must also be organized in such a way so as to facilitate understanding. This means the overall computer screen or display area must be well composed in a unified manner. Much has been said in Web design circles about Miller's law of 7-items ±2. Some have wrongly drawn a parallel to Web interface design with Miller's experiments. Miller concluded that there is a limit to the amount of items the immediate memory can retain: (7±2). However, he was not studying how many items humans can perceive, which can be thousands. Moreover, with their Web-site navigation people are generally not required to use their short-term memory. It would be simply unfair to expect users to memorize items in a menu. In fact, most Web-site navigation is presented on all pages at all times for continuous reference. Therefore immediate memory doesn't play a significant role.

To this end Wileman[21] has identified seven visual design considerations to mark clarity of meaning issues:

- Are words and images large enough to see conceptual size and weight
- Are the words bold enough, conceptual size and weight
- Is there enough good contrast
- Is the visual appropriate, read, interpret and understand
- What are the visual cueing devises
- Does the visual contain only essential information
- Are visual sequencing techniques used to present complex concepts

To identify the unity of composition issues Wileman [21] has identified six visual design considerations:

- Are the visual elements well laid out
- Does the margin detract or unify
- Does the entire message fill the page
- Do the words fit the pictures
- Is reader directed to centre of attention
- Is composition supportive of message

Figure 14 shows an example of how line thickness provides different emphasis.

Figure 14 : Visual Clarity

Figure 15 : Visual Unity

White Space

To draw a reader's eye to conceptual key points, good design in desktop publishing will contain substantial white space *(Figure 15)*.

This phenomenon represents areas around type, intentionally left empty. Such spaces can physically be white or tinted. White space is important for the structure of a page [15]. This also means the balance of four margins: header (or top margin), footer (or bottom margin), inner, and outer margins. Knowing how to apply white space is often left to basic judgement and intuition. Too much can make the message unattractive and difficult to read, while too little may jam the words and lines together such that the message is destroyed making reading and comprehension a daunting task.

While on the issue of white space, it is timely to bring in the printer's term, *'leading' (pronounced ledding)*. Leading originated when thick strips of lead were used between lines of metal type as spacing material [22]. A printer may require a paragraph to be leaded out. This simply means there needs to be more space between the lines.

Planning for white space should therefore allow graphical elements to stand alone. Finally, reducing the number of concepts on a page provides a cognitive rest for the reader. Research has shown that individuals process information differently [23]. Surprisingly, individuals who may perceive they learn best from pictures, may actually require more textual display [24], because icons are usually not self-explanatory.

Figure 16 demonstrates how the deliberate placement of text and graphical elements enhance the effectiveness of a desktop published advertisement[25]:PM F-23.

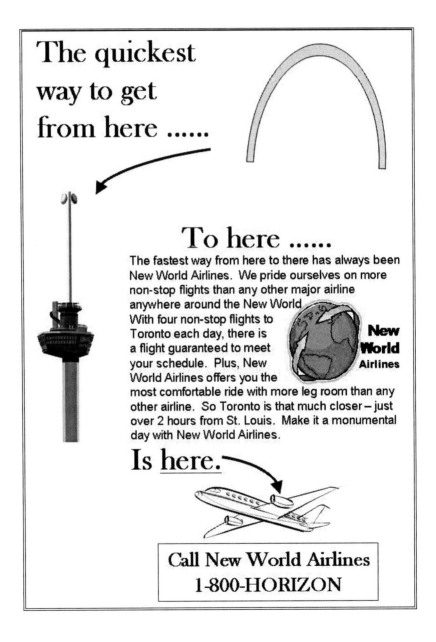

Figure 16 : Designing in White Space

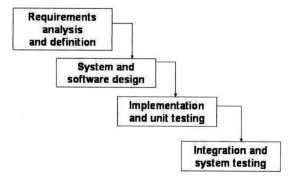

Figure 17 : Partial Waterfall Model

There Are Many Interesting Ways to Capture Ideas

For some of us, dreaming up good ideas is easy. What's more difficult is finding ways to get those new ideas out of our heads and on to paper or into a computer. Can we then say that we have captured our knowledge; or are these rough notations just more information?

At this point it's timely to expand a little on how information systems specialists differentiate information from knowledge. IT professionals take a firm stance on defining raw data as pure facts and figures. These facts are stored as unprocessed data Particularly in the IT genre, once raw data has been processed, like numbers in a spreadsheet for example. When these stored figures are processed (calculated), the data is considered to have become information. If we can accept this definition, where then does knowledge capture fit into our scenario? It is held by some people, that knowledge representation is quite different from data and information. According to this view, knowledge is structured information which stands in the place of commonly known entities in the real world. Once again we run into the territorial disagreements that swirl around the various disciplines that encompass HCI. To maintain our knowledge repositories we need shared linguistic agreement to ensure our library classification and processing of concepts remains robust. This is especially poignant for computer science, where much of their work involves *'artificial intelligence'* (AI).

How then can ordinary folk capture their ideas? Some people resort to using orderly models, to follow a logical progression of the way they generate their fledgling ideas. While others capture their creativeness by making doodles on paper and sketch the relationships among and between concepts. Another method, which comes from the computer scientists, is to follow a traditional linear process. This means, to develop a comfortable sequence of consecutive phases that include: Phase-1: the problem definition, Phase-2: the feasibility study, Phase-3: the (information) systems analysis, Phase-4: the systems design, Phase-5: the system's construction. These 4-phases reflect a rather simplistic use of the well known information systems modelling technique. Other variations are more comprehensive; they include other components to deal with verification and maintenance. Through the years software developers have used a drop-down approach they call the Waterfall Model *(Figure 17)*.

This Model still reflects a highly logical approach towards a creative activity which should be as free flowing as possible. The definition of creativity can be taken to mean idea generation that is associated with implementation as described by Kirton [26] [27]. People need to constantly think outside their square, by taking conceptual fishing trips to discover new relationships among and between what is already known. The important thing to remember about this knowledge/idea capturing activity is to write everything down, up front and ugly as some of our ideas may seem. It's very important to keep all one's early scribbles, especially during the initial stages of one's idea capturing process, however one goes about it. One simply cannot tell when an idea turns out to be valuable, so noting them means they stand a better chance of not being forgotten.

In this chapter on the human-dimensions of HCI, it is proposed that using computers is not as easy for some people as others [13]. Such an apprehension may be due to the highly visual nature of the techno-environment, and this graphical context may prove to be too difficult for particular sections of our computer users. Targeted training should therefore be given to novice-learners to increase their hand-eye coordination when manipulating graphics objects rather than text input. The Internet presents us with many extra opportunities for drilling into worldly knowledge on just about any topic. It's relatively easy to go info-surfing. Difficulties remain in the lack of effective HCI knowledge navigation, and this may account for the social context, or human-dimension. Consequently effective HCI should be a fusion of both human beings and their machinery, with their digital artefacts. To further explore this argument, the next chapter describes the machine-dimension of HCI.

However, in the light of this chapter's discussion, on the *human-dimensions of HCI*, there are a number of special areas to remember:

- Using a computer is not easy for everyone
- People want their techno-information in small chunks – maintaining concentration is tricky
- While the Internet opens many extra opportunities – it provides a virtual platform for abuse
- The dualistic nature of powerful thinking spaces – nurture wholistic windows for information
- The iPod revolution empowered a new set of techno-advocates – any age, anywhere
- Groovy ICTs are entering the workforce – shaking the traditionalist in-house trainer
- The surge in visual communication promotes shared mental models
- Desktop publishing emerges as an exciting and successful home grown industry. This means more people are delving into knowledge engineering to think outside their conceptual square to capture interesting ideas

Chapter Reference List

[1] Pettersson, R., *Literacy and Visual Learning*, in *Visual Information*. 1993, Educational Technology Publications: NY. 121-200.
[2] Wallace, P., *The Psychology of the Internet*. 1999, UK: Cambidge University Press. 264.
[3] Riding, R.J. & Rayner, S., *Cognitive Styles and Learning Strategies*. 1998, UK: Fulton. 217.

[4]   McKay, E., *Instructional Strategies Integrating the Cognitive Style Construct: A Meta-Knowledge Processing Model (Contextual components that facilitate spatial/logical task performance): An investigation of instructional strategies that facilitate the learning of complex abstract programming concepts through visual representation*, in *Applied Science (Computing and Mathematics Department)*. 2000, Deakin University, Available online from http://tux.lib.deakin.edu.au/adt-VDU/public/adt-VDU20061011.122556/ Waurn Ponds, Geelong, Australia.

[5]   Disability-Rights-Commission, *We Want a Society Where all Disabled People Can Participate as Equal Citizens*. 2007: Retrieved 01/06/08 from http://www.drc.org.uk/employers_and_service_provider /education/higher_education/senior_managers_guide.aspx

[6]   Sonwalkar, N., Demystifying learning technology standards Part I: Development and evolution. 2005, Campus Technology: 101 Communications. http://www.campus-technology.com/article.asp?id=6134.

[7]   Chan, A., *Communication technology and theory: Research into the interpersonal and social interface*. 2003, Gravity7,Viewed18/08/07 http://www.gravity7.com/articles_investigation_toc.html.

[8]   Richardson, S., Employers' contribution to training. 2004, Formal Report: National Centre for Vocational Education Research (NCVER). ISBN 1 92086 00 7.

[9]   McArdle, G., et al. Conceptual agent models for a virtual reality and multimedia e-learning environment. Paper *Presented at* the *14th IASTED International Conference on Web-Based Education. Held February 21-23*. 2005. Puerto Vallarta, Mexico. Conference Web-site Retrieved 19/01/08 http://www.iasted.org/conferences/2006/mexico/wbe.htm: IASTED.

[10]   Izard, J., Impediments to sound use of formative assessment (and actions we should take to improve assessment for learning), P.L. Jeffrey, Editor. 2004, Paper presented at the Australian Association for Research Education (AARE 2004): Positioning education research, held Nov 28 - Dec 2, in Melbourne.

[11]   Hung, D., Design principles for web-based learning: Implications from Vygotskian thought. Educational Technology, 2001. 41(3): 33-41.

[12]   Kang, M. & Byun, H.P., A conceptual framework for a Web-based knowledge construction support system. Educational Technology, 2001. 41(4): 48-53.

[13]   Bradley, G., Social and Community Informatics: Humans on the Net, 2006. NY: Routledge.265

[14]   Rosen, B. & Jerdee, T.H., The nature of job-related age stereotypes. Journal of Applied Psychology, 1976. 61(2): 180-183.

[15]   Pettersson, R., *Visual Information*. 2nd ed. 1993, NY: Educational Technology Publications. 374.

[16]   McKay, E., Human-computer interaction: GUI raises targets for computer literacy. Computer Education, 2001. June(98): 12-22.

[17]   McKay, E., Human-computer interaction: Introducing the desktop publishing world. Computer Education, 2001. Nov(99): 5-15.

[18]   McKay, E., Human-Computer Interaction: Effective multi-media presentations. Computer Education, 2002. June(101): 2-10.

[19]   Sewell, E.H., Visual symbols, in Visual Literacy: A spectrum of visual learning, D.M. Moore & F.M. Dwyer, Editors. 1994, Educational Technology: NJ. 435.

[20]   McNamara, S.E., *Designing Visual Analysis Training for the Individual Learner: An Examination of Individual Learner Differences and Training Content and Procedures*, in *Faculty of Education*. 1988, Monash: Victoria, Australia. 543.

[21]   Wileman, R., *Visual Communicating*. 1993, NJ: Educational Technology Publications.

[22]   Conover, T.E., *Graphic Communications Today*. 3rd ed. 1995, MN: West. 517.

[23]   Riding, R. & Cheema, I., Cognitive styles - an overview and integration. Educational Psychology, 1991. 11(3&4): 193-215.

]24]   McKay, E., Measurement of cognitive performance in computer programming concept acquisition: Interactive effects of visual metaphors and the cognitive style construct. Journal of Applied Measurement, 2000. 1(3): 257-286.

[25]   Proot, K.G., *Adobe PageMaker 6.5 : Illustrated Series*. 1998, MA: ITP.

[26]   Kirton, M., Adaptors and innovators: A description and measure. Journal of Applied Psychology, 1976. 61(5): 622-629.

[27]   Kirton, M.J., *Adaption and Innovation in the Context of Diversity and Change*. 2003, London: Routledge. 392.

Chapter-3

The Machine-Side of HCI: Foundations of HCI and Artificial Intelligence

The next part of our techno-saga covers the *machine-side of HCI*. Remember that the telling of this tale is through a social-contextual lens [1]. Nevertheless our clever computer machines didn't invent themselves. Moreover they still require special techno-people to maintain them – keeping alive the vision for binary opportunities; without them computing would remain rather ordinary.

In the Beginning There Were Bits and Bytes

To explain the evolution of the computing age, we'll return to our Mother Nature, to retell a celestial tale from the sea. Ever since the 17th century, people have been pursuing ways to capture information as logical knowledge elements. It all began with the German astronomer Johannes Kepler, and his theory that is commonly known as Kepler's laws. Kepler described the orbits of the planets in plain language that allowed ordinary people to understand his celestial *'world'*. Ever since this interest in calculating planetary orbits and the like, we have wanted machines to carry out our calculative chores. At first people were mainly interested in human computational logic and applying their skills by studying the motion of stars and planets to solve the mysteries of the universe. It took many years to understand that our Mother Earth and other planets revolve around the sun. A spin off from all this effort was the development of a mariner's navigation table from which it was possible to determine vessels' positions at sea from lunar positions.

Not surprisingly at that time, there were difficulties in predicting the effects of gravity on the moon (from both the earth and the sun). Then, following a major 1714 maritime disaster for the British Fleet, caused by faulty navigation charts, a prize was offered to anyone who could discover how to calculate longitude at sea. In 1767 a series of tables were developed to show the midnight and noon locations of many of the celestial bodies. Every year since, these tables were updated and revised. However, it was the pendulum clock that Christiaan Huygens invented much earlier in the Hague in 1656 that revolutionised the calculation of longitude. His innovative spiral balance is also known as the *'hairspring'* was a very fine spring, coiled flat, that controls the speed of oscillation of the balance wheel of a clock. Ultimately, they could be used by navigators wishing to check the accuracy of their nautical chronometers during long sea voyages.

Understandably, due to human error, the original nautical almanac was error-ridden. Apparently the calculations were made by elderly clergymen of the time, receiving low wages for their computations. Seven-figure logarithms were required to improve the original calculations. It was only after World War I that a young New

Zealand PhD student named Leslie John Comrie, conducting work on computations of celestial mechanics for the British Astronomical Association at Cambridge, completely changed the nautical computational genre. In 1926, Comrie's expertise for dealing with enormous quantities of numerical calculations was recognized, leading him to be appointed as deputy superintendent at Greenwich.

Comrie was convinced that machinery could be employed to calculate scientific computations more efficiently than humans. He wanted to replicate the census calculator, which Herman Hollerith invented. This punch-card calculator was used in 1890 to alleviate the drudgery of adding the US Census data. Data was represented on these cards that were punched with holes to convey personal information much the same as we would expect to see in any database record these days, with age, gender, country etc. As the cards travelled across a bath of electrically conductive mercury, many metal brushes pushed lightly against them; wherever there was a hole, a brush would sweep up a little mercury, closing the electrical circuit, causing one count to be added to a total (register). Comrie rented Hollerith tabulators to compute his beloved lunar calculations from 1935 through to the millennium. Even Comrie was surprised at the speed at which these 100 million figures were processed. Moreover, he possibly made the first eBusiness observation when he conveyed the cost benefits of these computations at a speed of 20 to 30 per second.

During 1929 IBM were on the scene as one of the largest manufacturers of mechanical calculators. They set up the first bureau, free of charge, at Columbia University to provide computation service for social scientists. Here they could deal with 150 additions per minute, sorting 20,000 cards per hour. Then in 1934 a second bureau was set up at Columbia University, also sponsored by IBM, to compute Wallace Eckert's celestial mechanics.

Word spread quickly, and other astronomers flocked to utilize the technology. Just why this happened remains a mystery, because it wasn't until World War II that other information genres began to appear.

These days if we look at the types of machines that were delivered to Eckert, some of us (mostly the baby boomers) will be able to see the emerging digital components that represent the modern computer processing unit, so often referred to in basic level education and training courses as an introduction to computer literacy during the 1990's!

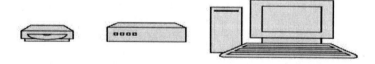

IBM at Columbia University, 1934

The machines that were installed by IBM at Columbia University for Wallace Eckert included:

Table 3 : Early IBM Computer Machinery

MACHINE	PURPOSE
card punch	Transfer data from paper records to punched cards.
verifier	Check the initial data on the cards against a second keying from the manuscript.
sorter	Automatically sorting the cards into groups at the rate of 20,000/hour.
tabulator	Perform additions – reading number from 9,000 cards/hour – when equipped with a printer, could print information from cards or provide accumulated totals.
High-speed recorder	Transfer information from one card to another at the rate of 6,000 cards/hour.
multiplier	Built to Eckert's specifications – automatically multiply numbers together at a rate of 730 cards/hour for eight-digit-by-eight-digit multiplications.

These days we have everything under the one lid, so to speak. It is interesting to note the linguistics that we now use to identify the component parts. When we buy our computers they generally consist of hardware, software, people-ware and procedures.

The term hardware relates to the equipment that does the computing:

- the basic input, processing and output, some devices may be controlled by the computer to be considered as online, while others may be offline, working independently (like a printer that is shared by other computer users in a network).

The term software relates to the sequence of internal (machine related) instructions that are designed to direct the functioning of the computer. Firstly the operating system software manages the computer's resources. Secondly the systems software (or utility programs) facilitate computing by directing the machine to respond appropriately when commanded by the user, usually through a mouse-click or when they press the *[ENTER]* key. These utility programs include such things as:

- organizing and maintaining data files
- translation of the variety of coded instructions written in a number of specialized computer-languages
- scheduling the jobs that the computer must attend to (like running the printer, while the user continues surfing the Internet)

Then there is the applications software that is designed to perform your everyday computing activity like: word processing, desktop publishing, spreadsheet calculations, database management etc, etc. Meanwhile, the term people-ware these days refers to all the IT personnel that are required to design, program, and operate a computer installation. These people they may perform the following supportive IT roles:

- information systems' end-users: they should be included in all information systems design teams to ensure their needs are met. In addition, end-users also serve an important role on application software design teams to ensure that accessibility evaluation remains on track.
- system analysts: they make a study of the information processing requirements, providing expertise for defining software applications problems, determining system specification, recommending hardware and software updates, design information processing procedures. They may also devise and

implement data verification procedures, design logic diagrams and data logic to be translated by programmers into computer code (software).

- interface programmers: they are at the centre of the software application's usability. They take their directions for designing the program code from the system analysts.

Procedures bind all the computing operations together. Most often they exist as sets of specifications that describe each aspect of data processing. In days gone by such procedures were sold with each computer. These days the user manuals may be filed to a CD or accessed online through your Internet Browser, once one has registered and accepted the manufacturer's licensing requirements.

The Quest For Artificial Intelligence

Less than a decade after IBM/Eckert's success at Columbia University another group were trying to find solutions to some very tricky problems. It was felt by some that since computers could be designed to seemingly absorb, store and process enormous quantities of data and the subsequent information, that when computers were fed enough historical data, they could also be designed to find more workable earthly theories than would otherwise be discovered by mere human beings. Some visionary scientists understood during the 1940's that machine intelligence would see the advent of robotics, which would perform tasks shunned by people as being repetitive, dull and often dangerous (like handing atomic fuel rods at a nuclear power station). While others knew it would be possible to build machines that would respond to the human voice and eventually, perhaps, respond to the needs of a user. However to really do this, scientists need to fully understand the nature of how humans learn, and how humans use language and their perception senses. In fact there are some scientists who acknowledge that understanding the inner workings of the human mind are quite insufficient when attempting to replicate these humanoid attributes. So doing could arguably be the most difficult challenge left within the field of science.

Another group of scientists were willing to go along with Alan Turing's test of machine intelligence in the 1950's. He boasted that a computer deserved to be described as intelligent if it could deceive a human being into believing it (the machine) was human. This belief remains evident in some AI circles to this day, and suggests that replicating humanoid-machines; that is, devices that think, move, hear, speak and appear to behave like we do, is entirely possible.

Who Cares if Computers Aren't Easy to Use?

Shifting away from the lofty aspirations of the AI purists with their energies set on bringing forward the perfect humanoid, we should pay homage to the large number of backroom techno-boffins who work very hard at keeping up their interest in HCI. These devoted individuals are to be found in IT digs all around the world. While some of these techno-geeks may have acquired their specialist skills by fiddling with computers from their baby-strollers, they work from an intensely intuitive experiential techno-training background. Many do, however, belong to the baby boomer generation and have taken degrees in computer science, software engineering, or information systems. As these techno-gifted people continue to tunnel away at their individual projects, each new piece of the HCI-jigsaw adds value to our collective knowledge of what is possible, and what is not – for the moment.

Techno-Geeks and Back Room Boffins

Our techno-progression in less than a decade is simply stunning. First, there was the early serial (data)-processing days with the limitations of those fledgling machines that could only do one thing at a time, albeit at lightning fast speed. Next came the parallel processing genre where multiple data calculations could be performed simultaneously. (Some call this mega-flopping). Because of this innovation we can now employ super-computers that some people believe will eventually shift us from the more familiar data-processing of today into more intelligent processing of worldly knowledge of the future.

Within the field of knowledge engineering, which is a branch of the AI genre, the focus is to automate human expertise. These expert, or knowledge-based information systems derive their conclusions based on computerized or stored data-sets. Some IT researchers believe these data-sets represent human knowledge that has been captured by technicians while interviewing the real experts: people. Unfortunately these expert information systems suffered from a rather slow up-take by more ordinary folk, over the last decade. These days, however, expert systems are found in many places. Some believe they are particularly useful in solving problems that previously required human intelligence.

An expert system may involve the following techno-features:
- store facts and their associated rules into an (expert) knowledge base, which then acts like a mega-knowledge repository
- perform logical reasoning, with uncertain data-sets
- reveal results from their logical reasoning, using everyday linguistics

Unlike the more ordinary database that many of us use, expert information systems' knowledge base also provides the relationships and the contexts in which the data-rules must operate. In some larger expert systems installations, there are a number of computers that are dedicated to specific computational/reasoning tasks. This means the expert knowledge repository may be in one machine, while the control or inference engine is in another. As such, software applications that have been stripped of their knowledge-files are called expert-shells. These shells form the basis of reusable control engines that can apply the rules and reasoning to interpret other data-sets.

The good news is that these days, ordinary people can build their own expert systems, However, the bad news for some others may be that they will need to know how to program. The most popular programming languages are considered to be the List Processing languages, such as LISP and LOGO, and PROGgramming in LOGic, known as PROLOG. LISP has been in existence for over two decades. A feature is that LISP programs can process their own '*lists*' of program code. A program can appear to '*learn*' from '*experience*' in a quasi human fashion. LISP is relatively easy to use, and utilizes logical inference techniques that underpin the expert information systems functionality. It achieves this by searching and analysing large, nonnumeric repositories to produce conclusions. While PROLOG is a much younger computer programming language, it was designed in 1970 especially for expert information systems. PROLOG therefore has inbuilt routines to communicate with the inference engine to perform high powered searching activities. Some AI people believe that PROLOG will outclass the earlier LISP language due to the manner in which it can deal directly with the logical relationship of the stored informational objects, rather than merely performing high powered calculations.

A truly *'intelligent'* system should be able to generate new concepts from what is knows. Some systems thought to be intelligent, such as knowledge-based expert systems, cannot do this.

It's the Way it Should be

Unless you happen to be a techno-geek or backroom boffin, the odds are that you may not be in the slightest way interested in emulating their techno-skills.

"Leave that geeky techno-stuff to them", seems to be the common approach, *"aren't our lives stressful enough!"* This disparate attitude is quite understandable if you consider the tonnes of Q&A sitting in cyberspace awaiting the much revered pearls-of-wisdom that may help the rather more ordinary computer-user out of a tight spot. This is especially relevant these days when it may be oh so inviting to develop one's own Web-pages. It has been said that the World Wide Web is the Gutenberg press of our time [2]. Almost anyone these days thinks they can make a Web-site that is published on the Internet for the whole world to see.

Yet look at the mess these rather ordinary people find themselves in when developing new Web-pages. Many brave people try using CSS (cascading style sheets), which should remain in the realm of people with more techno-savvy. CSSs provide both Web-site developers and their users more control over how their Web-pages display. The term CSS relates to the multiple nature of applying the same style sheet to any number of Web-pages. These CSSs are a brilliant way to keep track of things like screen-based headers and hyperlinks. The concept may be simple enough. However, unless people have experience with a basic computer programming language, a tangled muddle may result. It is indeed clear from such muddles; they should, at the very least have a working-knowledge of the HTML (hyper text mark-up language). In case you are not aware, HTML is a subset of the standard generalized mark-up language (SGML) that is the specific standard for electronic publishing for the Internet.

It's all very well to say there are many software applications that write up the HTML code in a seamless context to the novice-user. Watch instead how difficult it is to unravel all those HTML tags that are generated automatically by over zealous operating systems (or indeed, even by MS Word!). Moreover, why become stressed with the plethora of techno-events that cause your new Web-page to not behave the way you intended. Some of these issues relate to the type of machine that is being used and the monitor displaying the Web-page, the speed of the Internet connection, and the browser being used to view your page.

This is a vexatious HCI issue. Modern day computer programming seems rather attractive to some of us, except for those who may lack the ability to perform instant problem solving, to keep cool and to think logically. A lot of valuable time can go down the techno-drain pipe unless such unfortunates can get help immediately. Moreover there's a strong possibility they may well be left believing that venturing out from the comfort of their techno-Luddite-ness was not such a good idea. Indeed, they may never attempt Web-page development again. If this sounds like someone you know, chill out, sit back and relax. Enjoy your HCI instead, and leave the back room stuff to the boffins and techno-geeks. That's just the way it should be.

Standards Keep Everyone on Track

There is an emerging international trend for researchers to focus on workforce accessibility to digital information. While there are many types of human functional disability some of which are the result of the aging process, the focus of most research projects seems mainly aimed at catering for the more definable functional limitations of work seekers. Only limited research is evident, which is specifically designed to assist those recovering from concentration and motivation disabilities.

Australia is following a movement brought about by the Disability Discrimination Act 1992, with some work that is looking to improving general accessibility to information. Current initiatives include the draft *'Schools Online Curriculum Content Initiative'* (SOCCI) accessibility standard. There is also a review by the *'World Wide Web Consortium'* (W3C) to develop enhanced technologies that include specifications, guidelines, software, and tools.

Then there is the *'Web Access Initiative'* (WAI). In coordination with business organizations around the world, they are pursuing accessibility of the Web through five primary areas of work: technology, guidelines, tools, education and outreach, and research and development (http://www.w3.org/). The W3C are developing interoperable technologies that define the specifications, guidelines, software, and tools, to lead the Web to its full potential. Moreover, the W3C is a forum for information, commerce, communication, and collective understanding. Some corporate bodies are actively engaged in the development and dissemination of the W3C and WAI standards. However, this collective understanding still mainly addresses the issues surrounding the interactive effect of physical impairment and accessibility to information. Lack of programs that are specifically designed for individuals dealing with an intellectual or psychiatric disability leave a glaring gap in our techno-environment.

These days the IEEE, which is a non-profit organization, is one of two of the world's leading professional associations for the advancement of technology. The full name of the IEEE is the Institute of Electrical and Electronics Engineers, Inc.; which is commonly referred to by the letters I-E-E-E and pronounced Eye-triple-E. Serious techno-geeks and back room boffins are amongst the 100,000 members of the IEEE Computer Society, founded in those heady days of 1946. The *'Association for Computing Machinery'* (ACM), on the other hand, stakes their claim to be the first society in computing with their origins stemming back as far as the 1940s. Both these bodies share worldly attention as the peek informational bodies for computer professionals. They both ensure the cutting edge of technical information and community services to their membership. The ACM has recently had a shift in this regard, and away from main-stream research. Topics now include more of the *human-dimensions* or social context of computing. For instance: in ACM TechNews, Volume 6, Issue 681: Friday, August 13, 2004, the table of contents reveals a renewed research interest in the following issues that include: *"students saying no to computer science"* and the *"when machines breed"*.

By comparison, the *'Australian Computer Society'* (ACS) is a much younger society that represents the voice of the Australian ICT professionals. Together with a wider reaching body called *Professions Australia*, their combined membership of 14,000 presents an informed forum that interacts and negotiates with government and other peek industry bodies. The ACS fosters individual career development for employees by offering accredited IT related courses and special interest groups. These aim to convey best practice, experiential knowledge and skills to their membership. Moreover they help their membership select potential employers by presenting companies committed to actively investing in the ongoing development and training of their staff through their Corporate Recognition Program.

Rich Internet Applications

Talking up the technology has become a favourite pastime for the discourse on life-long learning. Because this is a perfect chance to use the leverage and the power of the Web environment, it's not surprising to see a major push coming from AI experts and others with vested interests in the electronic communications machinery that drives the Internet. In this techno-melting pot, there are key corporate players maintaining dominance when it comes to end-user participation. Yet closer to the proverbial coal-face of ordinary computer users, help-desk people with enough strategic engineering knowledge and skills are required to help us navigate from a unilateral desktop environment to an interactive Web-induced environment. Here, one's computer is dependent upon a distant machine to perform quite ordinary tasks, and to network (communicate) with other machines. However, funding agencies seem oblivious of the need to back the more visionary techno-geeks so as to capitalize on the benefits of distributed server-based Internet applications. After all, these extend those higher-end users to innovate collaborative desktop software platforms for the Internet, which in the end make ordinary computer users' lives easier.

There can be little doubt about the added value of interactive online learning support systems that have shown there is an immense attraction towards implementing ICT tools to enhance our learning potential. Some believe this rather new approach to increasing our experiential knowledge is now achievable through an enriched combination of Internet technology products. By combining the best of both worlds; that is, the client-side (customized operation) with the server-side (providing wider connectivity), we can see an emerging field that is being described by some techno-geeks as the *'Rich Internet Applications'* (sometimes referred to as RIAs). The current Internet technologies provide a range of powerful ICT tools that include: easier access, updating capability, scheduling of tasks, and flexible environments for both learning facilitators (teachers, corporate trainers) and students. There are three ICT elements that represent an RIA: rich client technology, server technology, and development tools.

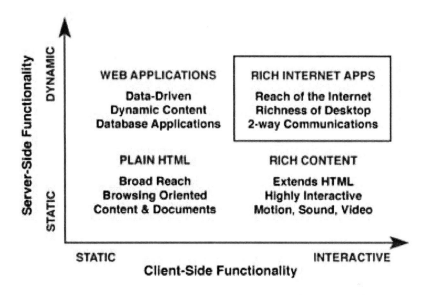

Figure 18 : Rich Internet Applications

Some believe that Rich Internet Applications are a natural progression from the earlier days of computing where the calculations, machine speed and logic were uppermost in software design. These days, the Neilsen heuristics, or rules of thumb that were developed for the (standalone) desktop environment in 1994, still apply in today's Web-mediated environment. *Table 4* shows how the Neilsen [3]heuristics that apply today.

Table 4 : Neilsen Heuristics and Rich Internet Applications

NEILSEN HEURISTICS Or rules of thumb	APPLICABILILTY TO RICH INTERNET APPLICATIONS (RIAs)
Visibility of system status – the system should always keep users informed about what is going on, through appropriate feedback within reasonable time.	RIAs should leverage the rich display capabilities to provide real-time status indicators whenever background processing requires the user to wait – including monitoring backend data processing, etc...
Match between system and the real world – the system should speak the users' language, with words, phrases and concepts familiar to the user, rather than system-oriented terms. Follow real world conventions, making information appear in a natural and logical order.	Understanding the user's vocabulary, context and expectations is key to presenting a system that matches their world. While RIAs offer novel metaphors, novelty often slows usefulness and usability – ensure they act consistently with their real-world counterparts. The user must remain in control.
User control and freedom – users often choose system functions by mistake and will need a clearly marked ‘*"emergency exit*’ to leave the unwanted stare without having to go through an extended dialogue. Support undo and redo.	Users are familiar with browser-based controls, including the back-button and location field. However using browser commands within an RIA may result in data loss. The RIA should include code that is aware and responsive to browser history.

Consistency and standards – users should not have to wonder whether different words, situations, or actions mean the same thing. Follow platform conventions.	All applications require consistency within their features, including terminology, layout, colour, and behaviour. Software branding guidelines also require solutions for a variety of customers.
Error prevention – even better than good error messages is a careful design which prevents a problem from occurring in the first place.	In forms, indicate required fields and formats with examples. Design the system so that it recognizes various input options (780.555.1212 vs 780-555-1212) rather than requiring the user to comply with an arbitrary format.
Recognition rather than recall – make objects, actions, and options visible. The user should not have to remember information from one part of the dialogue to another. Instructions for use of the system should be visible or easily retrievable whenever appropriate.	Limit the hide-and-seek approach with important interface elements. Don't hide controls that are key to user tasks. Revealing application controls on rollover or with a click can create exciting visual transitions, but will slow user tasks and create significant frustration.
Flexibility and efficiency of use – accelerators – unseen by the novice user – may often speed up the interaction for the expert user such that the system can cater to both inexperienced and experienced users. Allow users to tailor frequent actions.	RIAs can leverage the advanced functionality of the platform to provide accelerators such as keyboard shortcuts, type-ahead auto-completion, and automatic population of fields based on previously entered data or popularity of response. Less technical sophistication should also be available.
Aesthetic and minimalist design – dialogues should not contain information which is irrelevant or rarely needed. Every extra unit of information in a dialogue competes with the relevant units of information and diminishes their relative visibility.	For any given feature, style, or branding element, ask two key questions: *What is the return on investment for the business?* ; *what is the return on experience for the user?* ; *what value does the element contribute?* If a feature can be removed without seriously impacting ROI or ROE, remove it!
Help users recognize, diagnose, and recover from errors – error messages should be expressed in plain language (no codes), precisely indicate the problem, and constructively suggest a solution.	Error messages should hide technical information in favour of explaining in everyday language that an error occurred. References to *'missing objects'* or other development jargon will only frustrate users.
Help & documentation – even though it is better if the system can be used without documentation, it may be necessary to provide help and documentation. Any such information should be easy to search, focused on the user's tasks, list concrete steps to be carried out, and not be too large.	RIAs should contain simple and concise instructions, prompts, and cues embedded in the applications, prompts, and cues embedded in the application itself. More extensive help should be available from within the RIA.

However, ordinary people who are attracted to designing materials to take advantage of an RIA will need some guidance. Sadly, in the past the instructional qualities that are highly interactive, immersive and constructivist were ignored. Fortunately these days, there are many systems' developmental tools like Java, Flash, Dreamweaver, Virtual Reality Modeling Language (VRML) and X3D that have entered the web courseware design field. Because they are relatively easy to use, they re-establish the interest ordinary people have in taking the initiative to design their own information systems. The plethora of RIA attributes sit as a nexus between client-side technology and server-side functionality to include increasing the reach of the internet, and to enhancing desktop with two-way communications platforms.

Rich Client-Side Technology

The commonly used Flash player is a good example of how to provide all the benefits of the Web by keeping costs to a minimum (automatic compression and loading of components on demand). In addition, client-side scripting, high performance connectivity and real-time server communication are enhanced features. Refer to the previous table setting out how Neilsen's characteristics still apply in today's Internet environment, to explore the possibilities for capturing the efficiencies of *effective HCI*.

Server-Side Functionality

Normal mark-up languages connect the rich client-side technologies. For example, Web database language tools. Refer to Chapter-5 of this book for the full discussion on the dynamic server-side functionality.

Development Tools

Specialized tools offer an environment that provides the ability to create the various pieces of an application, from user interfaces to server-side logic. Staffing this type of ICT production event requires a mixture of IT professionals: an application architect to integrate the ICT tools into an existing environment, a multi-media expert to develop the interactive graphical user interface and communications service with the application server, and a web-designer in the initial stages of a system's development project: the latter to consult on the user interface specifications, and act as the conduit between the architect and multi-media practitioner.

Successful Rich Internet Applications can offer a range of benefits that include distributed, server-based internet applications that extend the interactive capabilities of desktop applications. As such, they should enhance the user's interactivity and manipulation of data, rather than behave as fancy graphical page-turners. They should provide the user with a real-time status check mechanism whenever background processing is underway. This way, informed users can understand and stay oriented during lengthy activities. Finally, because Rich Internet Applications can store client-side data, customisation of their interaction during a system processing cycle becomes possible.

Portability Devices

One of the most obvious changes in the techno-landscape is the wireless ability that enables us to go just about anywhere, taking our laptop devices to just about every corner of the planet. While many people have embraced the *'wireless fidelity'* (Wi-Fi) networks, there is still much room for improvement with the wireless connectivity standards and roaming technologies.   Wi-Fi is a *'local area network'* (LAN) technology, which the IEEE interoperability standard 802.11b applies to.   Products and networks which conform to this standard are built so that they will work together, regardless of make or model.   Anyone with a laptop or PDA that is complete with a network-card and within the 300-foot range, should be able to use the Wi-Fi network, to access the Internet for all the usual things ordinary people need to do on the Web. The Wi-Fi permits extraordinary portability.   The signal is generally stronger than a cell phone signal, and exhibit broadband connectivity rates that are far superior to the older dial-up (telephone-line) modems.   The trouble is, one has to be lucky to know where the effective hot spots are.   Notwithstanding homes with their own routers and businesses, the public places where you are most likely to gain access will be at airports, hotels, convention centres, cafés and shopping malls.   At such places there may be a substantial access charge.   Meanwhile, due to the enormous cost of fixing the roaming difficulties that users experience when they wander away from the hot spot, may take quite a long while to improve.

Techno-transportability is all very well as there is still a lot more to be done to secure our transmissions.   For instance: the *'Wired Equivalent Privacy'* (WEP) uncovered there are still many weaknesses in the standard security technology deployed with embryonic Wi-Fi.   To this end vendors are working on enhancing the security of wireless networks.   As a result, technologies such as *'Wi-Fi Protected Access'* (WPA) solutions are available as protocols to enhance cross-vendor support for wireless security.

Knowledge Squirreling

There can be no question that today's free ranging computing devices directly feed our tendency to hoard.   The delight we have for collecting huge amounts of information is hard to resist.   Like little squirrels, we collect our Internet tit-bits for that rainy day; because we know that we won't remember where we saw such-and-such.   The easiest place to find knowledge squirrels at their best can be seen in the corporate sector. Perhaps the reason is that someone else is paying for the storage vessels.   Nevertheless, knowledge-hoarding [4] forms part and parcel of the coercive power that often underpins organizational cultures [5].   In keeping with this is the notion that these days, we can easily buy data storage devices that either dangle off computers or are included with the regular system's architecture.   We have certainly come a long way since the storage capacity of the 8inch floppy disks that stored 80 Kb.   Look through the range of secondary storage devices these days.   It's mind boggling.   Even the ordinary user now describes their electronic filing devices according to the number of gigs (gigabytes). Where is all this hoarding leading us?

To the rescue, for the moment.   *'Universal Serial Bus'* (USB) technology has created quite a storm in the secondary storage industry.   A USB flash drive is a compact memory drive that acts like a portable hard drive, letting one store and transport one's most precious computer data.   These tiny devices can resemble anything from a rather flat clothes-peg to a piece of kitsch-jewelry.   They hold incredibly large amounts of information and are small enough, at about the size of a pack of gum, to slip easily into one's pocket.

Telework

A natural progression of the increase in portability of our techno-landscape means that people are choosing to not only play with their laptops anywhere, anytime, but also choosing to seriously change their work-habits, and work from a distance. Once again, and notwithstanding the cost of the equipment and *'Internet Service Provider'* (ISP) connection fees, the type of work one can do at a distance is only limited by the imagination. The linguistics for describing this include: remote access, remote work, mobilise, eWork, telecommuting, and of course plain old working from home. No matter what words are used to describe this environment, an equally new hypothetical attitude from the industry sector is to view working off-line as enabling them to maximise their profit and productivity, by supporting and effectively managing the performance of work in non-traditional work-places. Unfortunately, the reality is a little different. Working from home, on the surface may well be about (business) resilience in the face of change, and getting the most out of available resources. Nothing much is said about the possibilities of a wash-back effect, of the additional costs for the household. Remote help-desk facilities are often not geared to manage people working offline. As the equipment increases in sophistication, so do the number of things that can go wrong with the software. Printers need specialist care, Internet access can be difficult to set up, networking facilities can fail or be withdrawn, hard-drives can crash, etc, etc.

Mobile Phones

Walk down the street of a major city in Australia and you will soon see how the community relies on mobile phones. You wouldn't be blamed for thinking that virtually everyone carries a cell phone these days. People use them everywhere. Interestingly enough the Japanese transport system displays notices that ban the use of them, because they tend to disturb other patrons. No longer is a mobile phone just a mobile phone. Their digital enhancements include things like: mega-pixel cameras, *'quick-response-code'* (QR) code capability, and video functionality. People can buy a phone that virtually behaves as a mini-computer. Consider how easy it is to receive eMails, update your corporate diary to keep track of your appointments, and know that you have every phone number and personal details on your phone that also reflect your corporate address book. These devices are said to be on the threshold of metamorphosing the whole portable telecommunication landscape.

The mobile-technologies offer many opportunities for eBusiness. For instance, India is reporting 13 million cellular subscribers, around two million limited radius mobile users and close to 41 million fixed-line subscribers. They expect to have 120 million mobile users by 2008. However, service provision is problematic. Around the world there are duo-band, tri-band and then there is the Japanese system that won't connect to anybody else.

Podcasting

In the Beginning

Web-based broadcasting means the sending and receiving of audio files. To add to the excitement and perhaps more importantly for HCI is the distribution of visual information, through music video streaming and interactive synchronous online discussion. The term podcasting is derived from the combination of content (audio files) and delivery mechanism (casting or feeding the signal) for playback on mobile MP3 devices or personal computers. The podcast host or author is known as the podcaster. To access the most up to date information on podcasting readers of this book should access the Internet.

For instance: Web-sites like http://en.wikipedia.org/wiki/Podcasting, provide entries by techno-lay people writing interesting articles on the latest trends in this exciting ICT tool. To participate in a podcast you may need to download (or stream) the multi-media files. These days this process is automatic through software that reads the *'really simple syndication'* (RSS) or Atom web-feed technology. RSS now commonly refers to the following standards:

- Really Simple Syndication (RSS 2.0)
- Rich Site Summary (RSS 0.91, RSS 1.0)
- RDF Site Summary (RSS 0.9 and 1.0)

RSS formats are specified in *'Extensible Markup Language'* XML (a generic specification for data formats). RSS delivers its information as an XML file that can be called: an RSS feed, webfeed, RSS stream, or RSS channel.

It may be interesting to note that the editors of the New Oxford American Dictionary declared podcasting the 2005th word of the year, defining the term as a digital recording of a radio broadcast or similar program, made available on the Internet for downloading to a personal audio player.

Podcasting Mechanics

The publish/subscribe model of podcasting is a version of *'push technology'*, in that the information provider chooses which files to offer in a feed and the subscriber chooses among available feed channels. While the user is not *'pulling'* individual files from the Web, there is a strong *'pull'* aspect in that the receiver is free to subscribe to (or unsubscribe from) a vast array of channels. Earlier Internet *'push'* services (PointCast) allowed a much more limited selection of content.

Podcasting involves the latter *'pulled'* XML files to contain the Internet addresses of the relevant media files. In general, these files are transferred from a server to a client-computer. These files may contain audio or video, but could be any of the following file formats: images, text (and *'portable document format'* (PDF)s that use a postscript definition language to capture an image of your text).

A podcast is generally analogous to a recorded television or radio series. The content provider begins by making a file (for example, an MP3 audio file) available on the Internet. This is usually done by posting the file on a publicly available webserver. However, BitTorrent trackers also have been used, and it is not technically necessary that the file be publicly accessible. The only requirement is that the file be accessible through some known L (a general-purpose Internet address). This file is often referred to as *'one episode'* of a podcast.

The content provider then acknowledges the existence of that file by referencing it in another file known as *'the feed'*. The feed is a list of the URLs by which episodes of the podcasted how may be accessed. This list is usually published in RSS format (although Atom can also be used), which provides other information, such as publish dates, titles, and accompanying text descriptions of the series and each of its episodes. The feed may contain entries for all episodes in the series, but is typically limited to a short list of the most recent episodes, as is the case with many news feeds. Standard podcasts consist of a feed from one author. More recently multiple authors have been able to contribute episodes to a single podcast feed using concepts such as public podcasting and social podcasting.

The content provider posts the feed on a web server. The location at which the feed is posted is expected to be permanent. This location is known as the feed URL (or, perhaps more often, feed *'uniform resource locator'* URL). The content provider makes this feed URL known to the intended audience.

A consumer uses a type of software known as an aggregator to subscribe to and manage their feeds.

A podcast specific aggregator is usually an always-on program which starts when the computer is started and runs in the background. It works exactly like any newsreader someone would use to manage other web subscriptions. It manages a set of feed URLs added by the user and downloads each at a specified interval, such as every two hours. If the feed data has significantly changed from when it was previously checked (or if the feed was just added to the application's list), the program determines the location of the most recent item and automatically downloads it to the user's computer. Interestingly, it is estimated that perhaps only 20% of podcasts are actually consumed on portable media players. 80% are consumed on the PC on to which they are downloaded. Some applications, such as iTunes, also automatically make the newly downloaded episodes available to a user's portable media player.

The downloaded episodes can then be played, replayed, or archived as with any other computer file.

To conserve bandwidth, users may opt to search for content using an online podcast directory. Some directories allow people to listen online and initially become familiar with the content provided from an RSS feed before deciding to subscribe. For most broadband users the good news is that bandwidth is generally not a major consideration. It could fairly be stated that podcasting itself is a technology that came with the increases in global bandwidth and broadband popularity.

We are sitting at a digital threshold. Anyone with the right equipment is getting into this new way of receiving their information. Podcasts are popular because anyone with a microphone, computer, software and an Internet connection can produce one themselves.

Visionary Information Interface

Let there be no doubt about it, we are sitting at a digital threshold [1]. Businesses are quickly getting into the podcast-marketing act. They're installing Web-sites dedicated to promotional material that can be played and replayed. What a perfect way to distribute advertising material. Currently podcast-marketing is being used to sell anything from Starbucks, to marketing swimming events that promote the latest trend in swimwear. The more visionary marketing involves interactive podcasting, providing customers with the ability to search and respond to direct podcast mail-outs.

In the schools and Universities opinion varies on the effectiveness of podcasting-lectures, classroom events and the like. Surely when the dust does settle, and it will, a 40-minute lecture that imparts information in a passive absorption manner, will still be able to bore the socks off the students: especially if the instructional strategies really require a more exploratory architecture. In terms of the *human-dimensions of HCI* in an educational setting, the *machine-dimension* becomes a little more complicated.

Developing multi-media may not be so easy for some academics, who don't necessarily posses the IT skill to develop their own materials. As a consequence their support infrastructure needs to include one-to-one support by a Web-developer for the production of high grade digital learning materials.

ICT Tools

In the Beginning

Examine how the techno-linguistics change over time to describe our computing environment. At first, back at the beginning of the computer-age we used words to denote the pieces of a computer that carried out mathematical calculations and tabulations easier and faster than a human could. Often we associated the inventor with their machine; like the historical 1834 *Babbage analytical engine*, and the 1890 *Hollerith tabulator* that tabulated statistics with punched cards. Then we saw the age of automation that saw the processing machine shrink to give us a whole new set of terms to describe how a microprocessor could respond to electrical impulses, causing them to open and close circuits zillions of times per second. We looked on while this emerging microchip technology changed the techno-landscape for ever, for instance, microchip signals that generate the liquid crystal display in a computer-controlled (digital) watch.   There were endless discoveries that showed us how to use microprocessors to expand our data storage.   The electronic diary entered our vocabulary. Perhaps this was about the time we commenced the techno-dialogue about information, and where the discourse took different professional paths. On the one hand, computer scientists claimed the machine/operation level of HCI. However, they have remained in the hard-science fraternity alongside physics, chemistry, biology, etc. On the other hand, social scientists, known for their softer nomenclature, seem to accept the notion of information as a social entity. That seems to fit into the genres that relate to the humanities.

During the 1980's, 90's and onwards, we referred to the information-age as a term that applied to the period where movement of information became faster than physical movement. Under conventional worldly economic theory, the information-age also heralded the era where information was considered to be a scarce resource and its capture and distribution generated competitive advantage. At this time, the information system was recognized as a computerized system in which the data stored would be used in spontaneous ways that were not fully predictable in advance. This contrasted to a routine data-processing system that may be set up separately. Both are required, since needs are different in terms of speed of processing versus flexibility of access to data.   This is where the definitions become tricky, because the genre lines were beginning to blur. In some universities information technology (IT) courses were delivered from Business faculties while in others *'information systems'* (IS) courses were housed in the mathematics and computer science faculties.

These days information technology is a broad subject that is concerned with the use of technology in managing and processing information, especially in large organizations In particular, IT deals with the use of electronic computers and computer software to convert, store, protect, process, transmit, and retrieve information. For that reason, computer professionals are often called IT specialists or *"business process consultants"*, and the division of a company or university that deals with software technology is sometimes called the IT department. Other names for the latter are IS or *'management information services'* (MIS), *'managed service providers'* (MSP).

In the United Kingdom education system, information technology was formally integrated into the school curriculum when the National Curriculum was devised. It was quickly realised that the work covered was useful in all subjects. With the arrival of the Internet and the broadband connections to all schools, the application of IT knowledge, skills and understanding in all subjects became a reality. This change in emphasis has resulted in a change of name from *'Information Technology'* to *'Information and Communications Technology'* (ICT). ICT tools in the education sector can be understood as the application of digital equipment to all aspects of learning and teaching. It is present in almost all schools and is of growing influence. The growth of use of ICT and its tools in the field of Education has seen tremendous growth in the recent past. Although the educationalists refer only to *'technology'*, ICT tools have certainly entered the classroom in a big way, and have become part of a teaching and learning process.

The term *'ICT'* appears to have completely replaced IT and IS. Is this because finally we have dropped the genre ownership? Or is it just that the linguistics are now complete? People understand they don't need to talk at length about the bits and bytes. Speed and other technical aspects are only discussed by techno-geeks when it's a necessary part of the technical context. Instead ICT tools have a broader following. For instance there is a distinct government-level techno-ownership.   There are countless visionary ICT tool articles, without even a whimper of IT or IS.   The understanding has come of age.   Finally, we have the community's acceptance of *'information and communications'* (with its relevance to *'telecommunications'*) that brings forward the engineering fraternity to sit amongst the computer scientists.

Visionary Information Interface

ICT tools embody the full range of multi-media technologies. The ICT genre has arrived. ICT tools now extend to encompass the entire HCI domain. ICT tools are seen by the international community as an increasingly powerful set of techno-aids for participating in global markets, and promoting political accountability. It is well understood that the ICT tools are set to improve the delivery of basic services and enhancing local development opportunities. However, without innovative ICT policies, questions are arising among governments' policy makers.   Will many people in developing countries, especially the poor, be left behind? Because of this attitude, the *'United Nations Development Program'* (UNDP) was formed to help countries draw on expertise and best practices from around the world, in the hopes that they might develop strategies that expand access to ICT tools and harness them for development. Working in 166 countries, UNDP also relies on ICT solutions to make the most effective use of its own global network.

When Can We Banish the eWord?

We won't need to banish the terms: eBusiness, eCommerce, eLearning and e-everything else, because it will be understood by the majority of the community that they qualify the context in which ICT tools engineer the HCI. Maybe overtime, like the disappearing IT and IS words, the eWords will also vanish from our vocabulary.

To keep our narrative writing style free from heavily laden techno-terms, this chapter's '*machine-side view HCI*' was told through a social-contextual lens. Nevertheless, we can attribute understanding our clever machines to the following:

- never lose sight of the importance of historical context to explain machine-dimension of HCI
- IEEE standards do try to keep everyone on track
- '*Rich Internet Applications*' reflect the maturing machine-side of the IT industry
- portability and podcasting are the currently newest pins in the techno-landscape

Chapter Reference List

[1]   Bradley, G., *Social and Community Informatics: Humans on the Net*, 2006. NY: Routledge.265
[2]   Castro, E., *HTML for the World Wide Web*. 4 ed. 2000, CA: Peachpit - Addison Wesley Longman. 384.
[3]   McMullin, J. and Skinner, G., *Usability Heuristics for Rich Internet Applications*. 2007.
[4]   Walters, J., *Dismantling a Culture of Knowledge-Hoarding. Viewed 19/01/08 from*
      http://www.refresher.com/!jswhoarding.html. 2003, The CEO Refresher: Brain food for Business.
[5]   Luthan, F., *Organizational Behavior*. 1985, NY: McGraw-Hill.

Chapter-4

Problem Solving Through HCI

Thus far our introduction to *effective HCI* has been identified and treated as separate chapters. This was chosen as a deliberate strategy to highlight the emerging voice from the *human-dimensions of HCI* to strengthen the social context of applied computing. The book's narrative from this point on combines these often disparate views of HCI.

Interaction for Computer-Aided Learning

Our journey towards finding an information nirvana has thus far set out to convey the context of the *human-dimensions of HCI*. The saga commenced therefore with a retrospective glance at the past to understand why we might be doing particular techno-things that have otherwise become entrenched. In chapters-2 and -3 we hovered over the dualistic nature of the human-machine techno-carriageway, and teased out an argument for the largely forgotten *human-dimensions of HCI*. In chapter-4 I attempt to describe the ways people engage with their digital artefacts.

In the Beginning

In days gone by, computer aided learning *(or otherwise called CAL)* was one of the most commonly used terms to describe techno-learning environments. In reality nobody was really sure what it meant. It possibly came from the 1980's when people recognized that machines could be used to automate learning resources. Confusion continued through the 1990s where CAL was thought to mean practically anything from the single, monolithic computer program to sets of software programs designed to increase the reach of traditional delivery media. These might include, for example, a lecture series for the educational sector, or industry-based training courses. As time went on course developers were offering new terms to add to the confusion. *Table 5* represents how Gloria Gery showed that people were mixing and matching the possibilities of using technology in learning programs in their attempts to launch interactivity between the facilitation media and the participant.

The trouble is that we have many different ways to describe the techno-learning-vista. One way to understand the complexity of the computer-based training (CBT) environment would be to say:

> *"An interactive learning experience between a learner and a computer in which the computer provides the majority of the stimulus, {in which} the learner must respond, and the computer {then} analyses the response and provides feedback to the learner."* [1]:6

Table 5 : Interactivity of Media and People

MEDIUM	ACTION	ENVIRONMENT
Computer	Assisted	Instruction
	Aided	Learning
	Managed	Education
	Based	Training
	Enhanced	Teaching
	Mediated	Development
	Interactive	Study
Select one from each column		

Her explanation holds true even today. CBT is difficult to define because we still have not yet embraced the potential for effective human learning through well placed techno-pedagogies. These days we face even more choice through the advent of multi-media. As time progresses more techno-tools are added to the mix in a generic techno-grab bag. The trouble with this approach is that not enough people take the time to investigate whether their instructional strategies and delivery media align with the learning context. For instance, whether they are intending to implement an interactive learning experience; with no regard for the type of learning design, and much less for the architecture.

Setting up a Learning House

It is essential however to differentiate between the type of learning and the technical means that brings forward an instructional architecture to support it. Let us use the analogy of designing specifications for building a house. In this, we have an overarching purpose to provide specific prescriptions for the building process. We create different rooms for different purposes. For instance, we usually design a kitchen in which to cook, bathrooms where we can attend to body cleanliness, and bedrooms for sleeping. Similarly we can describe experiential learning environments, by taking a close look at the type of learning activities that are required to prepare a learner to develop their knowledge and skill.

Differentiate the Type of Learning

Some people say there are different views of learning. Nevertheless, let us look firstly at ways to think about types (or views) of learning. We will then discuss some learning architectures that can be implemented to support various types of learning experience.

The Absorption View of Learning

One prevalent view of learning is the passive absorption view. We need to be clear about how to differentiate between learning and instruction. Learning in this view, is about assimilating information; while instruction is about providing information to learners. Some call this a *'transmission'* view of teaching [2]. Courses that rely on lectures or videotapes to transmit information generally reflect this view. Why are transmission-type courses so common? I believe it's because: (1) they are the easiest to prepare, (2) they are a common teaching model that many have adopted from their educational experiences and, (3) some trainers lack an understanding of the active nature of learning.

The Behavioural View of Learning

In the first part of the 20th Century, behavioural psychology promoted a different view: one that considered learning to be based on the acquisition of mental associations. In this view learning is about correct responses to questions and instruction is about providing small chunks of information followed by questions and corrective feedback. In the course of making many small correct responses, learners build large chains of new knowledge. The behavioural view is reflected in programmed instruction and many traditional instructional design approaches that emphasize bottom-up sequencing of instruction, short lessons, and frequent reinforcement in the form of feedback.

The Cognitive View of Learning

In the last part of the 20th Century, learning was again re-conceptualized. This time the emphasis was on the active processes learners use to construct new knowledge. This construction requires an integration of new incoming information from the environment with existing knowledge in memory. In the cognitive view, learning is about active construction of new knowledge by interacting with new information, while instruction is about promoting the psychological processes that mediate that construction.

Differentiate the Instructional Architecture

Although the active construction of knowledge is commonly accepted today as the mechanism for learning, that construction can be fostered through four diverse instructional environments [3]. We can refer to these as the four architectures (receptive, directive, guided-discovery, and exploratory). Each of these unique instructional architectures reflects the different views of the learning context. They also require different prescriptions to enhance the effectiveness of their particular instructional architecture.

Receptive Architecture

Reflecting a transmission view of learning, a receptive architecture is characterized by an emphasis on providing information. The information may be in the form of words and pictures, both still and animated. A good metaphor for the receptive architecture is that the learner is a sponge and the instruction pours out knowledge to be absorbed. In some forms of receptive instruction, such as lectures or video lessons, learners have minimal control over the pacing or sequencing of the training. In other situations such as a text assignment, learners control the pace and can select the topics in the book of interest to them. Some examples of this architecture include a traditional (non-interactive) lecture, an instructional video, or a text assignment. Some eLearning programs known as *"page turners"*, which lack interactivity, also embody this architecture.

CD-ROM programs are designed to build awareness and enthusiasm for the new *Iridium satellite-supported communications system.* These programs can involve video, animated diagrams, and audio to describe the benefits and features of the new system. Very little learner interaction is involved since the goal is to provide information, not build skills. These include non-interactive lectures, instructional video, and text assignments. At the time this book was being prepared for publication the following Web-sites were available as good examples; see

http://www.swish22.com/flash.html .. basketball instruction
http://www.digidesign.com/disk/diskflix/ .. sound instructional modules

Directive Architectures

Directive architectures reflect a behavioral view of learning. The assumption is that learning occurs by the gradual building of skills starting from the most basic and progressing to more advanced levels in an hierarchical manner. The lessons present small chunks of knowledge and provide frequent opportunities for learners to respond to related questions. Immediate corrective feedback is used to ensure that accurate associations are made. The goal is to minimize the aversive consequences of making errors which are believed to promote incorrect associations. Programmed instruction, popular in the 50's and 60's, is a prime example of a directive architecture. Such lessons were originally presented in books but soon migrated to computer delivery. In programmed instruction, short content segments are followed by questions and corrective feedback. Many random eLessons designed to teach software skills use a directive architecture.

In this type of instruction there may be a sequence of lessons where the learner is guided step-by-step with a demonstration followed by a simulation practice. In some cases, if the learner makes a mistake during the practice, immediate feedback can be provided as a hint, encouraging the learner to try again. Typical of directive architectures, the lesson topics present small tasks and the lessons progress from simple to complex tasks. Directive architectures are based on deductive models of learning in which general principles or definitions are followed by specific examples and practice applying the principles. At the time this book was being prepared for publication the following Web-sites were available as good examples; see

http://www.candletech.com/ .. Candle making instructions
http://www.santosha.com/asanas/asana.html .. Yoga postures

Guided Discovery Architecture

Guided discovery uses job-realistic problems to drive the learning process. Learners typically access various sources of data to resolve problems and have instructional support (sometimes called scaffolding) available to help them. Unlike the directive architecture, guided discovery offers learners opportunities to try alternatives, make mistakes, experience consequences of those mistakes, reflect on their results, and revise their approach. The goal of guided discovery is to promote construction of mental models by helping learners experience the results of decisions made in the context of solving realistic cases and problems. Guided discovery designs are based on inductive models of learning; that is, learning of concepts and principles from experience with specific cases and problems.

Guided discovery eCourses can be designed to teach business processes, like instructing loan agents on how to gather information and make recommendations.

After getting an assignment to research a new loan applicant, the learner can access many sources of information. This may include, inter alia, literature on the industry, credit checks, references, and interviews with the client. In the screen shown, the learner is requesting a credit check. Coaching is available from a learning agent who provides tips and advice as needed. At any point the learner can compare their solution path to that of an expert and make adjustments. The learner continues to collect and record data, following a structured loan approval process. When they have collected sufficient data, learners write up a loan funding recommendation with supporting justification and submit it to the loan committee. At the time this book was being prepared for publication the following Web-sites were available as good examples; see

http://owl.english.purdue.edu/owl/ .. Online services
http://school.discovery.com/ .. Educational resources (free)
http://curriculumfutures.org/instruction/a02-04a.html .. Textual lesson plan
http://www.wavelengthmagazine.com/2005/dj05newdir.php .. Safe environments for skill development

Exploratory Architecture

Also known as open-ended learning, the exploratory architectures rely on a cognitive view of learning. Clarke identified that out of the four instructional architectures, the exploratory models offer the most effective opportunities for providing high levels of learner control. Instruction should therefore be designed to provide a rich set of instructional/learning resources including: learning content, examples, demonstrations, and knowledge/skills building exercises that are complete with the means to navigate the materials. Architectures of this type are frequently used for online courseware.

The Ongoing Lack of User Friendliness

Despite what we already understand as discussed above, the barriers to online learning remains a sticking point. People will say that Web-based instructional packages are poorly designed. They will call for a better understanding by the techno-educational designers, to lift their game and deliver appropriate specifications for increasing the usability of their learning materials. Generally speaking we need to improve the instruction strategies which drive these CAL environments. These days the industry sector leads the way with their expertise in interactive CAL. They champion better quality HCI products for the learning community per se. Chief among the industries concerned are, financial service providers, the automotive industry and general retailing to an ever-growing consumer public.

Constructivist Strategies Counterbalance Passive Environments

It doesn't take a rocket scientist to discover that people prefer their learning to involve active participation rather than taking a passive approach. In the latter, they may be expected to absorb the content of textual descriptions, video clips or a lecture about the learning task at hand. We all have different perspectives on how we participate. It is through this individualised approach for digesting the information that is put before us that creates and builds upon our sense of knowledge. As such the learner becomes the central player, casting out the context for their learning environment; that is, an environment that will work for them personally.

Current literature is awash with articles that promote the constructivists' strategies. These are designed to engage people with interactive activities to promote higher-level learning experiences. Much is known about the importance of developing personal meaning within an online learning context. Heinich [4] sums up this body of knowledge by saying that:

> *"Learning is the development of new knowledge, skills and attitudes as the learner interacts with information and the environment".* ([5] p:20).

Other constructivists speak about the different kinds of interaction that promotes learning at different levels. This approach is typical of the situated-learning environment whereby learners construct their knowledge after having received their techno-learning experiences through active participation at the appropriate level. With each interaction shown [5] *(Figure 19)* we can see the need for separate strategies for instructional experiences at each level:

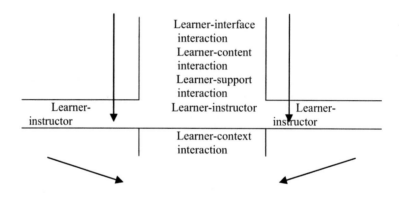

Figure 19 : Strategies for Instructional Experiences

Atsusi Hirumi [6] proposes a three-level framework for classifying eLearning interactions. This illustrates how the above framework may be used to design and sequence electronic learning interactions, and to analyze planned interactions that may reduce the need for costly revisions of instructional materials. Hirumi's level one finds the learner engaged in self-interaction, where the learner monitors and regulates their own learning processing. Level two interactions involve the learner with human and non-human interactions. Hirumi's level three reflects just the interaction with the instruction, consisting of activities that involve the learner in achieving the learning outcomes.

Two Modes of Learning

Notwithstanding the constructivists' emphasis on the need to create individualised knowledge discovery learning contexts, let us discuss the interactivity of the knowledge levels of the learning task at hand. We need to pause here, to think about the support that may be required in problem-solving experiential learning. In some instances a learner may face something in the HCI /types of problem solving tasks. The learner is expected to configure their own understanding of a new learning experience, to solve the task at hand. The HCI interface should therefore promote the learner's awareness for the need to reflect upon their existing experiential knowledge and to deal with solving the task at hand.

Such an environment requires the learner to adapt and accumulate an understanding of the subject domain. This while simultaneously acquiring the capacity for making efficient and sophisticated problem-solving decisions.

Context for Collaborative Problem Solving

In an ideal world, Web-mediated information systems should enhance dissemination and global accessibility. Furthermore, some of us believe the Internet should promote distributed people to work in a collaborative manner. In the past this type of distributed work group has required some form of physical collaborative system, usually configured to provide two ways of working together. First, through direct communication and collaboration, and second, by indirect communication through shared artefacts and common workplaces [7]. As such, collaborative systems can be created to run in different environments, adapted to cater for different groups of users, and made to be usable for various tasks. Moreover, small group instruction in a traditional face-to-face context can also be implemented with people over a distance using Web-mediated technology [8]. However, in drawing on an ICT tool-set as the vehicle for creating a successful collaborative climate, it should be noted that Web-mediated collaboration is very different from the collaboration in face-to-face instruction. For instance, face-to-face collaboration typically makes use of a rich variety of verbal and non-verbal cues, such as facial expressions, glances, tones, and hand gestures. By virtue of the enforced separation of people, Web-mediated collaboration will lack sufficient perceptual clues. It has been shown by many of the educational technologists who are the front runners in dealing with online collaborative learning, that this lack of the usual communication framework is not only awkward. It is also quite stilted and can be extremely frustrating compared to face-to-face settings [9]. In Web-mediated collaborative events, there should be some capacity for visual and audio communications to enable this seemingly natural tendency (at least in some cultures) that humans tend to eye-ball their communications partner for a conceptual acknowledgement and/or agreement/disagreement!

It has been proposed that one advantage of face-to-face group communication is the tendency for a more effective interaction to occur than in computer-mediated groups, despite the fact that the former tends to deviate from the task at hand. These breaks in concentration provide humans with the opportunity to relax and attend to the emotional needs of the group that may only be noticed through visual cues. Furthermore, people engaged in Web-mediated information systems have broader discussions than the face-to-face groups [10]. Face-to-face interaction can involve effective sequential problem solving activities. It is thus suggested that Web-mediated facilitation can become focused on solving general disagreements rather than on the questions at hand. Therefore, it should be understood when Web-mediated collaboration is applied to the education/training sectors, the instructional context is quite dissimilar to the collaborative context of a more traditional instructional setting. Because of this, carefully planned Web-mediated instructional strategies need to be devised to ensure that the people participating benefit as much as from the more traditional type of physical collaborative setting; that is, where face-to-face communication takes place [5].

In order to achieve the effective use of Web-mediated collaborative strategies, behavioural changes in the patterns of learning among group participants should be well understood. Further research is needed to determine how people learn in a technology based collaborative setting, and more specifically how they accomplish common tasks while involved in Web-mediated information systems. Much more work is needed on the effects of HCI and the interactivity of the learning process [11]. The key to understanding collaborative learning lies in understanding the rich interaction between individual students [12].

Collaborative Tools

When it comes to describing collaborative knowledge sharing on the Internet these days, people can become entrenched in the terminology. How easy it is to forget that we have all been using collaborative tools in our everyday lives for many years. Consider how accustomed we are to sharing our problems over the telephone with a friend. In the same sense, collaborative technology tools provide a shared digital experiential platform. Here, people can reconstruct their thoughts to generate new meanings. It's relatively easy to find techno-tools that enable people to come together using common off the shelf communication packages. It helps things along if one has a Web-camera to transmit an image of one speaking, while tapping into the computer. These live shows distributed through an Internet connection are becoming quite common amongst the techno-geeks as well as more common folk. The ICT tools are now so advanced that we can choose between real-time *'synchronous'* communication sessions where there is a two way flow of information, and the *'asynchronous'* ones that are delayed where the information is saved and may be received at another time. While it may be a new revelation to the IS/IT focused reader, at one point, educational technologists were filling up the literature with research papers that explain the differences between synchronous and asynchronous communication episodes.

Synchronous

Figure 20 depicts a typical synchronous communication model. Notice the continuous stream of data passing from the sender to the receiver. This is a reasonably typical way to describe the communication transaction leaving a sender, travelling directly to the receiver. On the phone for instance, it may become congested if two people talk together.

With synchronous communication, the talker mostly waits for some sign that their speech has been received. Over the phone, non visual acknowledgement from the receiver of the message may take many forms of hearable communication techniques; like uttering a *"Hmm"* or taking a breath. Over the Internet, synchronous feedback comes in many different forms. When using a camera attached to one's computer, there are all the usual ways that we can indicate agreement or otherwise; like raising an eyebrow and twisting one's head, or looking downwards while one thinks. The beauty of our digital communications landscape means that we can also store these precious moments for later retrieval.

Asynchronous

When the receiver's wait for a response extends to another communication session the flow of data/ideas becomes sporadic. This is known as asynchronous message transmission. The messages may leave the sender to be interrupted through a digital storage device, which means there may be a considerable passage of time before the receiver joins in. Typical asynchronous models can be found in threaded Internet discussion boards, where people take turns to respond in their own time. These delayed responses may also be sent to multiple people, who in turn respond at another time. eMailing is an example of this type of communication.

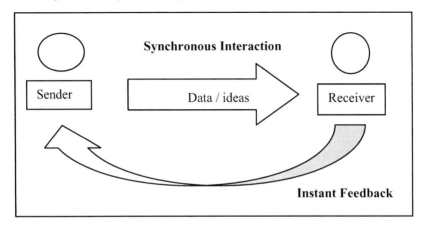

Figure 20 : Synchronous communication Model

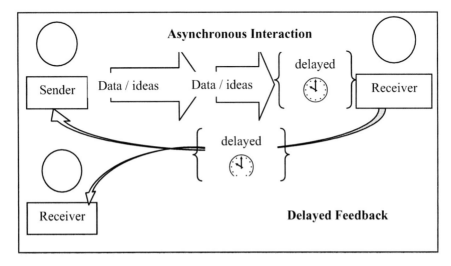

Figure 21 : Asynchronous Model

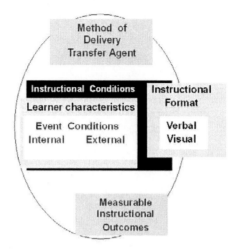

Figure 22 : Meta-Knowledge Process Model

Is There a Case for Blending Strategies?

Due to the iterative nature of interactive knowledge acquisition and online knowledge-sharing, collaborative problem solving promotes innovative solutions that may not be possible through a synchronous communication framework. One way to see what is happening is to model an eLearning environment using a high-level or meta-knowledge tool[13] *(Figure 22)*. In many ways we are facing a completely new educational paradigm.

   This model brings together the components of an online learning event. It shows how the *Method of Delivery* component directs the *Instructional Conditions* according to the results of a *Learner's Characteristics* (which could include cognitive style, or learning preferences), and the learning *Event Conditions*.   (These could include embedded strategies that help the learner cope with the complexity of processing the learning content).   In this model, the *Method of Delivery* component has a direct relationship with the *Measurable Instructional Outcomes* (which may change interactively throughout a learning session). It should be noted here that the directions for the choice of *Instructional Format* are given by the *Method of Delivery Transfer Agent* (which could be the learner themselves and/or a techno-agent).

   In one sense, online learning environments may facilitate a type of distributed cognition. Because of this, researchers must develop knowledge-mediation strategies permitting both the learning facilitators and the learners themselves to reflect and revise understandings. To this end, the online learning system they use will need to have a collaborative memory that can manage the communications. One method is to use an intelligent chat-type window, with a knowledge-sharing capacity to manage and edit information entered by learners and their instructors. Consequently, each learner can reflect on their asynchronous collaborative activities, which at times may involve other people as they participate in interactive knowledge sharing activities. The challenge for courseware designers is therefore to be engaged with information technologies. Technologies that will help find practical solutions to the dilemma of dealing with multi-media platforms. The range of media includes: text, graphics, and the newer digital streaming technologies which support video. However, while multi-sensory instruction is known to improve a learner's capacity to learn effectively, to-date the overarching role of knowledge-mediated HCI has been poorly understood.

A Matter of Gender

In the Beginning

Although it may not be so obvious unless you go looking through the gender balance literature, women have indeed been actively involved during the early history of computers. They leave an impressive trail commencing in the mid 1800's with Lady Ada Lovelace's pioneering procedure for the Babbage calculating engine to calculate Bernoulli numbers. The Bernoulli numbers B_n are a sequence of signed rational numbers that can be defined by the identity, the first two numbers are both 1 and any term further on than the second, is the sum of the previous two:

$$\frac{x}{e^x - 1} \equiv \sum_{n=0}^{\infty} \frac{B_n \, x^n}{n!} \, .$$

These numbers arise in the series expansions of trigonometric functions, and are extremely important in number theory and analysis. They are used in astronomy and biology as well. Although it may not have been recognized at the time, Lady Ada's calculation method was the first computer program. Further on, Grace Hopper developed the first computer compiler during the 1900's. She was also one of the developers of the *'Common Business-Oriented Language'* (COBOL), which to this day is still widely used. Although scientists were describing mechanical bugs in those early days, it was the moth that was caught in one of Grace Hopper's computer relays that became known as the original computer program bug. Throughout the history of computing, women (mostly self taught) were advancing the practical applications of the emerging digital technology. The *'Electronic Numerical Integrator and Computer'* now fondly remembered simply as ENIAC was programmed during World War II, primarily by six women. ENIAC was the first large-scale, electronic, digital computer capable of being programmed and reprogrammed to solve a full range of computing problems. Previous 'computers' had been built with only some of these properties. It was the ENIAC that was designed and built to calculate artillery firing tables for the U.S. Army's Ballistics Research Laboratory. The first problems run on the ENIAC however, were related to the design of the hydrogen bomb.

With this early success, it's not so surprising that women's involvement in computing continues today [14]. These days the inspiring line-up of women in IT sets an impressive bench-mark for gender balance in the business sector. As fine role-models they hold the top positions in business IT. Some examples are: Carly Fiorina of Hewlett Packard, Meg Whitman of eBay, Anne Mulcahy of Xerox and Patricia Russo of Lucen. Furthermore it's not difficult to see there are literally thousands of women engaged in some form of computing. Institutions founded by women for women include: the Anita Borg Institute for Women and Technology, the Association for Women in Computing, the Committee on the Status of Women in Computing Research, *'Association for Computing Machinery'* (ACM)'s, and Committee on Women in Computing. There are even some groups who adopt titles that reflect a more jovial stance: *"GirlGeeks"* and *"AusWIT"* (*Australian Women in IT*). These groups provide support, community and information for the women who are present in all aspects of computing. Unfortunately, although women are present in all facets of computer usage and IT, their presence is small compared to their presence in the workforce. For women, this situation is unfortunate. Women in IT are often paid less than men, even in communities which promote themselves as *'non-sexist'*. Surely the end result of following policies which discourage the employment of women in this way; it's the industry that is probably losing a substantial component of able people.

Is There Really Any Difference

Since those early days of people entering the age-of-computing, the records show a steady increase of girls' and women's interest and involvement with IT. Granted, the early pioneering decisions on the emerging computer technologies may have been made by males, with women's involvement being more towards implementing the techno-service side of things. These days, we see there is a progressive rise of techno-interested females from their school days (pre-college), through to their secondary college and higher education or university degree courses. Much has been written on this subject. The position people mostly take on techno-gender issues seems to depend upon their individual perspective towards the wider community. We appear to be captured by a gender-centric misunderstanding of women's technical aspirations for all things digital. For instance, why do men talk (and write) about their interest in technical aspects more readily than women? Is this because the balance of men to women in IT tips the scales heavily towards a male dominated workforce? Does the expectation that women remain on the softer-side of the techno-landscape, get in the way? Perhaps one way to explain how unbalanced the reporting of gender and things technical has remained with us today is to look at the tendency people have towards a pre-judged orientation for men's only understanding of techno-gender matters. Picture a group of men and women in coffee room conversations. How often do we see the men talking to the men, when the subject is techno-heavy, with the women participating in the conversation as onlookers? Moreover, it's interesting to see what happens at the dinner table, when a bloke wants to know something about computer usage? More often than not he'll ask another bloke when the female(s) present may have more knowledge and experience in the IT arena. So does it matter, and should we worry about it? In fact it does, and we should worry about it for two reasons: first, it is unethical to discriminate against any group; and second, such policies deprive the industry of potentially able employees.

Design Considerations

The trouble is, time seems to be running out already. Unless there can be a major turn around in our approach towards information systems design; we can expect the digital landscape to emulate the males' view of how things should operate. Perhaps it's timely and useful for this discussion to refer back to the interactive phases of change as they relate to gender and technology. For this purpose we examine how Justine Cassell has used a model disclosed by Macintosh in 1983. She draws on a feminist perspective to explain the lessons learned about designing IT for women [15]:

Are we not facing an age-old dilemma of how to manage the major differences between human beings? From our earliest days, boys and machines were deemed to be natural partners, while girls take the caring, nurturing roles in their stride. Have a look at the propensity for Web-designers to cater for the girly culture. Females too often are depicted as damsels in distress with body shapes that resemble a digital Barbie-doll. The digital boy- personae, on the other hand, reveal a stereotypical set of characteristics anchored to the quest to overcome all sorts of techno-morphed evil. Of course these video role-plays are quite understandable, given the entrenched habits of the earlier generation of parents. The trouble is, we now have enormous amounts of research which prove that girls are quite good at mathematics and things scientific. One might ask what all the fuss is about.

As Cassell [15] explains using the Macintosh model above, we can say that Phases-1 and -2 are long gone because it is no longer possible to build womanless technology. The public perception of the role women play was completely changed by Lovelace and Hopper's contributions to the scientific digital community.

Table 6 : Lessons Learned for Designing IT for Women

MACINATOSH PHASES		APPLICABILITY TO EFFECTIVE HCI
1	**Womanless history**	Earliest computers were mechanistic problem solvers.
2	**Women in history**	Ada Lovelace and Grace Hopper's contribution brought forward a newly acquired acceptance and respect for women's contribution to science and mathematics.
3	**Women as a problem, anomaly, or absence in history**	Highly paid Web-design consultants are hired to discover how to design ICT tools for women.
4	**Women as history**	Internet community is genderless; a one-user-population is seen as needing specially designed technology.
5	**History redefined or reconstructed to include us all**	A mature approach to multiple perspectives. Not only do the computer-interfaces become intrinsic to the nature of the *human-dimensions of HCI*, but also cease to be used as a type of techno-skin applied to a computerised information system once it's operational. Rather, the ICT tools are better equipped to adapt themselves to user requirements.

We can verify this aspect by looking around us. There is much evidence in current Web-sites for gender consideration in interface design. These days, consideration for the techno-savvy woman is posing a problem for IS-design. For instance, it is not unusual to find digital marketing hype that targets the lucrative teenage girls, while others offer digital advertisements that claim to know what makes women tick. Unfortunately these techno-marketing strategies resemble the glossy magazine sector where their tick-box surveys are designed with a narrow range of women's potential: this instead of extending women's intellectual range beyond everyday household chores.   There seems to be an implied worrisome-focus that maintains Web-site dependence, locking the more intellectually vulnerable inside their site forever.

Cassell [15] asks what is it going to take to progress us from the McIntosh Phase-3 to -4? How can we move on from the problem of women in the interface, to seeing women depicted as central to the design of the entire interface? She continues ……

> " ….. we will reach this phase when we consider the diversity of men as well as women in our design of the human-computer interface. That is, the users of technology must come to have many faces: men and women, young and old, American and Bangladeshi. Women are central to technology when all users are central to technology, when all users are diverse. Women are central when technology is designed for human needs. No longer will women be conceived of as having special needs any more than any other group. "Different folks, different strokes" might be the motto of stage four. When only one population is seen as needing specially designed technology, it is almost inevitably seen as external to the normal practice of technology. The marked is almost always perceived as the lesser. When only one population is special, one risks ghettoizing it."

Could we safely predict that reaching the McIntosh Phase-4 is possible? There's no doubt that reaching this level of techno-maturity would certainly enhance the current Web-design offerings. The Phase-5 seems to be still a long way off. These days, it's entirely possible to have the visual nature of the computer interface designed at the time by the users. Sadly, this is not the reality thus far.

Graphical User Interfacing

Following on from the previous section which ended with a prediction that reaching a computerised information system with multiple considerations is entirely possible, we now take a look at some of the usability issues that will ensure a more *effective HCI*. Before we do that let us confirm our understanding of a couple of terms: graphical user interface commonly referred to as GUI and another term that is sometimes incorrectly substituted for this acronym, *"graphical user interaction"*.

GUIs

Perhaps the best way to introduce this concept is to say there are many interface designs that we could employ to serve as a communication device between the user and the computer. For instance, these days the Microsoft Windows operating system provides a set of interfacing screens that most people have become quite accustomed to using.   The familiar Microsoft Windows interface provides easy access to the computer's system components. Once upon a time, before the advent of the graphical user interface tools we now expect as standard the user needed to know how to formally address or command the computer to ask for access to these components. Such commands were little beyond 3GL program code. These days, we no longer need to memorise an endless list of cryptic computer command strings, such as *"C:\Documents and settings>cd .."* to see a list of files in a directory. Instead we are treated by the Windows graphical user interface to little graphical icons known as thumb-nail pictures *(Figure 23)*.   These interface devices have become very sophisticated. As well as providing access to the computer system's physical operating components, they also serve to display other user file management and software applications' options. The days of memorizing how to use a computer's software package (or application) are long gone. Even if the user doesn't recognise a particular icon, the hovering cursor evokes a short explanation.

The advent of multi-media has enhanced user accessibility and navigation. For instance people no longer need to remember the procedure for generating an automatic index when typing up their word processing document. Instead they can simply move the mouse or position the cursor over the main menu options to expose the sub-level textual tags which describe the available options.

Figure 23 : Graphical Menu Icons

Graphical User Interaction

The way people and machines interact can be described in a number of ways. As we have seen previously, these days Menus are still the primary interface device that serves to assist people while they navigate their way through a number of computer interactions. For instance, the GUI in modern computers *"interfaces the interaction"* between the user, the computer, and the structured system of menus of the software application. At first when we are faced with a new GUI, we may need to stop and think about the options before us, and decide upon which course of action we should follow next. After a while without us really noticing, the way we respond to this particular GUI becomes more fluid; meaning our HCI response becomes an automatic cognitive interaction. Longer term, these interactions become habitual. For instance, ever noticed whether you stop and check that all your software applications are closed correctly and that you have removed that music CD, before you power off your desktop?

Habitual HCI Traits

Understanding the many ways people like to interact with computers makes for an interesting pastime. Although there is a wealth of excellent psychological research, picking the best theoretical model to apply to the *human-dimensions of HCI* remains difficult. This is because there are so many ways to describe cognitive style (see chapter-5 of this book for further clarity on this issue). Researchers in the professional practice of Management Information Systems (MIS), have taken a paradigmatic approach to investigate the interactive effects of system performance and end-user satisfaction with cognitive style. They draw on the famous Jungian typology to explain and validate their experimental constructs [16]. Because of this, there are still no conclusive findings in information systems research that explains the interactive effect of multi-media and human , on Web-mediated performance outcomes [17].

As we saw in Chapter-2, Richard Riding [18] suggests that the cognitive (thinking) preference of people can be measured on two separate scales. To recap, one scale reveals how we prefer to represent information while we think (verbal/imagery); while the other shows how we process information (analytic/wholistic). While it appears that we can adapt our thinking processing (perhaps to the task at hand), the way in which our brains process information is inherent and cannot be changed. However, this interesting topic relating to how people react to Web-mediated information is for another time and place. For the moment, our discussion on the *human-dimensions of HCI* turns towards the more physical aspects of human behaviour to differentiate a duality of cognition. If we say that responding to GUIs becomes habitual, let's think about how Gordon Lawrence describes the full range of patterns of mental habits. He suggests that there are eight (interacting) patterns, which some people reading this chapter may recognize as the core of the *'Myer-Briggs Type Indicator'*, known simply as the MBTI *(Table 7)*:

Table 7 : Core of the Myer-Briggs Type Indicator

INTERACTING MENTAL HABITS
Extravert
Introvert
Thinking
Feeling
Sensing
Intuitive
Judging
Perceptive

For argument's sake let us say for our HCI activities we may be able to further divide people's habitual thinking patterns into two categories: a preference for attending to the task, and problem solving. In the first instance, we may be able to say that while they carry out their HCI, these task-oriented thinkers are more concerned with the content of the interaction, than paying attention to their thinking patterns. Moreover they may enjoy perfecting their tasks and work diligently towards achieving tangible results. These habits, however admirable, can also be their down fall, as they may have unrealistically high expectations of themselves and others. For the implications for their HCI, this trait can make them on the one hand, over-critical, while on the other, slow and deliberate decision-makers. They expect their HCI interface to provide careful navigation. Some of these people may become intensely irritated by surprises and glitches, hence their cautious decision-making. They are also known for their skeptical attitude, which manifests when they insist on seeing all promises documented.

For the thinking-problem-solving oriented people, they enjoy taking an analytical stance during their HCI activities, knowing they will persist in a systematic manner to reach a workable solution. So saying, they may be very comfortable working with an unclear interface that may frustrate others. Online, these problem-solving individuals thrive in unstructured environments, making their own investigations when they encounter open-ended unexpected events. They are comfortable researching for a solution when things are uncertain. Moreover, they are very good at making comparisons, determining each risk as it arises. They seem to automatically calculate margins of error, and then to take action.

Tools of Thought

The GUI has certainly changed everything. These days, even the most ardent techno-geek will admit they have calmed down about Microsoft taking over the digital world. While the distance between the IBM compatible machines and the Apple computers is becoming less obvious, there is no prize for spotting the interface with the most user options. Most modern interface icons are structured so that mouse-overs easily display all the hidden content. Without realizing what's happened, computer users have been forced to systematize their thinking. Look at how easy it is to forget that Microsoft Word differentiates between the peripherals' management activities and the document formatting instructions. Could we not say that these days the interface designers assume that people are entering the world, able to read a computer screen much like they read a book, with effortless travel around a digital(screen)-page. For instance, try scrolling your eyes across the main Microsoft ribbon-menu (File, Edit, View, Insert, Format, Tools, Table, Window, Help). Most would speculate that there are many people able to visualize some of the things one can expect to find in the top-level options. Moreover, how may people have noticed that the choice of key-strokes for these menu options has a systematic hierarchy?

Visual Literacy

What then does this highly intuitive GUI do for our cognitive literacy? Once upon a time (but two decades ago) people were generally not considered to be visually literate. Researchers felt that people should undergo special visual literacy training to cope with the onslaught of graphic material that was entering their domestic landscape. Nowadays we are continually bombarded with little pictures of recognizable objects to overcome language difficulties. Just about everyone would know what these icons mean *(Figure 24)*:

Figure 24 : Common Visual Communication Tools

Universal Design Issues

As we have seen in earlier parts of this book, in days gone by some people felt that usability and HCI were central to computer science. This is quite understandable given the machine-centric issues that were prevalent while the supporting technology emerged. However, as time pushes us forward, we are improving our understanding of how to increase the *human-dimension* to enhance the usability of our interface devices. These days, it's more about what people can do, rather than concentrating on the machine-side of HCI.

Human Factors

These days we hear a great deal of rhetoric about user-focused technologies. Yet the reality of a personable techno-landscape still seems a long way off. The direction taken seems to have been championed by people who add a user component to their HCI almost as another machine-dimensional entity. This even though we often see nice diagrams that may reveal clever ways to interpret user-centric environments from a design perspective. Many of these user-focused systems do not include the social context [14],[19]. Clearly what is missing from many of these information systems is the *human-dimensional* design component. Instead the systems design concentrates on providing a unilateral utility. Why is this so? Perhaps the cause can be seen in the myth that customising information systems is difficult. According to Andy Smith [20], what is really required to progress human factors in HCI, are systems that deal with the more functional, aspirational and physical sides of people's requirements. In simple language, functional requirements relate to the specific machine-operational tasks that a user requires of a system, while the medium to longer term goals associated with job-satisfaction are *aspirational* aspects. In the end it's the expectation that a machine will perform the tasks in an appropriate manner that matches the physical characteristics of the user that remains foremost in people's minds when they approach their HCI.

    Figure 25 shows that the *human-dimension* actively involves users in the design of their information systems (adaptation from [20] p:85). Here we can see how easy it is to include the user in every stage of the design and development of an information system. What this diagram is really saying is that the ownership of the techno-landscape has broadened to such an extent that computer science and the mathematics professionals are no longer the main ideational gatekeepers. There has been a rather large shift towards a more balanced landscape that takes account of people's values, and indeed insisting upon at least some input from the social sciences.

    Once a few more information systems emerge that encourage the users to engage with the designers throughout the development process, we will start to see many others following this self-design approach [21].

Adaptive vs the Global Interface

The techno-front doors for many Internet sites offer a rather generic interface. Even rather good ones can become somewhat daunting for some techno-tender people. For instance look at all the features that a person must digest in a visual/verbal sense (Figure 26). Lack of consideration for information overload is taken from an important Australian government Web-site http://www.centrelink.gov.au/.

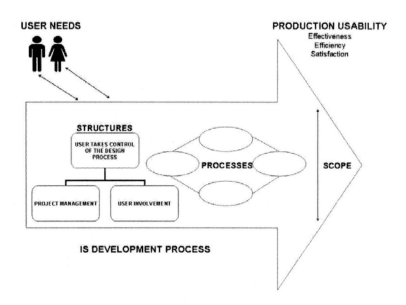

Figure 25 : Involving End-Users in Information Systems Design

Figure 26 : Cognitive Overload in Government Web-Site

This interface is the front door for a diverse range of people in the general community seeking assistance from the government in one form or another. Consider how difficult it might be for some people to conceptually wade through all these options. On the one hand, some may say this particular GUI is fantastic. For them, it may represent a one stop shop. Quite obviously, considerable energies by the Web-designers have been put into segmenting this interface. On the other hand, because of their cognitive processing style, some people may miss seeing where they need to go on the screen to get closer to the information they want. In any event, few people would argue that the visual real estate on this interface is quite amazing.

Let us take a moment to study the hierarchical nature of the navigation tools embedded within this interface. The top banner presents us with clickable government logos. Underneath there is a second ribbon-menu bar that presents an array of options. In the middle and to the left of the screen is a conceptual structure which offers a range of clickable government services (including an offer for the first time visitor to investigate through this special entry point). On the right hand, there is a further series of services. Towards the bottom of the screen there is an impressive set of languages that people are invited to use. Lastly we see another government banner, offering access to things like people's rights. More importantly, the Web-site offers help. At last this interface offers assistance for people who may not be really comfortable with the *'clickability'* of the techno-real estate. Too late, some may say…….

What is our response when we have to dig into a Web-site interface for what we want? How many times have you missed seeing a menu option or bread-crumb to progress your navigation? Does the age-old axiom work for things technological? Are first appearances really all important? For some, one of the most contentious issues for interface design relates to finding ways to scrub out the generic entrance and build systems that adapt according to the user's requirements.

Accessibility

Figuring out how to behave when faced with an unfriendly and cognitively cluttered screen is really off putting for quite a few people. For some the task of unraveling the information access rules is a major techno-barrier against which they do not survive. Even though usability standards have been set up to make life easier, these standards mostly relate to techno-tasking and process. The industry has been very slow in taking the next brave step: to go a little further to address people's cognitive difficulty when trying to access information through a seemingly unresponsive GUI. It has only been in the past few years that we have been able to see any progress towards designing uncluttered access tools. Shneiderman & Plaisant [22] provide an example of where such standards can relate to task and process. They try to account for techno-cognitive dissonance, including:

- keeping similarity of the task sequences in differing contexts
- taking care to name hyperlinks with a sensible description of the destination, application of carefully worded headings that relate conceptually to the content they describe
- providing binary check boxes when a simple yes/no is enough
- providing each screen load of information in printable pages, and letting people look at smaller images or thumbnails as a preview or taster ([21]p:62)

However, while accessibility standards exist for many forms of physical disabilities, confusion remains for how the industry proposes to account for people experiencing the many types of cognitive or intellectual difficulty. Moreover the existing US Rehabilitation Act Amendments of 1998 (known as simply '*Section 508*') appear to be devised to direct equipment procurement, instead of providing a workable framework that guides the design and development of accessible information systems. It is very important that someone comes forward to champion systems development for the intellectually disadvantaged in our general community. Presently, there is a pressing need for making a concerted effort on the part of information system designers. This to enhance accessibility to existing electronic information media in general, as well as improvement of emerging ICT tools. Ubiquitous computing is no longer acceptable because it does not allow for the plethora of differences in the way human beings' like to interact online. There is no excuse for allowing the current troublesome access processes to continue.

Projecting a Fear of Technology

Overtime, instead of creating inclusive ICT tools, unless something amazing happens to the contrary, there will be permanent damage inflicted on to the techno-landscape, shutting out many people from experiencing the joys of digital-information awareness. Why would anyone willingly expose themselves to being told over and over that because they cannot use a digital device like the rest of the community they are somehow wanting? No wonder certain people run a mile when faced with a techno-gadget. It is quite possible that negativity towards technology can be reversed by more joyful techno-experiences. Here's where the innate nature of our physical and non-physical awareness combine to cause trouble with our HCI. For some, it is simply too much to ask to stay cognitively focused when using a computer, to complete a task without any extra assistance.

Although it may be related, this is not so much about curing computer phobic tendencies. It is more about making sure that more people can engage with ICT tools that are easy to use, and fun to play with. The trouble is that affecting a change to the professional practice of information systems design is problematic, as the notion of awareness and digital gadgetry design is still in its infancy. The market for such devices is moving quickly with new gadgets entering the techno-landscape with every new sunrise. Sadly, for those who are rather scared of technology, the chance that they will remain in the techno-wilderness is quite high. Even if they wanted to, unless they have a reasonable level of technical know how, the fear of trying something new may prevent them from experimenting with new technology.

Once again there is plenty of rhetoric about improving HCI, but nothing of practical value has arisen to alleviate the abject fear some people experience. For instance, in the corporate world these days, we need strategies to help some employees relax when they are required to retrain for new computer-based tasks. For some, this type of HCI can be really confronting for all sorts of reasons. Not everyone can *"get it"* the first or second time they are shown a sequence of procedural steps in a long process. At times, making techno-mistakes in public is doubly confronting. It can be very uncomfortable for us when things go wrong using a computer, even in our own offices.

Here is where the interactivity of humans' physical coordination with the highly conceptual nature of techno-dissonance is extremely delicate. Information systems researchers are having plenty of fun investigating new ways for people to interact with computerized devices. However, when will we see some of these products made available for ordinary people in the community?

Overcoming the Browser Barriers

As the ICT tools developed sophistication, the techno-landscape adjusted to reflect the emerging push for access through the Web to rich information sources. It was necessary to have software applications developed for everyday people in the community to afford them easy access. These days, most of us don't think twice about Web browser technologies. Most of us are now quite familiar accessing the Internet through our favourite browser. As most of us know, Web browsers are simply the GUI that enables quick interactivity with the Internet through text and graphics displayed as Web-pages on our computer screens.

For those who have ever wondered about how all this works, a Web-site usually comprises sets of interconnected pages. The connectivity one takes for granted when *"surfing the Net"*, is provided by techno-links (or clickable objects) in each page, directing one through the embedded location details or Web-addresses of another Web-page or related material. These techno-navigational links are now commonly known as hyperlinks, because they allow us to traverse seamlessly through cyberspace, hitting upon information without our immediate intervention. A further embellishment is that a Web-site can also be activated in *'local area networks'* or LANs that are not necessarily connected to the Internet.

In the Beginning

These days, it is really difficult to imagine the world without browser technologies. A team of programmers in the USA at the National Centre for Supercomputing Applications produced the first one to become popular, naming it *"MOSAIC"*. They developed the first commercial Web browser calling it the *"NETSCAPE NAVIGATOR"*. Those of us who can remember, NETSCAPE dominated the techno-browser-landscape until 1999 when Microsoft launched their now famous *"INTERNET EXPLORER"* or IE. However in 2002, *"MOZILLA"* was released as an open source version of NETSCAPE for non-windows platforms. It was released again in 2004 as the more popular *"FIREFOX"* browser, which purports to be faster and more secure. Over time there have been a number of excellent GUI browsing tools invented, often by students, as special purpose interfaces.

Some of the more interesting non-Windows browsers were developed to work on any device, providing Internet access for everyone. Access was even possible using the older teletype machines. The line-mode browser that interacted with anything from Unix to Microsoft disk operating systems was one example of these. There were a number of other browsers like Hewlett-Packard's *"ARENA"* interface that was developed in Bristol, England. Its powerful features were designed to enable positioning of tables and graphics. Then there is the innovative *"OPERA"* browser that originally was developed in 1994 by two telecommunication researchers in Oslo, Norway. These days OPERA-9 is freeware, and well known for its lightening fast speed. It is downloadable for use in mobile devices such as Mobile telephones, set-top boxes and portable media players.

Microsoft vs Apple

As we have seen in earlier parts of this book, the super quick number cruncher that IBM and the techno-founding fathers (and a limited number of significant techno-females) innovated the beginning of the techno-era. All things digital sailed along quite nicely for all the IBM-compatible techno-geeks until the Macintosh engineers emerged to threaten IBM-compatibles' *"Quick and Dirty Operating System"*. The latter is still known today as the DOS (disk operating system). Unfortunately for our techno-Luddites the earlier attempts to launch the first GUI failed. At the time, for the Apple corporation, the failure of their Apple Lisa was strictly a commercial one. It was the largest since the Apple-III disaster of 1980. The targeted business end-users balked at Lisa's high price and largely opted to run less expensive (and more familiar) IBM PCs. The largest Lisa customer was NASA, which used Lisa-Project for project management and which was faced with significant problems when the Lisa was discontinued.

Which side of the *'digi-fence'* do you sit? Ever wondered why there is a distinct division of opinion these days as to what constitutes a *real computer*? Until quite recently it was thought that any respectable business corporation's preference has been to adopt the IBM's number crunching abilities for managing their business operations. They would never admit to knowing anything about the Apple Macintosh machinery. Conversely, it would be unusual to find an educationalist or designer using an IBM-compatible computer. Such professionals have preferred to leave aside the number crunching activities of the IBMs, to lovingly acknowledge the ease with which they can manipulate a fully graphical environment.

Picture a digital boxing ring. In the techno-geekish corner sit the IBM compatible experts, quietly feeling quite superior because of their technical prowess for issuing stylized commands directly into to a digital-operating system. In the other corner, sit the Apple-GUI proponents having survived those heady days, where they were laughed at for getting their earlier GUI machines with those funny mouse devices so wrong. This was the techno-scenario for most of the 20th century. There were many law suits issued as the players fought in the digital boxing rings over who would produce the standard operating systems as we know them today. Some would say, and his opponents sadly, that Bill Gates won enough of those early techno-battles to emerge as a strong market leader and trend setter.

Alternative Methods

For those who may not be aware, the most important software program for a computer is its operating system. Without one a computer will not function. Like in the olden days when computers took up vast amounts of space, modern day operating systems still perform many basic computing tasks. The operating system is expected to keep track of all the files and directories on the computer's internal hard-disk, as well as controlling the peripheral devices like the secondary storage disk-drives and printers.

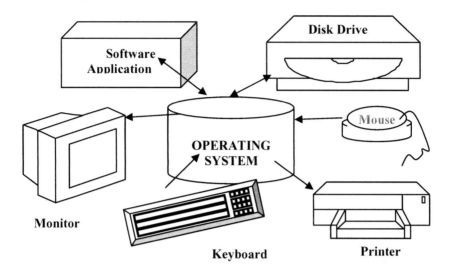

Figure 27 : Computer Operating System Maintains Control

Large operating systems are required to deliver more *"processing grunt"*: or put more formally, to take greater responsibility for the machine's computational powers. Essentially in these bigger capacity computers the operating system acts more like a traffic cop, making sure that each software program running alongside the user's requests can occur simultaneously. Moreover, the operating system is responsible for the overall security of the whole system, ensuring that unauthorized users cannot access the system. Operating systems can be classified as:

- multi-user - to support two or more users at the same time. In some large systems this means there may be hundreds or even thousands of concurrent users.
- multi-processing – supports running a software program on more than one central processing unit.
- multi-tasking – allows more than one software program to run concurrently.
- multi-threading – allowing different parts of a one program to run concurrently.
- real time – means responding to input instantly. For instance, the older DOS and UNIX operating systems, cannot be considered to support real-time processing.

This mini-lesson on computer operating systems would not be complete without mentioning that operating systems provide the basic machine core or software platform upon which other programs and ICT tools can do their work. These software programs are called applications programs. They enable everyday things like word processing, spreadsheets and database software, to mention the most common. In the past a basic knowledge of the DOS commands was essential for people to work a computer. These days, people can use a computer without really being aware of the operating system.

Leaving it all to the Robots Again

For a long time now people have been talking about and wishing for machines that can truly act like us! Although it may sound far fetched, in many ways we have already arrived at the position on the techno-landscape that was marked out for artificial intelligence many years ago. Think about all the wonders of science that are already performed only by machinery. Take space exploration for one. Look at the marvelous activities that are carried out by machinery thousands and thousands of miles away from our Mother Earth. I don't believe that many of us stop very often to marvel at the range of outer space operations occurring independent of human input. Nor do we really take much notice of how computerized our plane rides are. These wonderful techno-tasks and other equally fantastic life-saving routines are performed daily by robots. Robots in turn draw on high-speed processors imbedded in machines that process visual data as rapidly as it enters the system.

Towards Adaptive User Support

With all this outer space techno-wizardry one might be forgiven for supposing that modern information systems adapt to a user's preferences as a matter of course. Instead, we can say that outside the military where systems cater for volatile operational environments, we do not have the same degree of automation for systems used by the average person.

For this to happen we need to have machines that can learn from us. Some researchers call this type of ICT tool a learning apprentice. This type of seminal work has been carried out for the automotive industry where people can install a car navigation system. As the reader may know, these enable a personalized service based upon the decisions it learns from the user when travelling in the car. Another example is the ability to provide a dialogue in spoken language to aid decisions with regard to suitable locations. A nice restaurant, for instance. Such adaptive systems can update their user profiles to be ready for the next requests. In a way this is machine learning. These days, adaptive user interfaces can be developed for a plethora of tasks many people find boring, like sorting electronic mail, turning on the garden sprinkler system when there has been no rainfall and recommending the best movie of the week for you. Perhaps insufficient is being done for people who require adaptable information systems that respond appropriately to a given user.

Interactive Adaptive Information Systems

According to Paramythis & Weibelzahl [23], currently there is a considerable amount of unsolved research projects that fall within the domain of *"interactive adaptive systems"* (IAS). These researchers suggest that there is much being attempted in the IAS domain because nobody knows how to evaluate IAS outcomes. The few empirical studies that evaluate interactive adaptive systems tend to provide ambiguous results [23]. In fact what this is really saying is there are many *fuzzy* logic projects that investigate the systems design and development of interactive adaptive systems. Researchers' goals evidently are opportunities to play with the ICT tools rather than serving the waiting public. Rather than evaluating IAS projects by decomposing the adaptation and then evaluating in a piece-meal manner, Paramythis & Weibelzahl [22] propose a layered evaluation approach that seems to have merit. They maintain this model reflects a better approach to understanding layered evaluation of interactive adaptive systems. *Figure 28* identifies 5-places where researchers need to concentrate [23], including:

- Collection of user input data – mechanical sensors may also be used for this input.
- Interpretation of this collected data – to acquire meaning of relevance to the system. Here is where researchers should differentiate between the previous stage of the data input which is intended to identify, and conceptually dissociate the two stages to address them in isolation.
- Modelling of the current state of the world – derived new knowledge of the user, and the interaction context, as well as introducing the knowledge from other dynamic IAS models.
- Deciding upon the adaptation requirements. This step is too often missed in most research [23]. They propose that things like usability will be highly relevant. Other issues relating to timelines, obtrusiveness, and level of user control should be accounted for.
- Applying the adaptation. This stage is often neglected by researchers. Instead it should be varied independently of the decision making process, to take account of adopting different adaptation strategies.

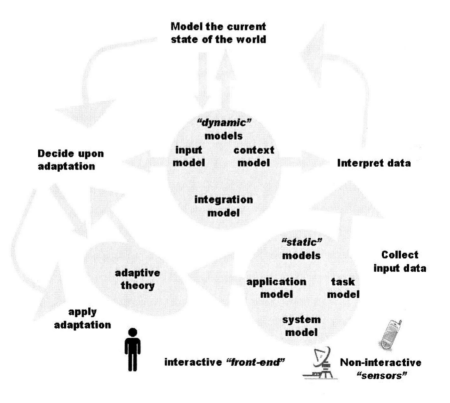

Figure 28 : Adaptive Decomposition Model

Looking at this simplified explanation for the purposes of this chapter may throw some light on why we cannot find these badly needed adaptive ICT tools yet *(Figure 28)*. The reason may be due in part to work which does not undergo this layered or piece-meal approach to finding out what is going on with certain adaptation strategies. Such strategies can provide valuable insights into the adaptation stages which an IAS passes through [23].

Machine Learning and Knowledge Discovery

For years we have been hearing about machines that can be taught. Well this may already be so, depending upon your definition of teaching and learning. Which ever way you wish to argue the point, at the moment, the process of machine learning falls directly within the field of artificial intelligence. When it all boils down to it, machines will only ever *'learn'* what human beings tell them. Throughout this book we have and will continue to observe that humans can tell a machine whatever they like through software programs. If we look a bit closer at the machine-side issues of this techno-phenomenon, we'll see there are two types of learning: inductive (where rules and patterns can be extracted from enormous data files), and deductive reasoning (where the conclusion is deduced from previously known facts). The problem with both these digi-learning decision-making tools is, there really isn't any guarantee that the human derived programming logic that is applied to the data inside the computer by the interrogating software program is correct. Trainee programmers find only too soon that computers don't do what we want them to do. They only do what we tell them to do!

For instance: a rule which says that *"since it is raining, the street must be wet"* may be true, yet you may also be able to say *"If it's raining then the street gets wet."* Let's use the premise that *"If it's raining then the street gets wet"* it could be argued that *"since it's raining the street is wet"* but not *"the street is wet so it must be raining."* Let us assume for one moment here, that because the wet street would be unavoidable because of the rain; the truth of the matter may well be that it may not necessarily be from the rain!

These basic statements *"if something then something else"* can logically (according to machine-programming speak) be followed by *"something is; so something else must be"* and *"something else is not; so something else cannot be"* are both valid machine-reasoning programming statements.

Bayesian Belief Networks

At this point the world of artificial intelligence looks towards inferential statistics for its advanced computational logic. To fully explain how this works would go way beyond the scope of this little book. However, we should look into the importance of this powerful mathematical approach to focus the importance for knowing how to articulate the relationship between the *human-dimension* of computer interactivity and the effectiveness of HCI. It would not be difficult to generate many real world examples where the probability of one event is conditional upon the probability of a previous situation. Therefore in keeping the variables to a manageable number regulates the discrete random variables. For instance, in an expert system designed for monitoring an event with 37 variables would result in a joint distribution of over 2^{37} parameters and would not be manageable
(see **http://www.niedermayer.ca/papers/bayesian/bayes.html#limitations**).

We'll take a rain-check on the probabilities for all eventualities that would occur if we returned to our earlier problem about raining and the probability of what caused the road to be wet! However we could draw nice Bayesian Networks which show the logic that look much like decision trees. Using this approach offers many useful reasons for following this approach rather than the more traditional methods to determine causal relationships. It is much easier to spot where the conditional relationships are likely to occur. When masses of calculations are required for instance in designing information systems for outer space, Bayesian inferences are considered to be useful. This is because the inference-engine can draw its own meaning on the behaviour of the data.

Apart from some worries relating to human intervention within the inference engine's processing, Bayesian networks afford incredible power. They permit qualitative inferences which previously were open to human error with regard to computational error. Because of this they provide robust support for causality analysis that through statistical induction support a form of automated learning involving parametric, network and causal relationship discoveries.

Usability Issues

Travelling through this book you may be discovering some common threads are surfacing when discussing *effective HCI*. One of these relates to the inevitability of techno-territory wars that emerge from time to time. Each side takes up their position in the battle field, perceiving a unilateral ownership of techno-terms. For the rest of us looking on, without an understanding of the paradigmatic context, much confusion can follow. For example, how does one think about usability? Take our previous conversation on HCI. What does usability actually mean? On the one hand, the designers of information systems may say it's about compliance with heuristics; or rules relating to behaviour of digi-objects or screen real-estate items. On the other hand, we could think of usability as providing principles that convey a user's perspective and set guiding principles to evaluate prototype and existing systems [24]. For a little more clarity, *Figure 29* demonstrates how some people refer to the issue of describing usability in terms of user expectations [24]p:19.

Figure 29 : Usability Expressed in Terms of End-User Expectations [24]

It is also no secret these days, especially in computer science circles, that the usability issues of HCI have become a contentious topic [24]. Previously not much has been said in their domain about how well the functionality of software applications must fit a user's needs and expectations. Instead, they've been concentrating more on maintaining the logics for (machine related) task processing flow. These days, generally speaking we are witnessing an increased awareness for putting forward the *human-dimension*, and to such an extent that the demarcation lines that previously surrounded disparate disciplines are becoming less obvious. One of the places where we see an overlapping of professional practice happening today is in the synthesis between computer scientists and information systems practitioners. In a recent study carried out primarily by computer scientists, respondents were asked to concentrate on user perspectives when evaluating information system's security. These researchers combined computer science (for designing their security for Web-based services), human factors and the social sciences (to understand the behavioural aspects of system security) [26].

Or take the group of information systems researchers who were recently looking at the usability of online grocery system. Their research focused on defining human error in terms of novice and experienced users. Novice-users will need to be assisted with every step of their knowledge navigation because the task processing is unfamiliar.

The more experienced user will only require a refresher. Moreover, experienced people will become very frustrated when they are stopped from jumping ahead when they need to bypass basic steps [27].

Trust

Although the techno-landscape awakening occurred in the mid 90's, eLearning has only gained prominence in the last few years. Because of this, and the rush to get materials online, there has been a tendency by courseware designers of Web-based materials to ignore the practice and methods of the past. Some have described this oversight as ignoring the power of trust [14]. This notion of trust is especially important when developing eLearning programmes. Trust is a primary enabler that involves the development of widespread agreement, consultation, collaboration and knowledge sharing [28]. Moreover, with the increased awareness for usability as we have been discussing in this book, *"computer-supported collaborative learning"* (CSCL) modelling in eLearning environments within a semantic Web architecture, requires new advances in knowledge engineering, offering revitalized ePedagogies for novice-learners [27].

It may well be easy to describe elements of trust when we think of HCI. The trouble is, with all this talk about trust in ICT tools, we still know nothing about the interactive effects of the five elements of trust identified by Mason & Lefrere [28], which are:

- consensus
- building
- consultation
- collaboration
- knowledge-sharing

These elements form the nexus of the complicated array of processes and outputs involved with any viable eLearning marketplace [28]. These days it would no doubt help things along if we developed a knowledge base that depicts the socio-cultural factors necessary for the knowledge-channels that categorize the ways of knowing that are applicable in the business/corporate context to the educational sector. They involve:

- **political** (agreeing to goals and rules for mutual benefit)
- **jurisdictional** (mapping the legalities and regional interests)
- **semantic** (reaching common understandings)
- **cultural**, **syntactic** (communities of practice, shared knowledge units and workflows) and **technical issues** (systems that exchange data and learning resource services) [29].

Some time soon, and because of the interest in trust and ICT tools , we are going to see a real *Knowledge Exchange Market* entering the techno-landscape. This enterprise will involve a new ICT tool that acts as an interactive learning grid operating either as an individual or distributed collaborative learning agent. The grid's objective is to follow the information gathering for the ordinary computer users' knowledge gathering (some may call learning) resources. Also attached to this new learning grid will be activity logs that feed data into a knowledge management component. The penultimate techno-gadget emerging from this grid technology also includes a component dedicated to mentoring and facilitation during each learning event.

In this chapter we brought forward some of the ways people relate to their digital artefacts to enhance their problem solving abilities. Therefore an important aspect of *effective HCI* as it relates to the learning/education/training domain is to differentiate between the type of learning and the instructional architecture. Due to the interactivity of effectiveness, efficiency and satisfaction in an online learning environment, complex usability issues arise whenever people engage with digital artefacts.

This chapter has raised issues which surround people and their computer use in everyday problem solving. Now then, in the light of this discussion let's reflect on the following:

- we should differentiate the type of learning people set out to do – and provide appropriate instructional architectures
- systems designers need to provide the online environments and tools that promote collaborative problem solving
- gender issues are alive and well – expecting ubiquitous interaction should be a thing of the past, we need proactive and adaptive information systems that encompass the principles of universal design
- GUIs often assume most people are visually literate – when the reverse remains true

These human-dimensions intertwine. Because of this, the next chapter of this book introduces the complexities of the conceptual nature of the *human-dimensions of HCI* within online learning. A conceptual model is proposed as a framework to understand the complexity of the techno-humanoid landscape.

Chapter Reference List

[1]   Gery, G., *Making CBT Happen: Prescriptions for successful implementation of computer-based training in your organization*. 1987, NY: Harper & Row.
[2]   Mayer, R.E., *Multimedia Learning*. 2001, NY: Cambridge Press.
[3]   Clark, R.C., Chapter 1. Expertise, learning, and instruction, in *Building Expertise, Second Edition*. 2003, Intern'l Society for Performance Improvement: ISBN 1-890289-13-2; ISPI No.5103: MN. 256.
[4]   Heinich, R., et al., *Instructional Media and Technologies for Learning*. 2002, Upper Saddle River, NJ: Person Education.
[5]   Anderson, T. & Elloumi, F., eds. *Theory and Practice of Online Learning*. G. Sanders, Editor. 2004, Athabasca University. ISBN: 0-919737-59-5.
[6]   Hirumi, A., A framework for analysing, designing, and sequencing planned e-Learning interactions. *The Quarterly Review of Distance Education*, 2002. 3(2): p. 141-160.
[7]   Koch, T., *Unpublished Diploma Thesis*. 1998, Technical University.
[8]   McKay, E., Garner, B.J., & Okamoto, T. Understanding the ontological requirements for collaborative Web-based experiential learning. Paper in the proceedings of the *International Conference on Computers in Education 2002*. 2002. Auckland, NZ: IEEE Computer Society.
[9]   Gutwin, C. & Greenberg, S., The effects of workspace awareness support on the usability of real-time distributed groupware. In the *ACM Transactions on Computer-Human Interaction (COCHI)*, 1999. 6(3): 243-281.
[10] Benbunan-Fich, R., Hiltz, S.R., & Turoff, M. A comparative content analysis of face-to-face vs. ALM-mediated teamwork. Paper in the proceedings of the *34th Hawaii International Conference on Systems Sciences (HICSS)*. 2001. Hawaii.
[11] Riel, M. & Harasim, L., Research perspectives on network learning. *Machine-Mediated Learning*, 1994. 4(2 & 3): 91-113.
[12] Dillenbourg, P., What do you mean by collaborative learning, in *Collaborative Learning: Cognitive and Computational Approaches*, P. Dillenbourg, Editor. 1999, Elsevier Science: Amsterdam. 1-19.
[13] McKay, E., *Instructional Strategies Integrating the Cognitive Style Construct: A Meta-Knowledge Processing Model (Contextual components that facilitate spatial/logical task performance): An investigation of instructional strategies that facilitate the learning of complex abstract programming*

concepts through visual representation, in *Applied Science (Computing and Mathematics Department)*. 2000, Deakin University, Available online from http://tux.lib.deakin.edu.au/adt-VDU/public/adt-VDU20061011.122556/ Waurn Ponds, Geelong, Australia.

[14] Bradley, G., *Social and Community Informatics: Humans on the Net*, 2006. NY: Routledge.265

[15] Cassell, J., Genderizing HCI. *The Handbook of Human-Computer Interaction*, J. Jack & A. Sears, Editors. 2002, Manwah, NJ: Laerence Erlbaum. 402-411.

[16] Carey, J., The issue of cognitive style in MIS/DSS research, in *Human Factors in Information Systems*, J.M. Carey, Editor. 1991, Ablex Publishing Corporation. 337-348.

[17] Myers, M.D. & Tan, F.B., Beyond models of national culture in information systems research. *Human Factors in Information Systems*, E. Szewczak & C. Snodgrass, Editors. 2002, London: IRM Press, 1-19.

[18] Riding, R.J. & Rayner, S., *Cognitive Styles and Learning Strategies*. 1998, UK: Fulton. 217.

[19] Singh, S., Smart personal agents: The users' perspective: A discussion paper from the *Centre for International Research on Communication and Information Technology CIRCUIT @RMIT*. 2001, RMIT, Melbourne, Australia.

[20] Smith, A., *Human Computer Factors: A Study of Users and Information Systems*. 1997, Berkshire: McGraw-Hill. 375.

[21] Law, C.M. & McKay, E. Taking account of the needs of software developers/programmers in universal access evaluations. Paper in the *Universal Access in HCI, Part-1, HCII 2007, LCNCS 4554*. 2007. Beijing, P.R.China: Springer-Verlad, Berlin Heidelberg. 420-427.

[22] Shneiderman, S. & Plaisant, C., *Designing the User Interface: Strategies for Effective Human-Computer Interaction (4th ed.)*. 2005, Reading, MA: Addison-Wesley.

[23] Paramythis, A. & Weibeizahl, A., *A Decomposition Model for the Layered Evaluation of Interactive Adaptive Systems*. 2005, Retrieved 20/01/08 from http://www.fim.uni-linz.ac.at/staff/paramythis/papers/paramythis_weibelzahl_UM2005_final.pdf.

[24] Preece, J., Rogers, Y., & Sharp, H., *Interaction Design: Beyond Human-Computer Interaction*. 1 ed. 2002, Harlow - UK: Addison-Wesley. 544.

[25] Bradley, G., *Social and Community Informatics: Humans on the Net*. 2006, NY: Routledge. 265. ISBN: 0-415-38185-1.

[26] Nosier, A., Connor, R., & Renaud, K. Question-based group authentication. *Paper in the conference proceedings of the OZCHI* held November *20-24*. 2006. Sydney, Australia. ISBN: 1-59593-545-2.

[27] McKay, E., Cognitive skill acquisition through a meta-knowledge processing model. *Interactive Learning Environments*, 2002. **10**(3): 263-291.

[28] Mason, J. & Lefrere, P., Trust, collaboration, e-Learning and organisational transformation. *International Journal of Training and Development*, 2003. **7**(4): 259-270.

[29] Norris, D., Mason, J., & Lefrere, P., *Transforming e-Knowledge: A Revolution in the Sharing of Knowledge*. 2003, Society for College and University Planning. Viewed 20/01/08 from http://www.scup.org/eknowledge/.

Chapter-5

Conceptual Learning: ICTs – Media – acknowledging cognitive performance

One of the chief motivations for writing this book is to fill a gap in the literature. This relates to the *human-dimensions (social context) of human-computer interaction (commonly referred to as HCI,)* with particular relevance for *effective HCI* applicable to the education and training sectors. Earlier chapters of this book were devised to provide a potted historical context of HCI in a narrative style to appeal to a broad audience. The intention in reaching beyond the techno-comfortable in this manner is to awaken those who may not pick up a more technical text. This fifth chapter brings forward the techno-humanoid landscape as a way to model the interactive components that bring about *effective HCI*. To explain the many facets of the *human-dimensions of HCI*, it is therefore important to synthesize the richness of the existing body of knowledge found in disparate professional practices. It is necessary to search beyond the techno-literature. This is why the reference list for this chapter is more extensive than with previous chapters.

Concept Learning

Given all the rhetoric on ICT usability over the years, we can say that using a computer hasn't yet reached the perfection that we would expect to see. However, to take the *human-dimensions of HCI* more seriously, surely means to take more notice of the differences in how people think during their information seeking dialogues with ICT tools. Sadly nothing has really happened yet in the techno-landscape to devise HCI strategies that acknowledge the variety of ways people respond to computers [1][2] [3]. By now clever GUIs should be providing multiple knowledge access strategies to cater for the rich diversity of a human-dimensioned techno-landscape. It's almost impossible to list the thousands of insidious techno-humanoid things impacting on our HCI. We can split this pervasive interference into two categories that combine to cause severe trouble for some computer users. In the first instance, let's call these trouble makers the external techno-humanoid contributors. In the second, we'll say they are our personal digital-awareness characteristics. As such, cultural dogma and professional practice are good examples of external influences that affect HCI [4]. At the very same time, simmering away almost unnoticed, are our individual characteristics like cognitive capability and physical digital-awareness. For the moment let us leave aside a discussion on the cultural nuances that affect our HCI, and look more closely at the contributing influence of professional practice *(Figure 30)*.

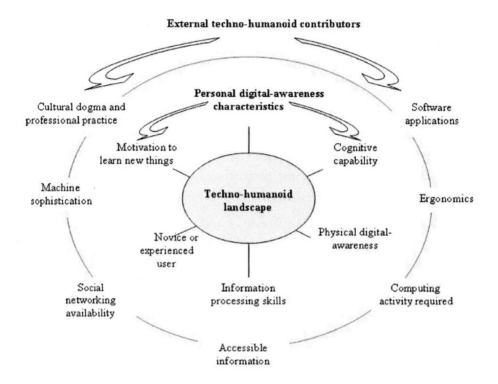

Figure 30 : Techno-Humanoid Landscape

We know for instance there are fundamental differences between the visual preferences of artists and non-artists, with interesting implications concerning the influence of their artistic background on their cognitive development. For some individuals, thinking is actually seeing. In fact, Kossyln [5] reports that such people, when asked to describe a specific attribute of that object, make an image in their mind of an actual object. Do not however, confuse the *thinking mode* of an individual, which can be changed according to the task at hand, with the way they may *process* this information. According to Riding [6] this is inherent and cannot be changed. However we need answers for the effect of multi-media on human beings' performance outcomes while using Web-mediated ICT tools [1]. To this end the nature of the effect of cognitive style differences on information systems usage and design has been explored [7] and more recently in Canada and the USA [8].

These days the highly graphical nature of the full range of ICT tools that are deployed through the Internet, enable us to deliver exciting courseware. The digital enhancement of worldly concepts that can be replicated for all to experience would appear to be never ending. However things do get a little tricky when these informational concepts are given to us through a GUI only, in a pictorial mode. At times, explanatory text for the graphical content of the concept to be learned may be limited, if not completely replaced by images (or pictorial representations). When this happens, it would appear there is an implied expectation by the courseware designers that people are all visually literate. Simply adding pictures to Web-pages does not always mean they can expect to be adding comprehension. This is where things get really awkward. As we have discussed earlier in this book, not everyone deals with the pictorial content of the GUIs in the same manner. This even though the literature has been showing a need to provide for individualised courseware for at least the past 3-decades. The problem of how to increase the usability of GUIs for those folk who have difficulty absorbing graphical concepts still remains largely unsolved.

Defining Techno-Age Concepts

It's far too easy to splash a GUI with colourful pictorial content upon the user's screen. Just think how more powerful the online instructional strategies would be if we were to take account of what is already known about how our minds work, and have that foresight applied to facilitate the techno-landscape. Here is where the dilemma of unsuitable HCI manifests. By not paying attention to the interactive effect of the external techno-humanoid contributors and the personal digital-awareness characteristics, many people will suffer degraded HCI experiences. For instance, to make sense of their world before the advent of the techno-age, people would differentiate between public and personal concepts in a systematic manner. In defining a newly experienced concept a person would automatically set out to build their own mental construct by comparing their personal thoughts towards this new concept (or thing) with those of others, by using one or more words to share their understanding. These shared "*mental constructs are the critical components of a maturing individual's continuously changing, enlarging cognitive structure [that] are the basic tools of thought.*" [9]:22).

Now, this may have been all very dandy when our lives were uncluttered by technology, but how do these pre-digital age learning traits translate into an *effective HCI?* Well for starters, there's something very public about sharing knowledge through the Internet with people you don't really know well. When people encounter a new concept in a Web-mediated learning environment, don't expect everyone to '*get it*' straight away. Some quickly assimilate newly defined concepts with their own experiential awareness and respond immediately. Others do not and appear to give up. Instead the latter should be encouraged to wander off in a cognitive sense into their own private thinking space where they can seek out their own understanding of the concept in question. As such, we may ask whether the new found techno-age can innovate opportunities for bringing forward a new type of techno-transparency that will reduce some of the inhibiting consequences of cultural dogma. Surely it is about time we were able to leverage the external techno-humanoid contributors of cultural differences with sensitive software applications to increase our personal digital-awareness. Moreover, surely it is incumbent upon us to use technology in new ways to increase the sharing of our knowledge about the world around us.

This means we need to find new ways to motivate some people towards learning new things when using the Internet. We know for instance that regardless of their experience elsewhere with other tasks, when trying something new for the first time we are describing a novice learner. In keeping with the dichotomy of the novice/experienced learner profile, it is very important to differentiate what a person knows from what they do not. For instance, a novice will require very specific instructions for learning a newly encountered task, whereas a mere overview of the same task will satisfy a more experienced person. When learning online, it's about time we had better ways to navigate our way straight to the information we need. It is a tremendous turn-off to have to wade through an exhaustive procedural list if we don't need it. By the same token, it is very useful to be able to return to the basic instructions should we only need a refresher.

Concept Classification and Characteristics

If we look more closely into definitions of concepts and with more detail, we will eventually find ourselves thinking about classes of concepts that fall into rather neat hierarchies. Some people may tend to do this automatically. For instance, we know there are four categories or groupings of concept types based on: the structure of the concept's attributes, perceptibility of the concept example, ease of the concept's definition, and the relationship to other concepts in a hierarchical sense [10]. Some people will relate easily to a particular class of word that is used, making the choice of unambiguous trigger words really important. This is a common technique these days. Think of some of the catchy advertisements we see on TV. In the thinking space of a few short seconds, some people can be convinced they are hungry, and follow the suggestion that they must dial up immediately for a *'delicious'* pizza. It is similarly easy to convince people that they must have the latest techno-gadget.

With screen-based information, the way that concepts are displayed is critical. As we have discussed earlier in this chapter, people invent concepts as arbitrary characteristics to make sense of the world [11]; [12]. There are four types of concepts that we constantly deal with everyday. They can be classified as: concrete, abstract, rule and process *(Figure 31)*.

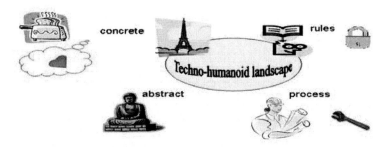

Figure 31 : Four Types of Concepts

Concrete concepts are by far the easiest ones to represent in a GUI using ICT tools, because of their commonly recognizable and definable attributes. They represent tangible things that have common physical features. Things that people can readily see (like buildings), or may be heard (like laughter), or they may be felt (like emotion), or smelt (like burnt toast)!

However it's the abstract concepts that do make things a little bit tricky, because there are no recognizable attributes that can be pointed to. In fact, people have to be shown the abstract-ness of these concepts (like religious belief). Another example of this type of abstract relationship is between family members (son, daughter, uncle and aunt). While exact words do not have to be employed, these definitions must be clearly defined.

Rule concepts represent the notion of basic facts or the meaningful information about certain worldly things. As such the learning of rule concepts has been previously treated as the lowest level of intellectual skill development. Think of how often you see Web pages that are full of unrelated facts and figures. Yet when a person fully understands a rule concept (like knowing that a key opens a lock), they move toward a deeper empowerment because they can recognize relationships between one or more concepts. Therefore, it is very important to show these interactive relationships between concepts.

Process concepts are very special because they combine all the other concept attributes we have seen in the concrete, abstract and rule based concepts. Although many researchers have differing opinions of problem-solving activities, they all agree that problem-solving research is rule-based. Process concepts draw on our knowledge of two or more previously learned rule concepts to solve unfamiliar problems.

Instructional Strategies Under Constant Review

There can be no doubt that the fantastic capabilities of digital processing have spilled over to completely alter Instructional Science forever. Over the last decade, we have experienced several paradigmatic shifts as the instructional designers of the time struggled to come to terms with the techno-landscape. Let us first take a quick look backwards, to understand our emerging position on the instructional design for ICT tools. This little journey sits comfortably alongside any story which depicts the developmental progress of available IT tools from the early computing era into the new millennium. Accordingly, we can see a developmental saga that travels through 3-distinct phases, that include theoretical views on behaviourism, cognitivism and constructivism. For those who may need a quick reminder, behaviourism is based on observable changes in behaviour. The distinctive approach of behaviourism was (and still is) the belief that new behavioural patterns become automatic if they are repeated often enough. Cognitivism on the other hand, reflects the human thought processes behind the behaviour. Practitioners believe that changes in behaviour can be observed to explain what is happening within the learner's mind. Constructivism however relies on the premise that we utilize individual experiences that become personal schemas. To construct our own particular perspective of the world, a central focus of constructivism is to prepare people to strengthen their capability to solve ambiguous problems.

Constructivism and Knowledge Acquisition

Given the ever shifting state of the educational techno-landscape, and considering the popularity of ICT tools utilized for online learning, it is quite understandable that Instructional Science is constantly changing. Some may say that the traditional work on concept leaning has only taken on a techno-cloak to become knowledge acquisition.

Examining the literature during the previous decade, it is easy to see that the constructivists believe that *"learners construct their own reality or at least interpret it based upon their perceptions of experiences, so an individual's knowledge is a function of one's prior experiences, mental structures, and beliefs that are used to interpret objects and events."* Moreover, that *"what someone knows is grounded in perception of the physical and social experiences which are comprehended by the mind."* [13]. It is perhaps not very wise to try and take an overall approach in describing how constructivism should work in today's ICT context. Recall at this point our earlier discussion on concept development. This now becomes critical to our discussion. From the rhetoric in the literature, it would appear there may be a common misperception about constructivism. A suggestion that people develop their own (knowledge) schemas totally isolated from others (socially shared knowledge). Surely it is only sensible to conceive that humans prepare their own knowledge based upon their two-way checking routine? We were discussing earlier where they drift off into their own cognitive space to align newly presented concepts with their own *'experiential rememberings'*. Instead it is more acceptable to note that constructivism is achieved through a process of social negotiation.

As we have seen in the opening chapters of this book, the techno-landscape was undergoing massive expansion of machine capacity and software development, throughout the previous decade. Consequently, while ordinary folk in the community have been reinventing their understandings of new ways to implement more powerful ICT tools for online learning, the paradigmatic divisions between the well known proponents of cognitivism and constructivism has blurred. For instance, locating 1990's issues of *Educational Technology*, it is useful for our discussion to bring forward a well known cognitive psychologist Dave Merrill's assumptions [14] of constructivism. He suggests that:

- knowledge is constructed from experience
- learning is a personal interpretation of the world
- learning is an active process in which meaning is developed on the basis of experience
- conceptual growth comes from the negotiation of meaning, the sharing of multiple perspectives and the changing of our internal representations through collaborative learning
- learning should be situated in realistic settings; testing should be integrated with the task and not a separate activity

Efficiency and Effectiveness of Techno-Automation

Let's put aside the importance to remember to always draw on basic theories of learning when generating online courseware. A more pragmatic approach is required to ensure the *human-dimensions of HCI* moves forward. Even with the advantages afforded by hindsight, it's no longer good enough to simply rely on the lessons learned by others. Not even from those who have passed through the literature to illuminate a new generation of Instructional Science. We have reached the point where more innovative educational strategies that can cope with ICT tools in a techno-landscape are way overdue. Despite the call from Diana Laurillard [15] to rethink our use of educational technology in higher education, there's still way too much bad stuff on the Internet. One of the causes for this proliferation of worldly techno-crap is that it's relatively too easy for ordinary people to make their techno-materials and mindlessly launch them into cyberspace. If those of us who know and understand what is happening, even if we don't respond at this point, online learning is forever doomed.

Instead, the techno-humanoid landscape requires careful planning to invoke the richness of our inherent cognitive capabilities. So saying, we are well advised to rethink those founding basics of knowledge construction. One example of this would be found in the prior work on concept learning by Tennyson and Cocchiarella [16]. These researchers took a rationalistic approach to describing the learning process as a 2-phase process (formation of conceptual knowledge and development of procedural knowledge). Their view of concept teaching was based on direct empirical validation from a programmatic line of instructional systems research. As before, these researchers also proposed that conceptual knowledge is formed in an individual's memory, and is more than just the storage of declarative knowledge. Remember that earlier in this chapter, we saw how people evaluate their personal experience in terms of cognitive-fit with social acceptance of newly presented concepts.

ICT tools should be carefully deployed to promote an understanding of a concept's operational structure within itself, as well as between associated concepts. Surely there is absolutely no harm in adopting this type of HCI to emulate our natural cognitive processing? An individual develops procedural knowledge when using their conceptual knowledge to solve domain-specific problems. Apparently two cognitive processes interact when an individual exercises their procedural knowledge during a problem solving exercise, which in turn further elaborates their conceptual knowledge. The second phase of the Tennyson & Cocchiarella [16] model deals with the instructional design variables for teaching concepts. They explained that these instructional design variables are directly related to specific cognitive processes in concept learning. They claim that this component has three cognitive processing stages:

- to establish connections with necessary knowledge in memory
- for the formation of conceptual knowledge
- the development of procedural knowledge

Although they suggested more research is needed to investigate ways of adjusting the presentation strategies to account for possible differences in conceptual learning, we are no further ahead.

Mental Constructs

Another way to describe how people adjust their thinking when using digital devices and the Internet can be explained using the interaction of external techno-humanoid contributors and the personal digital-awareness characteristics. In this sense we can use the term concept to refer to both the cultural meaning given to the concept name and to an individual's mental construct. The Learning and Development Theory shows how concepts have been defined with the lowest entity as an item, when referring to an object, event, action, quality or relationship [17]. Apparently, as an individual attains a given concept at successively higher levels of understanding, their mental constructs change. People go on to use their mental constructs to identify all examples and non-examples as well as using the concept in an expert manner. Therefore we see yet again, where the literature has shown us that mental constructs are considered to be the building blocks of a person's cognitive structure. The latter can be thought of as the fundamental agents of all thinking processes. Sadly, the present instructional materials that involve ICT tools leave the learner to stumble their way through a self-discovery learning tour (more often than not tinged by disaster).

Because of this, some groups of people do not succeed! Effective instructional strategy must direct the learner to the general and critical attributes Merrill et al [18](1992) identified the concept's attributes as providing the information with which the student must become cognitively engaged [19]. However, instructional strategies for the computerized learning context must include both perceptive and non-perceptible attributes of the concept according to Merrill (1998), and the cultural meaning given to the concept name [20].

Relationship Modelling

As we have seen the difficulties in the knowledge acquisition of abstract concepts has been to find ways of showing people the relationships between several other concepts (or knowledge domains). The more traditional methods would be to draw on familiar story-like scripts to do the job. For instance, one could use the familiar scenario of eating in a restaurant to explain the relationship between price of dishes on the menu and the quality of food, or visiting a doctor to explain the trust relationship between practitioner and patient. In order for these scripts to make any sense, the script's properties must have the culturally agreed upon attributes and instances of the newly encountered concept. However it has also been noted that people often have difficulty remembering the script-based texts. People can become confused about what was actually said, with what the script strongly implied [21]. Furthermore, people preferred to learn event sequences that preserved the scriptal order. Interestingly enough they were also best at recalling brief obstacles or distractions which caused a block or temporarily suspended pursuit of the script's goal. Props or events, on the other hand, were least recalled.

Once again, it's about time we had access to the richness of this type of knowledge acquisition or learning context expressed through ICT tools as an important feature of the *human-dimensions* of our HCI. Also that such tools draw on the interaction of external techno-humanoid contributors and the personal digital-awareness characteristics. Not only do we now have the media to generate meaningful examples, we also have the ability to customize the GUIs for cultural sensitivity. The trouble is that while the techno-philes have been struggling with the newness of the techno-landscape, rudimentary pedagogy as it applies to online learning has missed its share of attention. Consequently, for us to understand how this could be done, it is useful to compare the *"Script Theory"* [22], against the much older *"Gestalt Theory"*. *Table 8* shows where the ICT tools can be implemented to facilitate knowledge acquisition in an online learning environment.

Table 8 : Script Theory and Implications for *Human-Dimensions of HCI*

Script Theory	Implications for *human-dimension* HCI
Script generation	Promotes the interaction of external techno-humanoid contributors with the personal digital-awareness characteristics for improved learning outcomes.
Constituent structure of scripts	Enables the exposure of the concept attributes.
Script recall	Facilitates the over all meaning.
Script recognition	Quickens the individual's cognitive checking process.
Script action reordering	Stimulates memory recall.
Script expectations and comprehension time	Strengthens the predictability of the instructional design process.
Remembering deviations from scripts	Enables recognition of implied relationships between one or more interrelated concepts.

The Gestalt Theory originated in Austria and Germany toward the end of the 19th century. Since that time it has continually evolved as a reaction to the Associativist Theory and the school of thought that became fundamental to several disciplines, including instructional design and learning theory. While the Associativist theorists broke down and analysed individual stimuli, or the constituent parts of the mind, the Gestalt theorists were known to be more interested in the grouping of these stimuli, and the viewing of the organized wholes that produced a different view. For the readers who may not be aware the term *'gestaldt'* is German for *'being' 'figure'* or *'configuration'*. For many people, Gestalt psychology is a well known school of psychology. It teaches that psychology should study the whole pattern of behaviour instead of analysing it into elements, since the whole is more than the sum of its parts.

To help see what may be driving our thinking while working on a computer, let us now look at a Gestalt grouping technique [23] that may explain how we make sense of our world *(Table 9)*.

Table 9 : Gestalt Theory and the Implications for *Human-Dimensions of HCI*

Gestalt Theory – Laws of Organization		Implications for *human-dimension HCI*
Proximity	Elements tend to be grouped together according to their nearness	To facilitate the interaction of external techno-humanoid contributors with the personal digital-awareness characteristics, for improved understanding of newly encountered concepts; all grouped items and elements must be identified with pictures and text to ensure the exact meaning is conveyed by the ICT delivery media. Examples provided in an online learning context must enable people to generalize and discriminate.
Similarity	Items similar in some respect tend to be grouped together	
Closure	Items are grouped together if they tend to complete some entity	
Simplicity	Items will be organized into simple figures according to symmetry, regularity, and smoothness	

In saying we need to innovate *effective HCI* strategies to facilitate online learning, it simply does not make sense to throw the metaphoric (learning theories) baby out with the bath-water. When it all boils down to it, cognitive processes involved in concept acquisition are well known in the educational technology community as generalization and discrimination [14];[18]. Educational research has shown that generalization occurs with a particular response in a stimulus situation, which was acquired in an earlier, but similar stimulus situation. When processing stimuli information presented by the new instance, people attempt to make a precise *"if ....* *then"* inference. Discrimination on the other hand, occurs when a learner exhibits a particular response in one stimulus situation, but a different response in another stimulus situation [18] . When, for instance, a generalisation from one instance to another does not produce the expected result. For example, an individual can *"acknowledge that a small dog, which is roughly similar in size and is also hairy, may in fact actually be a cat!"* Therefore, the first procedure in analysing a content area is to determine the relationships between concepts.

Information Processing

There are a vast number of well respected theories of intelligence in the literature. Opinion is divided according to the personal orientation of the researcher. Several researchers propose new and unsettling explanations about human information processing to completely refute the traditionalist approach [24]; [25]; [26]. There have been several supporters of the notion that contextual considerations play a vital role in the information processing operations of the human mind [24]. While there are others who propose a purely internal orientation [27], describing the human mind in terms of a closed processing system receiving continual input from the world around us. Artificial intelligence research is driving the focus of Instructional Science research to find the means to replicate the information processing of the human mind (Tennyson & [28]. However, there are a growing number of prominent researchers who no longer want to follow the traditional attempts to depict memory as a box in a flow diagram [29].

Baddeley [30] for instance has written several books and many papers on human memory. According to Baddeley [30], memory is a collection of interacting systems, which combine to store and subsequently retrieve information. It is our capacity to learn and remember, that has enabled us to develop tools, communication skills and technologies. Consequently, it is through this interaction of communication with technology, that humans now have an even greater capacity to store and retrieve vast quantities of information. The progression of our ability to communicate through writing, film-making and indeed television can thus be regarded as an extension of the human memory.

Trying to categorize human memory becomes too theoretical [30]. Baddeley [30] suggests that there are no true answers, only interpretations of available evidence. In organizing information mentally, however, one of the most common techniques humans draw on is their visual imagery ability. He demonstrated the effective use of peg words to recall sequences of unrelated items in an appropriate order.

Cognition and Instruction Format

Most of the past research on memory was highly controlled, with results reflecting the contrived experimental laboratory conditions. In reviewing memory models and research, Baine [25] warned against generalising laboratory findings from past research on memory to the natural environment, unless the exact nature of the experimental procedure is known. Mnemonic strategies are practical techniques which have the potential to make information more memorisable and easier to retrieve. For example, there is well known research that proposes a principle of cognitive economy [31]. This identifies labeling, visual imagery, and maintenance rehearsal as effective mnemonic strategies. The notions of Rosch's [31] cognitive economy are once again relevant to explain human cognitive categorization systems. Her first principle, called the cognitive economy, is related to the automatic way humans conserve their cognitive energies. It was seen as a method, which balances our need to discriminate between the infinity of things we wish to know, and those things of lesser importance. Her second principle, relates to the highly correlated relationships which occur in the material objects of the world. Rosch [31] defined this principle of categorization, as the perceived world structure. However, she warns, this must not isolate the knower from the notion of the perceived world. In addition to this, Rosch[31] suggests that the influence of the culture at any particular point in time determines the human category system.

Process-Oriented Learning Resources

Engaging ICT tools for educational activities are one method to alter previous traditions. In the past these have been passive and overly prescriptive, concentrating on discrete and disconnected measures of student performance. The instructional method believed to improve student learning was the design of process-oriented learning resources. These were first described by McDermott Hannifin [32]:77 as *"teaching and learning activities which engage students cognitively in analyzing and transforming information."*. Process-oriented resources promote cognitive functions and operations to orient themselves to the new information. While thus engaged, they are able to retrieve related material from their long-term memory; thereby constructing and transforming information. This in turn becomes encoded into new understandings which can then be stored into their long-term memory. Such processes become particularly relevant when process-oriented outcomes are expected. Teaching methods should reflect the critical thinking, reasoning or problem solving that is required as a learning outcome.

McDermott Hannifin goes on to reveal that when learners are given a cookbook of steps to follow for solving particular types of problems, they would rather pay attention to the application of the steps, than to the understanding of the principles behind the steps themselves. The danger may be that they only experience their learning at a surface level, without ever developing the necessary insight to solve problems in general. Moreover there are benefits when the facilitator uses instructional strategies in which they verbalize, describe and model their thinking processes. Learners are then better able to model the facilitator's problem solving strategies, as well as the reasoning processes underlying the problem solving strategies.

Table 10 : Researchers' View of Cognitive Abilities

Terms describing cognitive differences	Researchers
Levellers-sharpeners	Holzman & Klein, 1954 [33]
Field dependence-field independence	Witkin, Dyke, Patterson, Goodman & Kemp, 1962 [34]
Impulsive-reflective	Kagan, 1965 [35]
Divergers-convergers	Guilford, 1967 [36]
Holists-serialists	Pask & Scott, 1972 [37]
Wholist-analytic	Riding & Cheema, 1991 [38]
Adaptor-innovator	Kirton, 2003 [39]

Cognitive Style

Notwithstanding the psychologists, for most people, fully understanding the literature relating to individual learning attributes is challenging to say the least. There are many terms describing how individuals process information that change according to the researcher's professional paradigm. Early attempts during the 1950's and 1960's by psychologists researching cognitive abilities and processes produced a fragmented list of models and labels *(Table 10)*. These were derived mainly from single experiments [6].

Riding and Rayner argued however, that cognitive style should be understood to be an individual's preferred and habitual approach to organizing and representing information. Be that as it may, it was Pask [40] who first proposed the existence of the *"holist/serialist"* distinction, as an example of different learning strategies, rather than the presence of a learning style.

Visual Perception

Current cognitive theories of perception and imagery do not really clarify how people react to using ICT tools for knowledge acquisition. There has of course been a considerable amount of earlier research which shows differences in recall for pictures and words in adults [41]. However it was Ritchey [42] who suggested that memory activations within the semantic domain would vary on 2-dimensions, both between-meaning representations and within-meaning representations. Pictorial stimuli therefore, because of the additional information they contain about the physical properties of an object, would tend to give rise to more extensive activations within-meaning representations than their verbal counterparts.

One technique to facilitate perception of those precious abstract relationships can be shown effectively using block-word diagrams. Let us take an example of showing the relationships between concepts that deal with the processes of a food chain using arrows [43];[44]. Whereas class inclusion relationships like mice are herbivores,

herbivores are consumers; can be shown by placing appropriate concepts in the same visual rectangle, and then perhaps shading it [43].

Placing concepts together, such as this in the one square, helps the learning of generalizations, because it facilitates the perception of similarities between them. At the same time, placing each concept in its own square, assists the novice learner to discriminate between concepts, as it facilitates the perception of differences. The ordering of the squares and the concepts within them sequentially, or by means of arrows, contributes to the formation of associations and chains. This process assists the novice learner perceive logical, causal and sequential relationships.

Visual Literacy

Once again, the use of the term visual literacy will also differ according to the researcher's professional paradigm. Many researchers have shown that measuring an individual's visualization ability is a very difficult research area. Consequently more work is needed to unlock the mysteries surrounding the interactive effects of peoples' cognitive processing capability and online performance outcomes. In 1991, James & Moore investigated whether the level of field dependence affects a student's ability to profit from either imposed visuals or instructions to form visual images, to aid immediate recall of concrete pared-associate nouns. They believed there were possible changes in the relationship between field dependence and visual strategy as students move from elementary to high school. Their three-way analysis of variance showed that all three main effects (grade level, cognitive style and visual strategy) were significant. This means there was no interaction! However, this result is not at all surprising, given that the purpose of their study was to investigate the relationship of cognitive style and the efficacy of imposed visuals and instructions to form visual images, as aids to immediate memory recall.

Knowledge and Learning

Instructional systems rely on the analysis of learning content; that is, the specific knowledge requirements within a domain of information. Knowledge has been identified by Gagne [11] as concrete or declarative (that is knowing the specific facts and rules), and abstract or procedural (that is knowing how to apply declarative knowledge in new situations). However it was Gibbs [45] who argued there was enough evidence from linguistics and psychology to conclude that people construed many concepts in terms of metaphor. He/she? called for more research to see if, when and how, certain concepts were metaphorically represented.

Researchers have refined their attitude towards the relationship between knowledge and learning since the 1960's. For instance, a comprehensive schema acts as a basis for classifying types of learning [46]:267. Romiszowski [46] suggested that *"knowledge is 'information stored'' – it is something an individual possesses. Either he has it, or he has not – a go/no-go quality. Individuals differ in the quantity of knowledge that they posses."* He argued that individuals would always differ in the quality of the results they achieve when they apply knowledge to practical tasks, because of the innate individual differences between people. Instead of reporting on an individual's cognitive differences, Hummel & Holyoak [47], argued that the cognitive architecture embodied in their computational model, called *"Learning and Influence with Schemas and Analogies"* (LISA), to represent the human thought process. Consequently their approach to cognitive individuality is generic, investigating the mechanistic side of the HCI equation. They maintained that LISA may help us understand why human thinking was superior to the constraints of machine generated memory capacity.

Knowledge Acquisition

The inter-relationship of the human mind with the ability to learn and make decisions that change the person and the world, has been a focus of educational researchers for many years. Literature on acquiring knowledge covers a broad spectrum, with each researcher concentrating on their particular professional paradigm. To support the *human-dimensions of HCI* as the primary conceptual framework for our discussion here, we shall look at a mere portion of the expertise that has gone before us, that is relevant to the techno-landscape. For a more complete discussion on this interesting topic see McKay [26];[48].

Let us begin with the Bruner's [49] explanation that the task of teaching a task should represent the structure of the subject-to-be-learned in terms of the learner's way of viewing things as a series of habits and associations. While another view reveals that the learners should be encouraged to play with problems [50];[51], making a distinction between knowing and understanding is important. Understanding it was said, takes time, and was achieved by allowing the novice learner to become immersed in a problem. It was held that the way the learner can encounter intricacies and subtleties of the concepts-to-be-learned, enables them to explore the learning domain in rich and meaningful ways, thereby progressing from simply knowing to understanding.

Another view conveyed is that multi-sensory instruction improves a student's capacity to learn effectively [52]. This instructional approach maximized the learner's skills brought to the learning task, while minimising the experiences where their ineptitudes are emphasized. Meanwhile, Sternberg's [53] approach was to concentrate on the basic information processes in analogical reasoning. Stages of skill acquisition involve 5-steps from novice to expert [54]:

- Novice
- Advanced beginner
- Competence
- Proficiency
- Expertise

Constructivism

Most of the literature reviewed above has focused on instructional frameworks and cognitive processes. During the 1980's however an alternative voice emerged from the research, which placed an emphasis on the importance of the individual in the learning and memory domain. Although there is still much debate amongst instructional theorists and instructions designers, the constructivist approach has continued to gain respect and support through to the present day. It was said that learners do not learn in a passive manner [55];[56]. They must actively engage in their learning [52]. This means they will proceed through 3-learning stages:

- Interpret the topics to be learned
- Elaborate these interpretations
- Test these interpretations

Describing how human cognition reached beyond an automatic response as a reaction to input, Bruner [57] defines the *"BIG (beyond-the-information-given)"*; while the contrasting *"WIG strategy (within-the-information-given)"* holds back on direct instruction. It was Perkins [55];[56] who explained the issues that surround the notions of technology meeting constructivism. He argued that on the one hand, BIG constructivism allows students to be fully engaged in a number of thought-oriented activities, which directly challenge them to apply and generalize their initial understandings, and refine their learning strategies along the way. Furthermore, he believed that *"BIG"* instructional strategies are able to produce contrasting concepts (like showing the distinction between heat and temperature) through implementing computer based imagistic metal models. While on the other hand, *"WIG"* produces learning by concepts rediscovered (like not offering the official characterization of heat versus temperature). Under a *"WIG"* strategy, the student would be encouraged to provide an intuitive explanation, with the instructor only stepping in at the last moment. These days, ICT tools can provide simulations that utilize both instructional strategies.

Anchored instruction is another constructivist approach to instructional design that we need to touch upon here. This is the term that the *"Cognition & Technology Group at Vanderbilt"* [58] (CTGVB) applied to their instruction. It means the instructional strategy engages the learner in problem-rich learning environments. Anchors create a macro-context [58], in which all the stakeholders are involved in the learning programme. For instance, the subject matter experts, teachers and students from diverse backgrounds combine to communicate in a collective learning experience. They have also proposed that the macro-experts provide the potential to facilitate experimental studies for further research.

Knowledge and Cognitive Style Differences

Notwithstanding our earlier mention of Richard Riding's [38] thoughts on cognitive style and their reference to other important work relating to cognitive strategies people employ, it is important to discuss some conflicting evidence in our quest to enhance the *human-dimensions of HCI* for the educational and training sectors. The importance of this work relates an otherwise forgotten reason as to why some people are able to *"get things"* when using educational ICT tools more quickly than others. Due to the highly visual nature of most multi-media it is necessary to give some thought to the number of people with perfect eye-sight, who nonetheless may not be able to see various attributes in a visual sense unless they are directed to look at them specifically.

The original work was conducted by Lowenfield [59] with further research taken up by Howell [60] and Moore & Bedient [61]. However, the latter researchers mixed the presentation of visual stimulus in a sequential manner, with the cognitive characteristics of visual material. This was an unfortunate mistake, because it blurred the understandings of *"haptic/visual types"* and *"field dependent/independent"* individuals. For instance they claimed that field dependent individuals may have difficulty in retaining a visual stimulus, when the materials are presented in sequence. Furthermore, that it would be reasonable using multiple (or simultaneous) imagery, to reduce the visual task for the field dependent learners, as well as the field independents. To settle this argument Riding & Cheema's [38] ability to condense the earlier style constructs into their two families of cognitive style, has unlocked the looming stalemate for explaining how people may respond to verbal/visual stimuli. Researchers often working in isolation use similar labels from the literature that groups their work into one (or both) of the following schools of thought: *'wholist-analytic'* and/or *'verbal-imagery'*. The resulting deadlock occurs through a misunderstanding of which grounded theory the researcher follows. To this end, the *"wholist-analytic"* and *"verbal/imager"* continua reflect an integrative model of cognitive style [38]. It is worth noting here that Richard Riding has devised a computer-based tool, known as the Cognitive Styles Analysis (CSA), to measure an individual's position along these 2-cognitive dimensions [6].

Transfer of Learning Outcomes to New Places

Prior to most people entering into a skill development programme involving some form of HCI, the learning outcomes are usually proudly displayed for all to see. As such there is an implied expectation that the skills and knowledge gained during the training/educational programme as meta-cognitive abilities will be transferable to another context. Sadly, this is often not the case. Usually the training session may have been organized into segmented block(s) of time – say two or more hours. These instructional programmes often involve concentrated rhetoric on the part of the trainer/facilitator, interwoven with an opportunity for hands-on practice. Upon returning to their own environment away from the training room, people are left lacking any form of unilateral meta-cognitive ability, without the one-to-one facilitation of the training room.

It may be interesting to note here that meta-cognitive abilities that involve logical problem solving skills are essential for business decision making. Because of this the teaching of introductory computer programming skills can be a valuable exercise. However, in the highly analytical learning domain of computer programming, the novice is frequently left to develop procedural (or abstract) knowledge on their own. As such, while learning initial concepts they never have the opportunity to experiment with generalized procedural (or conceptual) knowledge processes [62]. Moreover, they are often exposed to worked examples that are generated by expert programmers. Bagley [62] argued that in this circumstance, the novice may not be able to retrieve the appropriate personal schemata without being taught the rules (declarative knowledge), the abstract processes or general procedural knowledge associated with the programming language. Novices were therefore left to rely on common sense, to extract the necessary procedural processes (conceptual knowledge) necessary to build relevant schemata. When this happens, they may regress, due to their failure to draw any benefit from the learning experience [63].

Instructional Format

Now that we have discussed some of the factors which affect knowledge acquisition, we shall move on to some ways we can innovate instructional material to enhance learning through carefully designed ICT tools. In the past is has been noted that instruction was not helpful when students' preferred mental representations (verbal, spatial) were not taken into account. Therefore learners instructed in a way that does not match their preferred mental representation will use the strategy that is easiest [64]. Even though earlier research tried to link instructional format with individual differences in learning mode, many subsequent researchers appeared to lose sight of these individual differences. The common belief that pictures will enhance learning performance for all was consequently promoted across the (learning) board.

However, there was evidence of agreement in the Instructional Science research community two decades ago that still holds relevance today for the *human-dimensions of HCI*. Earlier, Merrill et al., concentrated on 4-primary instructional design variables, for organizing learning content into a single presentation strategy *(Table 11)*. It is still necessary these days to translate these instructional design principles to the online learning environment:

Merrill & Tennyson [65] demonstrated that the structural form of the information to be learned has an effect on the form of knowledge an individual codes into their memory. It was much later that the Klausmeier's *"Concept Learning Development"* (commonly called the CLD) model was advanced as another fine example of an empirically based instructional design (Tennyson [16] representing 4-levels of conceptual development *(Table 12)*.

Merrill admits however that his original *'Component Display Theory'* CDT did not show people how to implement computer-based instruction. While the original CDT advocates learner control, it did not include prescriptions for online learner guidance concerning different transactions or different content representations. Instead, his second CDT extends the original CDT to include 4-cardinal principles of instruction that provide for both tutorial and experiential instruction [12]:358) *(Table 13)*.

However it is Laurillard [15] who takes the notion of autonomy in learning materials one step further. According to this, we should be able to design curriculum materials, such that a student never encounters materials that they are cognitively ill-prepared to learn.

Table 11 : Merrill's Four Primary Instructional Design Variables

Instructional Design Variables	Implications for *human-dimensions of HCI*
Definition	Whenever a lesson requires a definition, you probably should implement a concept lesson (eg: mass, force and acceleration).
Expository instances	Use ICT tools to demonstrate to a student that each given instance as a set of matched example/non-example pairs in which subsequent examples are divergent from the preceding examples and which range in difficulty from easy to hard.
Interrogatory instances	Present information to facilitate the student's question answering. A story is a good example; where the story is merely the vehicle that provides context in which to couch questions that require a response.
Attribute elaboration	Identify each critical attribute and the most common potentially confusing attributes of the concepts that are being taught.

Table 12 : Tennyson & Cocchiarella's Four Levels of Conceptual Development

Original CLD model	Implications for *human-dimensions of HCI*
Concrete: **Recall of the critical attributes**	Individuals have attained the concept as an object only. People can discriminate the concept from other objects and represent it internally as an image, and remember the representation. For instance: someone possessing an image of a clock. The identity level was inferred by the individual's recognition of an object in another situational context, or sensed in a different modality such as hearing or seeing.
Identity: **Recall of learned examples**	People not only discriminate, but they also need to generalize the forms of the particular object as equivalent across the different contexts in which the same object is experienced. For instance: a person recognizing the clock in a different setting.
Classificatory: **Generalize to newly encountered example**	An individual responds to two or more different examples of the same class of objects, events, or processes. For instance: when the clock on the wall and the one on the desk are recognized as being different visually but have the same functionality. At this level, the attributes cannot be clearly distinguished. An individual may not be able to express the differences between the objects verbally at the classificatory level.
Formal: **Discriminate between newly encountered instances**	An individual can discriminate the attributes of the concept, and name the defining attributes giving an acceptable definition of the concept. It is only when people can accomplish all four levels of concept attainment that it is inferred that they have learned the concept.

Table 13 : Merrill's Four Cardinal Principles of Instruction

New CLD model's 4-cardinal principles of instruction	Implications for *human-dimensions of HCI*
Cognitive structure	The purpose of the instruction should be to promote the *development* of that cognitive structure which is most consistent with the desired learned performance.
Elaboration	The purpose of this type of instruction is to promote *incremental elaboration* of the most appropriate cognitive structure to enable the learner to achieve *increased generality and complexity* in the desired learned performance.
Learner guidance	The purpose of this element is to promote the *active cognitive processing* which best enables the learner to *use the most appropriate cognitive structure in a way consistent with* the desired learned performance.
Practice	The purpose of this instruction is to provide the dynamic, ongoing opportunity for monitored practice that requires the learner to demonstrate the desired learned performance, or a close approximation of it, while the instruction monitors the activity and intervenes with feedback both as to result and process.

Mnemonics

Humans have been using drawings to convey meaning since the beginning of time. The concept of *"notationality"* was devised way back in 1968 by Goodman [66]. This notion provided one end of a continuum that can be used for classifying symbol systems, placing non-notational systems at the other [67]. The characteristics of a notational system are a one-to-one matching of the (learning) element, and its referent. Similarly the characteristics of a non-notational system are revealed as not having a one-to-one relationship between the element, and its referent. *'Non-notational'* systems can lead to multiple meanings due to ambiguous mapping with the field of reference. The kind of information an individual extracts from a non-notational symbol system varies, according to the way the individual reads them [67]. It is this very issue where ICT tools can play an important role: through sensitive design practice, to assist with this process. When a learner with a particular cognitive style cannot cope with the GUI, it is now possible to develop these characteristics into software objects that act as *'notational transfer agents* [68]. For people to be able to map their own understanding of the images conveyed, textual captions are absolutely necessary to address the explicit and implicit features of the information.

Visual Information Processing as an Instructional Strategy

As we have seen throughout this chapter, educational researchers have shown there are important relationships between learning and instruction. Instruction involves the control of the learning processes, inducing learners to draw on their own learning strategies for particular tasks. However, instruction operates externally to the learner. Nonetheless, it is the learner's mental skills that must be used productively in learning events. It is thought that most people use imagery as a cognitive process. Sadly, only a few learners are mentally skilled in its use. When learners apply mental skills to a particular learning task, these skills are said to be functioning as learning strategies. The dilemma for devising effective learning ICT tools as learning resources is to know when and how to implement instructional strategies that provide sufficient information to interest learners. Instructional strategies are said to have two components [69]. The operating task is the first component, providing the way for inducing novice learners to adopt particular cognitive processes; for instance, when instructional materials explicitly require learners to form (mental) images. The second instructional component is the learner's capabilities.

At this point we should distinguish between learning and instruction to say that learning strategies have two origins. In the first instance, when learners are told what strategies to use, and secondly when learners are capable of deciding what learning strategy to adopt for a particular task. As such, instructional strategies have been distinguished between detached and embedded *(Table 14)*. Detached strategies [70] and detached activators [71] are independent of the subject matter. Embedded activators can include pictures, diagrams, mnemonics, and analogies [19]. These two instructional strategies occur when novice learners are told to use a particular cognitive process. For instance, when instructional material requires a learner to recall information previously presented. A requirement of this type of instruction is that the learner should follow a particular strategy to complete a certain task.

Table 14 : Detached and Embedded Instructional Strategies

Detached strategy	Embedded strategy	Implications for *human-dimensions of HCI*
As the DOWHILE loop is a leading decision loop, the following strategy takes place. The logical condition p is tested, with a specific question. eg: are there any family members who need to clean their teeth	BACKGROUND: All computers have three main functions: data input, data processing, information output. Data is given to the computer via a keyboard or another input mechanism. The computer program performs or processes, whatever function it was designed for and the result is printed on the computer screen or printed by the printer is commonly referred to as the output.	Visualization in learning involves representations and processes that are picture like, contain form, size, pattern, and even colour (Kosslyn,1980). While visualization in instruction, on the other hand, comprises embedded and detached instructional strategies that promote internal visual processing of information.

Visualization strategies can include highly visual components such as pictures and diagrams as well as non-visual components. The latter include verbal instructions given to learners to form (mental) images.

Verbal Exposition as Instructional Strategies

In some cases, it can be shown that we are more comfortable using verbal rather than visual communication [72]. It can be further argued that this may be due to our early school days where the instructional emphasis was on reading and the use of the spoken word for learning subject matter [72]. Moreover, verbal exposition has been described as, the mere telling, an illustration, or the demonstration of an instructional event [73];[74]. Verbal exposition can also take the form of diagrams and charts [74]. This form presents logical relationships among concepts-to-be-learned in a spatial layout.

However, words are only the primary vehicle in instruction [75]. Learners need to transfer their knowledge by using a verbalised skill, received during the instructional event, to an appropriate skill in some other mode. There are other forms of instructional exposition, besides verbal, pictorial, and graphical in representing single words, whole sentences or labels. They are used to define objects and actions [72]. These verbal symbols are usually specific to a particular language, and as such, may be highly abstract in nature. Pictorial symbols on the other hand, are highly realistic and very concrete [72]. However, some graphical symbols may be very difficult to read.

Automated Learning Content Structure

As we have seen earlier in this chapter, representation of abstract concepts is difficult largely because they cannot be seen. This is of particular importance when considering the interactive effects of cognitive style on learning ability. For instance, *"wholists"* may not be able to locate the fine detail easily, while *"analytics"* may have difficulty correctly identifying the complete concept [6]. Furthermore there is an issue of fidelity. There should be a degree of correspondence between the learning entities shown in *Table 15* [76]:

Table 15 : Learning Entities that Should Correspond

Issues of learning content fidelity	Implications for *human-dimensions of HCI*
Actual object	The representation should usually include all of these defining characteristics that make the object or event a member of a particular class. For instance: if a mammal were defined as a fur-bearing animal that suckles its young, then it may not be sufficient to indicate that a cat was a mammal [31];[77]
Event	
Symbol and its representation	

Retention and Instructional Strategy

In highly abstract learning domains, for instance in the learning of computer programming concepts, the control structures (or logic flow) of a programming language are difficult concepts for novice learners to absorb. They may also be difficult to transfer to a new situation. Part of this problem is due to their knowledge subsumption being a cognitive process that is involved in learning and forgetting. According to Ausubel (1962) a cognitive structure was organized in an hierarchical manner, with highly inclusive conceptual traces. These traces can be used to describe the continuing representation of past experience and present cognitive structure, as being purely hypothetical constructs only. However, it is the new material that is likely to be subsumed under a relevant and more inclusive conceptual system; acting as an effective anchoring process to facilitate retention.

Meanwhile, Bagley [62] was able to confirm that instructional strategies that only focus on specific skills promote short-term retention only. She proposed that if the instructional goal is long-term retention (like remembering how to apply or use a newly learned concept in a different situation), structured instruction should focus on developing schemata of conceptual or procedural skills.

Building Electronic Learning Systems

Attaining an Information Super Highway

The physical global linking of individuals via ICT tools now provides us with the capabilities of instant access to information, and what should be effective eLearning programmes. So far, the notion of an information super highway remains a purely theoretical exercise [78]. To date there is no evidence, which suggests the building of such a system yet. As long ago as the mid-1990's researchers have been saying that integrated learning systems can be implemented to act as intelligent tutors.

Theoretical Learning Systems

Over the years there have been many attempts at building learning systems that have the capacity of adaptability. Among the instructional design community, are the better known examples of theoretical computerized learning environments such as the

"Knowledge-based Instructional System Design" (KISD) methodology by [79]. This involves adopting a systems design approach that concentrates on knowledge relationships and the learning context. In 1993, Tennyson devised the *"Minnesota Adaptive Instructional System"* he called MAIS, suggesting it links knowledge acquisition (declarative, procedural and contextual) to expository learning, practice and problem oriented strategies. Furthermore, MAIS does link the cognitive processes of recall, problem solving, and creativity to a complex system of self-directed learning strategies [80].

Capturing the Learning Environment

Much is known about capturing the learning environment. Each year around the world the academic conference circuit is brimming with eager educational technologists strutting about with their techno-stuff. However, while the presenting researchers choose to disseminate their findings in well written (peer-reviewed) scholarly papers, they are often constrained by their paradigmatic approach that may deter outsiders from adopting their work. Many of the papers that survive the peer-review process these days include healthy offerings of experiments that involve virtual reality to demonstrate theoretical learning environments in the high-end of educational technology.

Theoretical Offerings

For instance in an Australian based conference held in at the end of 2006, Simeon Simoff's paper on loose integration of building collaborative virtual environments is discussed as a collection of several underlying technologies [81]. Simoff maintains that his framework allows for an open integrated environment which supports HCI, while uniting existing supporting technologies at conceptual and interface levels. His proposed methodology is suitable for developing customisable learning environments, which include different computer mediated environments and different modes of delivery. Collings, Trevitt & Absalom [82] believe their work is an evolutionary process; they are working on providing information technology supported learning environments that involve active engagement in a new community of learning. To this end they are capturing their empirical data from course notes and seminars, as well as the reflections of designers and users. Graha, Pearce, Howard & Vetere [83] draw on existing taxonomies in human factors and educational technology to clarify their working definition of interactivity maps. These explore the relationship between individual scenarios, theories of action and levels of interactivity.

A Practical Approach

In a joint industry/academic collaborative research venture, McKay, Axmann, Banjanin & Howat [84] presented their project to an international audience of Web-based education experts at a conference held in Chamonix, France, March 2007. Instead of remaining within a theoretical framework this research extends the usual paradigmatic approach to deliver an advanced repurposing pilot system *(called ARPS)*. The mandate for this work is to disseminate a practical repurposing tool to the Australian Government that can be repopulated by anyone interested in sound instructional design principles. The foundation of this educational system development tool employs the instructional principles of David Merrill in a knowledge navigation methodology. This underpins a customizable Web-based designing tool that can adapt to a learner's skill level. It represents a new approach towards instructional systems design and stands to break new ground for novice educational system developers, wishing to enter the techno-realm of online learning.

Identify Learner Skill Levels

Concept classification performance can be achieved by using attention-focusing devices to direct the learner's attention. The critical attributes present a specific example and correct for under-generalization errors. To correct for misconception errors potentially confusing attributes can be presented in particular examples of non-examples. The absence of the critical attributes in a specific non-example is designed to correct for over-generalization [18].

They refer to this phenomenon as developing skills, while the transfer of principles and attitudes were represented as general ideas. They described a 2-fold approach explaining how construction curricula can be taught by ordinary teachers to ordinary students. The first issue is to keep the instructional materials focused. The second relates to matching the instructional outcomes of instructional material to the differing abilities of learners at different school levels.

Constructivist Learning Approach

As we have seen earlier in this chapter, the concept of active learning is central to the constructivist's approach to learning. There are 5-facets to a learning environment [55, 56] *(Table 16)*. They include:

Table 16 : Perkins 5-Facets to a Learning Environment

Five Facetted learning environment	Implications for *human-dimensions of HCI*
Information bank	The explicit information for the topic-to-be-learned
Symbol pads	The devices a learner will use to support their short-term memory while learning
Construction kits	The physical building resources
Phenomenaria	The variety of contexts used to situate the topic-to-be-learned
Task managers	Can be either textual or instructions from a teacher/learning facilitator

Table 17 : Bruner's Framework for Teaching People How to Use Computers

Bruner's Framework	Implications for *human-dimensions of HCI*
Action	ICT tools for the enactments and demonstration
Icons	Graphical imagery for summarizing pictures
Symbols	Words and numbers expressed in textual captions

The Perkins *"phenomenaria"* and *"construction kits"* are 2-learning environment categories, which actually situate the topic-to-be-learned in authentically complex and meaningful contexts. In other words, the learner is engaged in an active manner while learning the topic.

Knowledge Acquisition

In keeping with this book's genre for improving the *digital-awareness of HCI* it is fitting to include a small section here that explains two of the researchers' experimentation on knowledge acquisition. The first one is an empirical validation of a knowledge acquisition methodology using conceptual graph analysis for an instructional system's design. Gordon, Schmierer, & Gill [85] suggested using conceptual graphs as representational medium, which could be used to integrate and organize knowledge obtained from:

- Documents
- Verbal protocols
- Question probes
- Observation of task performance

They validated this method by presenting two groups of learners with text and graphics on a topic in engineering dynamics. One set of materials was written by a recognized subject matter expert (expert-generated text), and subjected to a conceptual graph analysis. The text was first translated into a conceptual graph structure, next the graph was revised via question probes and observational/induction methods. The final graph was then returned to a standard text format. Learners receiving the knowledge-engineered text solved significantly more problems than learners receiving the original text. Conceptual graph analysis is a generalised method that can be used for a broad range of training domains, providing a highly structured means of making explicit the knowledge base to be incorporated into instructional design.

However, it was Presno [86] who thought that the most comprehensive and effective way to teach people how to use computers was to follow Bruner's framework *(Table 17)*.

Tools for Computer Aided Instruction

The traditional instructional design view in the literature appears to have completed a full circle, with an introduction of the technical solutions proposed for computer-based training otherwise known as CBT. A powerful design approach also exists for generating rule-based instruction, particularly for *'computer-aided instruction'* (CAI); there is still little mention of individual learning characteristics. In 1998 Quealy & Langen-Fox [87] investigated attributes of CAI delivery using:

- Text and still image
- Text, still image and audio track of the text
- Video image and audio track of the text

Technology can offer the effectiveness of learning strategies, whereby the learner has control over their learning environment. This means that the learner can have control over the method for processing and recall of their knowledge, during an instructional event. Technology in the CAI environment, forces the learner to adopt a generalised set of mental skills, as opposed to the development of reactions (cognitive strategies), to the instructional strategies they experience, with the more traditional types of instructional materials. As such, although teachers will, and should, design their own software, teachers should not have to learn programming to do so [88]. Novice learners participating in CAI benefit from working through a textual workbook before entering code into the computer. The biggest difficulty learners encountered was distinguishing the proper instructional outcomes (rules vs concepts and rules vs problem solving). Other features of their approach include:

- To ensure explanatory feedback is provided with the right answers
- Use of individualised learning strategies as an option for tutorial programs
- An emphasis on verbal information in the CAI lessons and a preference for a textual approach

Conditions of the Learner

As mentioned in earlier sections of this chapter the *human-dimensions of HCI* is a synthesis of several disparate disciplines. Consequently, by drawing on the valuable contributions made by earlier researchers, it is now possible to isolate strategic research variables. This is a complex melding process, as it involves defining variables for discussion (and research) that have multiple points of origin. Therefore a theoretical framework can be devised for dealing with the ICT tools. Such a framework draws on the paradigms of Instructional Science and information processing to provide the primary context for the *human-dimensions of HCI*. Moreover, our discussion to this point forms the background for the most important variable in the techno-landscape: the conditions-of-the-learner.   Previously known among the instructional design community, the conditions-of-the-learner describes the various learning states of an individual learner.

Internal-Conditions

We use the term internal-conditions to describe the process of gaining a skill and the subsequent storage (committing to memory) or prior capabilities that are supportive of further learning. While there are many examples of outstanding work that relates to the functioning of human memory, it took the Doctoral Study of McKay [26] to actually connect HCI, and the interactive effect of instructional strategies with cognitive performance benchmarks. Because of this the McKay meta-knowledge processing model broke new ground *(Figure 32)*.

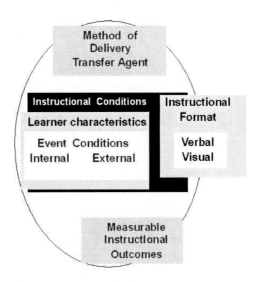

Figure 32 : Meta-Knowledge Process Model

Over time a number of memory models have been put forward. Two such models depict a *"mono-"* or *"dual-framework"*. A single memory system, verbal access times decrease more than pictorial access times [89]. They proposed that verbal access to a single semantic system was more rapid than in simultaneous representation in either verbal or non-verbal memory systems.

If semantic decisions regarding verbal material are made in a non-verbal system, then one was led to question the function of a verbal-memory system [89]. They proposed that a further dual-memory model could potentially account for their research data, and assumed that category decisions were made in a verbal-memory system. Such a model must also reflect differences in access time required for pictures to gain access to the verbal-knowledge system. They hypothesized that access and transfer times, can be summed to yield a measure of access time into semantic memory, and that this is functionally equivalent to a single-memory model. Therefore, they considered the processing differences between pictures and words as estimates of access times, related to a single-semantic memory. A single memory system seems more plausible, because a standard view that imagery as a right hemisphere phenomenon is incorrect [90]. It may only be that it is more important for that hemisphere. Moreover, objects were constructed in our minds, one piece at a time [90]. Convergent-divergent thinking has been a human-dimension of interest to many people. To this end, Hudson [91];[92] reported that learners who were *"convergers"* preferred formal problems and structured tasks demanding logical method. To identify those states within the learner, that facilitate learning it is necessary to delve into the following domains *(Table 18)*:

Table 18 : Learning Facilitation States

An individual's learning facilitation states	Implications for *human-dimensions of HCI*
Memory	While there certainly has been an ongoing debate; the jury is still out on this one. Nobody really knows how our memories work. Although experts are eager to expose the secrets of human-beings' brain functioning, it's probably safe to predict that two hemispheres control radically different styles of thought. Moreover, some individuals may be dominated by one hemisphere, producing different thought patterns.
Thinking skills	Within the learning domains that require high-level thinking skills, as we have seen earlier on in this chapter, Sternberg (1978) said that image (or abstract) concepts, occur in the human mind in sets of overlapping sub-spaces.
Relationship of instructional format and cognitive style	The issues relating to individual differences in the way we may process, store and retrieve information is affected by the interactive effect of instructional format (text and pictures) with cognitive style on learning performance outcomes McKay (2000).
Representation of information during thinking	As many complicated variables impact upon the way we think; therefore the Riding continuum can be used to explain that people decide whether they will think using text (verbal) or visual (images) as their thinking mode to complete a particular task.
Mode of processing information	An individual's mode of processing is inherent and cannot be changed. ICT tools should be configured for creating the greatest impact.

Gagne's Capability Categories

As there is an interactive effect of instructional strategies with cognitive style on the learning outcomes for knowledge acquisition, it is entirely appropriate to refer to the Gagne [11] learning outcome categories to provide a sound theoretical framework that supports the *human-dimensions of HCI (Table 19)*.

Table 19 : Gagne's Learning Outcome Categories

Capabilities	Implications for *human-dimensions of HCI*
Intellectual skills	Knowing how to program, involves many intellectual skills. For instance to understand the concepts of logic patterns requires both declarative knowledge (know the rules), and procedural knowledge (problem solving strategies).
Cognitive strategies	We regulate our own internal processes by attending, learning, remembering, and thinking. Forgetting can be explained in terms of what the individual decided as crucial in the given instructional strategy, and what information can be easily rediscovered [93].
Verbal information	This kind of information is described in many places as the most basic type of fact (or rote) learning. It can be thought of as pure verbalization, without any necessity for comprehension of the wider context.
Motor skills	The effective and efficient use of computer-input devices. For instance: operating a computer-keyboard and mouse as pointing devices require highly-developed hand-eye coordination.
Attitudes	The way people feel about a particular learning experience should be positive, if there is to be any lasting effect on the memory processing.

External Conditions

To facilitate the learning process, the (external) conditions-of-the-learner have the capability to unlock our prior domain knowledge, or previous intellectual skills. In the case of mature age learners, who now face an increasing need to undergo retraining later in life, this is an immensely rich knowledge base [94].

Interactive Effect of Internal/External Conditions

The mental skills used by learners require study as well as the learning outcomes. There have been a small number of researchers looking at the interactivity issues of the internal/external conditions-of-the-learner. For instance: McKay (2000) showed that people who choose to think in terms of pictures when they receive their information, but have an (inherent) *"wholist information processing mode"*, will not achieve their best learning outcomes. Moreover, Clark [95] proposed that only certain media attributes are more efficient for certain learners. Instead, research which follows this line of thought, will allow the mental set theorists to shift from focusing on media attributes as causal in learning, to media attributes as causal in the cost effectiveness of learning.

The reader of this chapter has certainly covered a lot of ground:

* concept learning

- instructional strategies *(should be)* under constant review
- information processing
- knowledge and learning
- instructional format
- building eLearning systems
- conditions of the learner

Understandably it is perhaps the most theoretical chapter of this book, presenting the reader with a *'techno-humanoid landscape'* upon which to model the complexity of the interrelating aspects of Web-mediated learning in terms of how to promote *effective HCI*. To facilitate more people reaching their information nirvana, we need to bring forward a revitalized view of the *human-dimensions of HCI* that has tangible outcomes [1]. To this end, the next chapter serves to present practical examples of the relationship between the external techno-humanoid contributors and the personal digital-awareness characteristics of the techno-humanoid landscape.

Chapter Reference List

[1] Bradley, G., *Social and Community Informatics: Humans on the Net*, 2006. NY: Routledge.265
[2] Huber, G.P., Cognitive style as a basis for MIS and DDS designs: Much ado about nothing? *Management Science*, 1983. 29(5): 567-577.
[3] Lewin, A.Y. and Stephens, C.V., Designing post-industrial organization: Theory and practice, in *Organization Change and Redesign: Ideas and Insights for Improving Managerial Performance*, G.P. Huber and W.H. Glick, Editors. 1992, Oxford University Press: NY.
[4] Myers, M.D. and Tan, F.B., Beyond models of national culture in information systems research. *Human Factors in Information Systems*, Editor. E. Szewczak and C. Snodgrass. 2002, London: IRM, 1-19.
[5] Kossyln, S.M., Information representation in visual images. *Cognitive Psychology*, 1975. 7: 341-370.
[6] Riding, R.J. and Rayner, S., *Cognitive Styles and Learning Strategies*. 1998, UK: Fulton. 217.
[7] Benbasat, I. and Taylor, R.N., The Impact of cognitive styles on information system design. *MIS Quarterly*, 1978. 2(2): 43-54.
[8] Zhang, P., et al., Human-computer interaction research in the MIS discipline. 2002, *Communications of the Association for Information Systems*.
[9] Klausmeier, H.J. and Sipple, T.S., *Learning and Teaching Concepts: A strategy for testing applications of theory*. 1980, NY: Academic Press. 228.
[10] Fleming, M.L. and Levie, W.H., *Instructional Message Design: Principles from the Behavioural Sciences*. 1993, NJ: Educational Technology Publications.
[11] Gagne, R.M., *The Conditions of Learning: And the theory of instruction*. 4th ed. 1985, NY: Holt/Rinehart/Winston.
[12] Merrill, M.D., *Instructional Design Theory*, D.G. Twitchell, Editor. 1994, NJ: Educational Technology Publications. 480.
[13] Jonassen, D.H. and Editor, C., Evaluating constructivistic learning. *Educational Technology*, 1991(September): 28-33.
[14] Merrill, M.D., Li, Z., and Jones, M.K., Instructional transaction theory: An introduction. *Educational Technology*, 1991. 31(6 June): 7-12.
[15] Laurillard, D., *Rethinking University Teaching: A framework for the effective use of educational technology*. 1993, UK: Routledge.
[16] Tennyson, R.D. and Cocchiarella, M.J., An empirically based instruction design theory for teaching concepts. *Review of Educational Research*, 1986. 56: 40-71.
[17] Klausmeier, H.J., Concept learning and concept teaching. *Educational Psychologist*, 1992. 27(3)(Fall): 267-286.
[18] Merrill, M.D., Tennyson, R.D., and Posey, L.O., Teaching Concepts: An instructional design guide. 2nd ed. 1992, NJ: *Educational Technology Publications*. 211.
[19] Reigeluth, C.M., Meaningfulness and instruction: Relating what is being learned to what a student knows. *Instructional Science*, 1983. 12: 197-218.

[20] Varela, F.J., Thompson, E., and Rosch, E., A fundamental circularity: In the mind of the reflective scientist, in *The Embodied Mind*, D.W.E. Massro, Editor. 1991, MIT Press: Cambridge, MA. 3-14.

[21] Bower, G.H., Black, J.B., and Turner, T.J., Scripts in memory for text, in *Human Memory: Contemporary readings*, J. Seamon, Editor. 1980, Oxford University Press: UK. 311-343.

[22] Schank, R. and Abelson, R., *Scripts, Plans, Goals and Understanding*. 1977, Hillsdale: Erlbaum.

[23] Kearsley, G., *Explorations in Learning & Instruction: The Theory into Practice Database*: Gestalt Theory. 1998, George Washington University.

[24] Jenkins, J.J., Remember that old theory of memory? Well, forget it!, in *Human Memory: Contemporary readings*, J.G.Seamon, Editor. 1980, Oxford University Press: UK.

[25] Baine, D., *Memory and Instruction*. 1986, NJ: Educational Technology Publications.

[26] McKay, E., *Instructional Strategies Integrating the Cognitive Style Construct: A Meta-Knowledge Processing Model (Contextual components that facilitate spatial/logical task performance): An investigation of instructional strategies that facilitate the learning of complex abstract programming concepts through visual representation, in Applied Science (Computing and Mathematics Department)*. 2000, Deakin University, Available online from http://tux.lib.deakin.edu.au/adt-VDU/public/adt-VDU20061011.122556/ Waurn Ponds, Geelong, Australia.

[27] Scandura, J.M. and Dolores, J., On the representation of higher order knowledge. *Special Issue: Cognitive perspectives on higher order knowledge. Journal of Structural Learning*, 1990. 10(4)(Aug): 261-269.

[28] Tennyson, R.D. and Spector, J.M., System dynamics technologies and future directions in instructional design. *Journal of Structured Learning and Intellegent Systems*, 1998. 13(2): 89-101.

[29] Ortony, A., *Beyond literal similarity. Psychological Review*, 1979. 86: 161-180.

[30] Baddeley, A., *Your Memory: A user's guide*, A.Baddeley, Editor. 1982, NY: Macmillian. 221.

[31] Rosch, E., Principles of cognition and categorization, in *Cognition and Categorization*, E.Rosch and B.Lloyd, Editors. 1978, Erlbaum: NJ.

[32] McDermott Hannafin, K., Designing process-oriented learning resources. *Annuls New York Academy of Sciences*, 1993: 77-82.

[33] Holzman, P. and Klein, G., Cognitive-system principles of levelling and sharpening: Individual differences in visual time-error assimilation effects. *Journal of Psychology*, 1954. 37: 105-122.

[34] Witkin, H.A., et al., *Psychological Differentiation*. 1962, NY: Wiley.

[35] Kagan, J., Individual differences in the resolution of response uncertainty. *Journal of Personality and Social Psychology*, 1965. 2: 154-160.

[36] Guilford, J., *The Nature of Human Intelligence*. 1967, NY: McGraw-Hill.

[37] Pask, G. and Scott, B.C.E., Learning strategies and individual competence. *International Journal Man-Machine Studies*, 1972. 4: 217-253.

[38] Riding, R. and Cheema, I., Cognitive styles - an overview and integration. *Educational Psychology*, 1991. 11(3&4): 193-215.

[39] Kirton, M.J., *Adaption and Innovation in the Context of Diversity and Change*. 2003, London: Routledge. 392.

[40] Pask, G., Styles and strategies of learning. *British Journal Educational Psychology*, 1976. 46: 128-148.

[41] Paivio, A. and Csapo, K., Picture superiority in free recall: Imagery or dual coding. *Cognitive Psychology*, 1973. 5: 176-206.

[42] Ritchey, G.H. and Beal, C.R., Image detail and recall: Evidence for within-item elaboration. *Journal of Experimental Psychology Human Learning and Memory*, 1980. 6(1): 66-76.

[43] Winn, W.D., The effect of block-word diagrams on the structuring of concepts as a function of general ability. *Journal of Research in Science Teaching*, 1980. 17: 201-211 (b).

[44] Winn, W.D., Visual information processing: A pragmatic approach to the imagery question. *Educational Communication and Technology Journal*, 1980. 28: 120-133.

[45] Gibbs, R.W., Why many concepts are metaphorical. *Cognition*, 1996. 61(3 December): 309-319.

[46] Romiszowski, A.J., *Designing Instructional Systems*. 1981, UK: Kogan Page. 420.

[47] Hummel, J.E. and Holyoak, K.J., Distributed representations of structure: A theory of analogical access and mapping. *Psychological Review*, 1997. 104(3 July): 427-466.

[48] McKay, E., Measurement of cognitive performance in computer programming concept acquisition: Interactive effects of visual metaphors and the cognitive style construct. *Journal of Applied Measurement*, 2000. 1(3): 257-286.

[49] Bruner, J.S., *The Process of Education*. 1960, NY: Vintage Books.

[50] Hannafin, M.J. and Land, S.M., The foundations and assumptions of technology-enhanced student-centred learning environments. *Instructional Science*, 1997. 25(3 May): 167-202.

[51] Jonassen, D., Instructional design models for well-structured and ill-structured problem-solving learning outcomes. *Educational Technology Research & Development*, 1997. 45(1): 65-94.

[52] Diana, E.M. and Webb, J.M., Using geographic maps in classrooms: The conjoint influence of individual differences and dual coding on learning facts. *Learning and Individual Differences*, 1997. 9(3): 195-214.

[53] Sternberg, R.J. and Grigorenko, E.L., Are cognitive styles still in style? *The American Psychologist*, 1997. 52(7): 700-712.

[54] Dreyfus, H.L. and Dreyfus, S.E., *Mind Over Machine: The power of human intuition and expertise in the era of the computer*. 1986, NY: Free Press. 231.

[55] Perkins, D.N., What constructivism demands of the learner. *Educational Technology*, 1991(September): 19-21.

[56] Perkins, D.N., Technology meets constructivism: Do they make a marriage? *Educational Technology*, 1991(May): 18-23.

[57] Bruner, J., *Toward a Theory of Instruction*. 1966, Massachusetts: Harvard University Press.

[58] Cognitive and Technology Group at Vandervit 2, Anchored instruction and situated cognition revisited (1). *Educational Technology*, 1991. March: 52-70.

[59] Lowenfeld, V., Tests for visual-haptic aptitude. *American Journal of Psychology*, 1954. 58: 100-111.

[60] Howell, A.D., *An Electroencephalographic Comparison of Lowenfeld's Haptic Visual and Witkin's Field-Dependent-Independent Perceptual Types*. 1972, Ball State University: Indiana.

[61] Moore, D.M. and Bedient, D., Effects of presentation mode and visual characteristics on cognitive style. *Journal of Instructional Psychology*, 1986. 13(1).

[62] Bagley, C.A., *Structured Versus Discovery Instructional Formats for Improving Concept Acquisition by Domain-Experienced and Domain-Novice Adult Learners, in Faculty of the Graduate School*. 1990, Minnesota: Minnesota. 280.

[63] King, J.M., Brain function research: Guideposts for brain-compatible teaching and learning. *Journal of General Education*, 1997. 46(4): 276-88.

[64] Sternberg, R.J., Principles of teaching for successful intellegence. *Educational Psychologist*, 1998. 33(2-3 Spring-Summer): 65-72.

[65] Merrill, M.D. and Tennyson, R.D., *Teaching Concepts: An Instructional Guide*. 1977, NJ: Educational Technology Publications.

[66] Goodman, N., *The Languages of Art: An approach to a theory of symbols*. 1968, NY: Bobbs-Merrill.

[67] Salomon, G., *Interaction of Media, Cognition, and Learning*. 1979 Reprint 1985, California: Jossey-Bass.

[68] McKay, E., Cognitive skill acquisition through a meta-knowledge processing model. *Interactive Learning Environments*, 2002. 10(3): 263-291.

[69] Winn, W., The role of diagramatic representation in learning sequenced, identification and classification as a function of verbal and spatial ability. *Journal of Research in Science Teaching*, 1982. 19(1): 79-89.

[70] Rigney, J.W., *Learning Strategies: A theoretical perspective, in Learning Strategies*, H.F. O'Neil, Editor. 1978, Academic Press: NY. 165-205.

[71] Meyer, B.J., Signaling the structure of text, in *The Technology of Text*, D.H. Jonassen, Editor. 1985, Educational Technology Publications: NJ. 64-89.

[72] Wileman, R., *Visual Communicating*. 1993, NJ: Educational Technology Publications.

[73] Merrill, M.D., Li, Z., and Jones, M.K., Second generation instructional design (ID2). *Educational Technology*, 1990(February): 7-14.

[74] Winn, W. and Holliday, W., Design principles for diagrams and charts, in *The Technology of Text*, D. Jonassen, Editor. 1982, Educational Technology Publications: NJ. 277-300.

[75] Gropper, G.L., *Text Displays: Analysis and systematic design*. 1991, NJ: Educational Technology.

[76] Merrill, M.D., *Component display theory, in Instructional - Design Theories and Models: An overview of their current status*, C.M. Reigeluth, Editor. 1983, Erlbaum: NJ. 279-333.

[77] Garner, W.R., *The Processing of Information and Structure*. 1974, NY: Wiley.

[78] DFE, *Superhighways for Education*. 1995, HMSO: United Kingdom.

[79] Duchastel, P., Towards methodologies for building knowledge-based instructional systems. *Instructional Science*, 1991-1992. 20(5-6): 349-358.

[80] Tennyson, R., MAIS: A computer-based integrated instructional system. *Behavior Research Methods, Instruments, & Computers*, 1993. 25(2): 93-100.

[81] Simoff, S.J. Dynamically constructed virtual spaces - the "Loose Integration" framework. *Conference paper in the proceedings of OZCHI*, held November 20-24. 2006. Sydney, Australia. ISBN: 1-59593-545-2, 136-142.

[82] Collings, P., Tevitt, C., and Absalom, M. Developing a Shared Understanding of IT-Supported Environments. in OZCHI held November 20-24. 2006. Sydney, Australia. ISBN: 1-59593-545-2, 19-24.

[83] Graha, C., et al. Levels of Interactivity and Interactivity Maps. *Conference paper in the proceedings of OZCHI* held November 20-24. 2006. Sydney, Australia. ISBN: 1-59593-545-2, 45-50.

[84] McKay, E., et al. Towards Web-mediated learning reinforcement: Rewards for online mentoring through effective human-computer interaction. *Conference paper in the proceedings of the 6th IASTED International Conference on Web-Based Education.* Held March 14-16. 2007. Chamonix, France, p:210-215, ISBN:978-0-88986-650-8.

[85] Gordon, S.E., Schmierer, K.A., and Gill, R.T., Conceptual graph analysis: Knowledge acquisition for instructional system design. *Human Factors*, 1993. 35(3 September): 459-481.

[86] Presno, C., Bruner's three forms of representation revisited: Action, pictures and words for effective computer instruction. *Journal of Instructional Psychology*, 1997. 24(2): 112-118.

[87] Quealy, J. and Langan-Fox, J., Attributes of delivery media in computer-assisted instruction. Ergonomics, 1998. 41(3): 257-279.

[88] Lee, D., Case Study: A systems approach to the design of a computer-based module for teaching BASIC. *Educational Training Technology International*, 1994. 31(I): 5-9.

[89] Rosinski, R.R., Pellegrino, J.W., and Siegel, A.W., Developmental changes in semantic processing of pictures and words. *Journal of Experimental Child Psychology*, 1977. 23: 282-291.

[90] Kosslyn, S.M., Aspects of a cognitive neuroscience of mental imagery. *Science*, 1988. 240(Articles): 1621-1626.

[91] Hudson, L. *Frames of mind*. Harmondsworth: Penguin Books, 1968. 1966, London: Methuen.

[92] Hudson, L., *Frames of Mind*. 1966: Harmondsworth: Penguin Books.

[93] Schank, R.C., The structure of episodes in memory, in *Representation and Understanding Studies in Cognitive Science*, D.G. Bobrow and A. Collins, Editors. 1975, Academic Press: NY. 237-272.

[94] Rosen, B. and Jerdee, T.H., The Nature of Job-Related Age Sterotypes. *Journal of Applied Psychology*, 1976. 61(2): 180-183.

[95] Clark, R., Media will never influence learning. *Educational Technology*, Research & Development, 1994. 42(2): 21-29.

Chapter-6

Shared Cognition: Seamless Learning

Don't be deceived by *Figure 33*. While this chapter does appear to leave the Earthly comfort of the book's previous dialogue to resemble a make believe fiction book, its main purpose is to mark the mid-way point of our techno-saga. So much of what we need to deal with when discussing *effective HCI* remains within the esoteric techno-community. As such it's high time that somebody brings the discussion back down towards the general population of computer-users.

On the Trail to Information Nirvana

Our journey through this book thus far has travelled across the techno-landscape in order to get a feel for the *human-dimensions (or social context) of HCI*. To commence the journey, we dipped our toes into the bygone techno-knowledge pool of computing history to set the context for understanding our place in today's digital environment. Though scientists don't have all the answers about shared cognition, it is really fascinating to conjecture on what happens to people when they communicate through a computer.

Figure 33 : The Road to Information Nirvana

Many people will conceptualize that an Internet highway could be much the same as an information highway. To sustain this belief, some of us may visualize there is a techno-digital means that transports electronic information and data into cyberspace. However, these metaphorical techno-visions do not necessarily mean the same thing. Unfortunately these understandings are not absolute. They are constrained by our previously encountered image schemas, together with an internal coherence of conceptual characteristics for each metaphoric term [1]. This interesting proposition comes from the cognitive linguistics literature that discusses the notions of a conceptual blending of the information highway [2]. For the full details readers are recommended to visit http://philosophy.uoregon.edu/metaphore/iclacnf4.htm .

Most people think of the information highway as something which allows us to move through cyberspace, to a variety of different physical locations [2];[3]. In keeping with this phenomenon it is likely some of us may have the thought (in some image schema) of projecting ourselves and our computer-machinery through cyberspace to other destinations. These techno-joy rides however are a little more complicated. Indeed, along these fibre-optic pathways of the Internet, to simply gather information from either local or far-flung places, we may experience rather bumpy rides. Moreover, these techno-bumps refer to the technology per se (that cellular transmission is not as reliable as cable transmission). Then again, our cyberspace turbulence may also relate to the hurdles of government infrastructure that corporations endure when trying to implement their cellular information highways.

Meanwhile, Rohrer [2] insists on adding an analogy of time to enhance our understanding of the information highway. As a consequence, if we don't keep pace on the information highway, and survive the turbulence, our place in the cyber-future will remain hopelessly stalled. Those that don't survive can expect to become *backward* in terms of nations, corporations or individuals. Just as those techno-bumps slow our travel through cyberspace, the way we negotiate turbulence through the cyber-future will reflect the way we manage to overcome those regulatory hurdles: hurdles which lie between us and our *information nirvana*.

Perhaps our travel towards an *information nirvana* is but a mere whimsical notion that some people will forever seek out, without ever realizing when they are there (like Dorothy in the Wizard of OZ). In seeking out the reason why this happens perhaps it is useful to extend Rohrer's [2] metaphor of the information highway as consisting of dual lanes: one that leads to cyberspace, and the other to a society transformed (in time) by information technology. Moreover, some of us are already capitalizing on ICT tools to provide our mode of travel into the cyber-future *(Table 20)*. The rate at which we travel is not, however, fuelled by techno-tools, but rather by the quality and amount of information. Another way to prepare for the techno-turbulence is to attend to the things that we know how to do really well.

Table 20 : The Trail to Reaching Information Nirvana

HIGHWAY - source	INTERNET – target	APPLICABILITY TO *EFFECTIVE HCI*
highway	Highway to the future	The Internet is better understood as a bioelectronic environment that is literally universal. It exists everywhere there are telephones wires, coaxial cables, fibre-optic lines or electromagnetic waves. This environment is '*inhabited*' by knowledge, including incorrect ideas, existing in electronic form. It is connected to the physical environment by portals which allow people to see what's inside, to put knowledge in, to alter it, and to take knowledge out. Some of these portals are one-way (TV receivers and TV transmitters). Others are two-way (telephones and computer modems) [4].
space	Time	
destination	*information nirvana* (techno-utopia)	
journey	travelling along the information highway in order to meet the demands of the future and arrive at *information nirvana.*	
vehicles	New technologies (computer, software, phone, TV etc)	
Fuel	Information	
goods transported	nations, citizens, corporations	
drivers	telecommunications experts	
Impediments to motion (roadblocks, bumps, mechanical trouble)	government regulations, intellectual property laws	

Continuing the notion that the Internet highway transports people and their bundles of information through cyberspace, we extend the techno-metaphor mentioned above to postulate that as we move towards our *information nirvana*, we are not completely alone. During our cyberspace journeys, some of those techno-bumps can actually be the interactive effect of encounters with other's information from particular travelers as they attempt to traverse the techno-turbulence. In reaching out to these others for confirming comfort, we share snippets of our information bundles. For instance, we may find out that a server is out of action, or whether we need to download a special piece of software to fix a mechanical defect. After a while we may develop an innate sense of trust with some of these cyberspace encounters. As we have seen in earlier parts of this book, an important part of our sensitivity for learning is closely tied to sharing our mental models with others. Over time we may collect various groups of people characterized by the type of cyberspace encounter we have with them.

In order to find some more clarification of the social context of the *human-dimensions of HCI*, let us now turn to the knowledge domain of organizational behaviour to see how people deal with situation awareness. People will tend to share mental models in two modes [5]: when they are working on a particular task by themselves or they are part of a team. According to the context of the task (unilateral or with a group/team of people); they may focus on knowledge structures or belief structures. Within the group/team tasking people do this by sharing their knowledge schemas. Consequently people gradually develop their own transactive memory together with the concepts of shared internal frames of reference, schema agreement, accuracy and group cognitive consensus [5]. Group learning therefore consists of information sharing and the use of an individual's transactive memory *(Figure 34)*.

Within an Internet environment, reaching a cognitive consensus becomes a little tricky. People still need to move through their knowledge sharing to reach a final decision [6], just as they do away from ICT tools. Consequently with this type of cognitive modelling in cyberspace it may be the collaborative coordination of shared ideas and their interpretations that will facilitate the consensus. Moreover, away from the Internet, according to organizational behaviour experts, group development involves 4-phases *(Figure 35)*. These are: forming, storming, norming and performing. A fifth stage however acts as an adjunct to the preceding stages to form closure: this remains relevant to the group-membership [3];[7]. It does not fall within the management and developing team-membership. While the overall process of setting the group dynamics isn't necessarily geared to follow chronological order, it may cycle through each stage with feedback loops and reciprocal actions. However, it is the actual sharing of mental models that affects team performance through improved team cognitive transactions like communication and coordination [5].

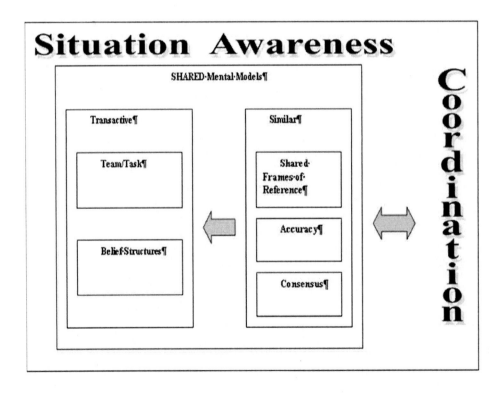

Figure 34 : Situation Awareness and the Coordination of Shared Mental Models

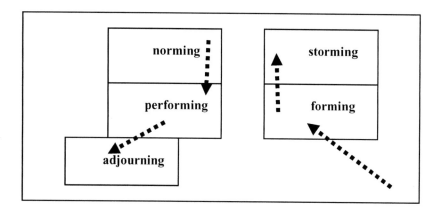

Figure 35 : Group Forming Process

Forming

The forming stage is the initial process of a group coming together with all the usual expectations, identity, preferences, beliefs, and knowledge to share. In cyberspace, this is where people must put their best techno-foot forward, so to speak. It is the most polite stage in which the team spirit may commence. If not handled to everyone's satisfaction, it will be seen to be one of those techno-bumps that may cause a real barrier to smooth flowing information . During this initial step, people actively engage in figuring out what the team concept is. Over the Internet there must be protocols for the order of speaking/listening or watching/reacting through the many forms of Web-cam techno-gadgetry. In addition, cyberspace meetings should also involve an exit strategy to facilitate people discontinuing. Failure to do this means the communication lines become disrupted when everyone speaks together, damaging any chance for effective listening. Moreover, maintaining the usual communication feedback we expect becomes quite tiresome. At this early stage, potential leaders may pop up and take over. However, the conveyed mood is generally positive with some people showing unbridled excitement. It may, rarely, offend others during this early formation stage.

It is usual to find some anxiety relating to defining the tasks and how they will be accomplished during this set-up stage. Apart from determining acceptable group behaviour (which is quite separate from the communications protocol for the Internet), group administrative decisions should be made for things like: defining the tasks of the group members, how each task should be accomplished, and when the task should be completed. Over the Internet, many of these set-up activities can be accomplished easily enough through shared files, including deciding what information needs to be gathered by the group members. Because of the excitement in this forming stage, many of the discussions may become abstract to the extreme, resulting in some people becoming quite impatient. Over the Internet such impatience is understandable behaviour, but becomes a real problem, because the usual body-language is not picked up by the rest of the group. Additionally, a plethora of distractions exist: a position only made worse with ICT tools to entice people's attention off course. If the reason for coming together as an Internet group is project based, it is perfectly normal for none of the project goals to have been accomplished during this *"getting to know you"* exercise. In these cyberspace encounters, it is helpful if a debrief mechanism is in place to flag the exit strategy for team-members. One that depicts them completing the forming stage of group development.

Storming

Expect high levels of techno-turbulence during the storming stage. This is where the group membership negotiates through communication and social interactions. This is when the processes that involve group learning and cognitive conflict become evident. Expect this stage of group interaction to reveal role differentiation, status of team members, experience with the team, and familiarity with team-mates, all coming into play. Basically the honeymoon that may have been evident during the forming stage is definitely over. Those potential leaders who may have remained silent during the earlier stage may come forward to clash openly, causing disagreement. The result of this behaviour could be to blame the general team concept. People who are showing tendencies for hostility may need some good old one-to-one counseling from a trusted facilitator to overcome past differences. It is usual to find feelings and behaviours [8], they include:
- resistance to the tasks at hand
- suggestions for quality improvement by other team members
- distinct fluctuations in motivation and attitude towards the team and the project's chance of success
- arguments arising amongst team members – even though they may agree on real issues
- defensiveness, competition, and choosing sides
- questioning the wisdom of the selected decision makers and other team members
- establishing unrealistic goals; disunity and increased tension, and jealousy

Although the behaviour of people during this stormy stage of group formation can appear to be very dysfunctional, they can begin to understand each other. The storming stage of an embryonic group is perhaps where cyberspace interaction is the most vulnerable: and this due to the tyranny of techno-turbulence. It is vital therefore, that management strategies are put in place to keep people on track. The lid should be kept on the rising eMail flame wars that are unfortunately an inevitable fact of how some people behave in cyberspace. Internet flame wars occur all the time because people may gradually misperceive a sequence of behaviours that begins with a disagreement and gets more heated [9]. At times there is a place where people's perceptions are likely to jump over to the flaming side, sadly bringing in character attacks and foul language. Luckily, we are able to insert smiley faces to help reduce the misperception of a flaming-message when the intention was plainly disagreement. However, when these techno-emotions are added to a terribly nasty message, those little discrete smiley faces look hurtful and even grossly ironic.

Unfortunately, when these flame wars erupt within a long-standing and normally peaceful cyberspace group , they may have very damaging consequences for the longer-term health and overall culture of the group. As such they become so entrenched that they resist outside intervention, even though this mediation is intended to defuse the negativity [9]. Similarly to the end of the previous group forming stage, it is helpful if an exit mechanism is in place to debrief the group-membership as they are entering a transition between the forming/norming stages.

Norming

Norming is where the group's grounding is achieved. Clever ICT tools can be put in place to encourage the team-members to increase their situation awareness and team knowledge, developing their own transactive memory system, schema similarity, and shared mental models. At this point in the group's development cycle, there is a noticeable shift in people's behaviour occurring, as they overcome the storming phase and start to work well together. One of the advantages of cyberspace affordances is to promote instant soft-copy feedback. When contentious issues arise during this transitional period, the team will notice they bounce back and forth between the storming and norming activities. Fledgling norming behaviour may motivate individuals to boast about their project to non-group members, adding positive praise for various group members. As the group culture matures through an inevitable series of regressive storming cycles, they spring back to more collaborative behaviours. Such cycles simultaneously become less frequent. Moreover, the earlier jostling for leadership gives way to an acceptance of a natural group-leadership, while overall the team acknowledges management direction. It is usual to find behaviours [8], they include:

- people expressing criticism more constructively
- acceptance of team-membership
- attempts are made to achieve harmony by avoiding conflict
- more friendliness, with people confiding in each other, and sharing of personal problems
- a palpable sense of team cohesion, spirit and goal
- establishment and maintenance of team-membership boundaries and ground rules

As people work through their differences, more time and energies are spent on achieving the project's goals. Basically, for a group to survive the norming phase means they have reached agreement and consensus among the team-members and respond well to leadership facilitation. Their team-membership roles and responsibilities are now quite clear and accepted, with important decisions made by group agreement in relative comfort. Delegation is directed toward individuals for the smaller decisions. Moreover, commitment and unity towards the project's goals is strong. The team-members begin to participate in fun and social interaction. There are team-level discussions as they collaboratively develop processes and working style. Once again, a debrief mechanism should signify that the norming activities are no longer relevant. Group cohesion is well established and it's down to business.

Performing

The fourth stage of performing entails completing the task, whether it's in making a decision, or efficiently performing an action. It's the level in which the team-members operate as a high-performance team. They have reached the stage where they can transfer their collaborative skills to new projects and tasks, with successful completion. There are very few lapses back to the storming phase. The group begins operating as a self-directed team. As they take on new work they may be inclined to market these activities towards other teams. It is important to note that new members can be confidently brought into the group. Reaching this stage takes time. It can be 6-months or longer.

It is usual to find feelings and behaviours [8], they include: -
- team-members having a better understanding of each other's strengths and weaknesses. They attain insights into personal and group processes
- they are willing to undergo constructive self-change
- people have acquired personal skills which prevent or help them to work through group problems as they arise
- they identify a close attachment to team-membership

The best indicator that the group has reached this stage is acknowledgement that they are getting through a lot of work. Moreover, all team-members are more strategically aware. They clearly know why they are doing things. Their shared vision means they can cohesively withstand interference or participation from the leadership. They are energized and at times focused on over-achieving project goals. They self-select and make most of the group's operating decisions based on criteria agreed with their team-leader. They are aware that they have attained a high degree of autonomy. Disagreements still occur. However they now get resolved in a positive manner. Any changes or adjustments that are necessary to their operating processes and structure are made by the team-members. They work confidently towards achieving the project goals, attending to relationship issues, and style and process issues along the way. Team- members look after each other. At times, they require newly delegated tasks and projects from their leadership. The team-members do not need to be instructed or assisted, although they may seek out assistance from their leader on issues that relate to personal and interpersonal development.

Adjourning

It can be said that adjourning is likened to a group break-up process, and usually occurs when all tasks are completed successfully with project related goals fulfilled. People should be able to move on to new things, feeling good about their involvement and their achievements. People usually value a final briefing that affords group sharing, with timely acknowledgement of the improved process during this reflection stage. Often there are **bitter**-sweet feelings about finalization of team-membership, with an understandable reluctance to bid each other farewell. Many team-membership relationships formed for specific projects do however continue long after the group disbands [8]. For instance, ICT tools make it easy to secure continued networking, utilizing information that can be directed to a database, for later retrieval. Meanwhile there are many alternative methods. People can converse through cyberspace utilizing the plethora of communications packages like Skype.

Eye-Mind-Imagination Pathways

Reaching an *information nirvana* sounds all well and good. However, once an individual recognizes they have got there, it is entirely possible that their humanoid senses will need a retune. For instance, look at how often we need to use our imagination. Look too at how much reading and scanning of various types of material there is to do through our voluminous computer screens. Coping comfortably with the highly pictorial Internet media will therefore be a new skill for some of us, requiring a shift from talking through visualizations - using our mind's ear - to knowing how to absorb screen content directly through our mind's eye. *"Not so fast"*, you may be saying as you read this text, "describing visualization in this manner is not entirely new. Recall Albert Einsten's familiar words, *"imagination is more important than knowledge"* ". It has also been said that to develop the ability to create and manipulate images in our mind offers more potential for mental leverage than anything else [10]. Moreover, Dharma Singh Khalsa MD[11] says that Einstein's brain:

"when compared to the brains of intellectually average men who had died near the same age (76), the only difference found was an enhanced Area 39, which researchers believe is the most highly evolved site in the brain. "When people have lesions in Area 39, they have great difficulty with abstract imagery, memory, attention and self-awareness," writes Dr. Khalsa. Einstein had an abundance of glial cells in Area 39, which serve as 'housekeeping' cells, as opposed to a measurable excess of 'thinking' cells. The job of the glial cell is to support the metabolism of the thinking neurons. The presence of these extra glial cells is what had enlarged Einstein's Area 39. Other experiments were performed that validated the hypothesis that Einstein had an enlarged Area 39 because he was in effect a "mental athlete" who had "trained hard" all his life. One of the ways he did this was via the extensive use of his imagination."

While some readers may argue there is evidence of a causal fallacy here (that *"Glial Cells imply genius"* is like saying that, *"Most people die in bed, so bed is a dangerous place!"),* this is nonetheless an interesting perspective to consider as a contributing factor for the *human-dimensions of HCI.* Moreover, Magee also describes how we need to pump the *"imagination-ions"* so as to develop our visualization muscle. As we have seen earlier; not everybody has the necessary cognitive ability to process visual/verbal information.

eReality Learning Environments

The converging techno-landscape is bringing forward many interesting possibilities for augmented reality. In terms of the *human-dimensions of HCI,* eReality takes on many guises. Let's revert once more to the machine-side of the HCI equation, where we see there is considerable work being carried out by the AI proponents. Typically these people are keenly interested in the coding of adaptive technologies that support industry-academia collaboration. Their work involves big projects that support eBusiness and eCommerce. There are also a number of experts emerging through the techno-landscape innovating software engineering approaches towards modelling learning environments. These techno-driven projects focus on the underlying technology to optimize efficiency. On the other side of the HCI equation, however, there are a significant number of people showing great interest in peeking into what other people are doing. The interest in reality television is immense. Unfortunately the marketers have captured this cyberspace to entice the unwary into signing up for so-called free gifts *(Figure 36).*

Figure 36 : The Free Gift Hook

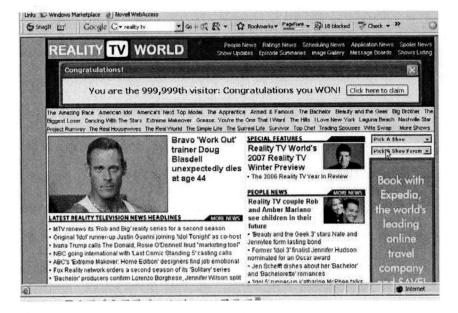

Figure 37 : Securing Your Personal Details

Sadly, to receive your free gift, the techno-trap for this type of techno-scam is to capture your personal information for a global repository, where there are no guarantees of security or control *(Figure 36)*.

Virtual Reality

"Virtuality reality" (VR) is a technology which allows a user to interact with a computer-simulated environment, be it a real or imagined one. Most current virtual reality environments are primarily visual experiences, displayed either on a computer screen or through special stereoscopic displays. Additionally, some simulations include sensory information, such as sound through speakers or headphones. Some advanced, haptic systems now include tactile information, generally known as force feedback, in medical and gaming applications. These VR systems track the user's hand and head movements. Users can interact with a virtual environment or a virtual artefact either through the use of standard input devices such as a keyboard and mouse, or through multi-modal devices such as a wired glove, the Polhemus boom arm, and omnidirectional treadmill. Any of several types of stereoscopic devices transform otherwise 2-dimensional image data into 3-dimensional images [12]. The simulated environment can be similar to the real world. For example, simulations for pilot or combat training. It can also differ significantly from reality, as in VR games. In practice, it is currently very difficult to create a high-fidelity virtual reality experience, due largely to technical limitations on processing power, image resolution and communication bandwidth. However, those limitations are expected to eventually be overcome as technology becomes more powerful and cost-effective over time.

It is unclear exactly where the future of VR is headed. In the short run, the graphics displayed in head-mounted displays will soon reach a point of near realism. The aural aspect will move into a new realm of three dimensional sound, including the addition of sound channels both above and below the individual. The VR application of this future technology will most likely be in the form of over-ear headphones.

With our technological limits today, sight and sound are the only 2-senses that will be able to be replicated almost flawlessly. There are however, attempts being currently made to also simulate smell. The purpose of current research is linked to a project aimed at treating post traumatic stress disorder in veterans by exposing them to combat simulations, complete with smells. Although it is often seen in the context of entertainment by popular culture, this illustrates the point that the future of VR is very much tied into therapeutic, training, and engineering demands. Given that fact, a full sensory immersion beyond basic tactile feedback, sight, sound, and smell is unlikely to be a goal in the industry. It is worth mentioning that simulating smells, while it can be done very realistically requires costly R&D to make each odour. Additionally, the machine itself is expensive and specialized, using tailor-made capsules. Thus far, basic and very strong smells such as burning rubber, cordite, gasoline fumes, and so-forth have been created. Something complex such as a food product or specific flower would be prohibitively expensive (consider the perfume industry as an example).

In order to engage the other sense of taste, the brain must be manipulated directly. This would move VR into the realm of simulated reality: not unlike in the movie, *The Matrix*. Although no form of this has been seriously developed at this point, Sony has taken the first step. On April 7 2005, according to Times Online [13], Sony went public with the information that they had filed for and received a patent for the idea of the non-invasive beaming of different frequencies and patterns of ultrasonic waves directly into the brain to recreate all 5-senses. While there has been research to show that this is possible, Sony has not conducted any tests as of yet and says that it is still only an idea.

Impact

There has been increasing interest in the potential social impact of new technologies, such as virtual reality (as may be seen in utopian literature, within the social sciences, and in popular culture). A Wikipedia Web-site in 2006 revealed that VR will lead to a number of important changes in human life and activity [14]:

- VR will be integrated into daily life and activity and will be used in various human ways.
- techniques will be developed to influence human behavior, interpersonal communication, and cognition (ie: virtual genetics) http://virtualreality.unversityvillagepress.com/index.php?intemid=25&catid=4
- as we spend more and more time in virtual space, there will be a gradual *"migration to virtual space,"* resulting in important changes in economics, worldview, and culture.
- The design of virtual environments may be used to extend basic human rights into virtual space, to promote human freedom and well-being, and to promote social stability as we move from one stage in socio-political development to the next.

Feral learning – Internet Spins Off a New Pedagogy

Many humans retain their inquisitive nature throughout life. We begin learning about our world before birth, outstripping other species for what we already know when we arrive on the planet. Human beings take a relatively long time to reach maturity. Extra developmental time is given over to learning – assimilating all kinds of information into our disproportionately large brains [15]. However, instead of gaining super strength, speed or size, our inquisitive disposition for learning and manipulating thoughts sustains us throughout life. In our earlier years, many commence traditional schooling, conforming to a formal educational setting for at least 12-years or more. Some young people during these years are completely alienated from their own learning process, which previously sustained them so nicely. Often, there are negative aspects to this imposed socialization process that discourages enquiry for the sake of it. Some of our young even give up their motivation for self enquiry altogether. Instead of pursuing knowledge because it's fun - just finding out about things - eventually they succumb to a set curriculum, which has been designed (by somewhere else) as a generic learning environment. Fortunately, many school-based learners do survive to proceed successfully through life. Those who do not become alienated, eventually dropping out of this formalized, or so called traditional learning system. Moreover, deviation from conventional schooling for extra curricula activity is not formally recognized. Yet despite the dilemmas of imposed curricula, by the time people reach postgraduate studies, they are expected to be self-motivated, reflective critical-thinkers [15].

Table 21 : ICT Tools Can Promote Feral Learning

Feral learning pedagogy		Implications for the *human-dimensions of HCI*
Holist	Acknowledges the validity of learning as and when it comes forth	Many educators see flexible learning as the direct consequence of the ways that ICT tools are altering education [16]. As a consequence the flexibility of these new delivery tools promote a new type of feral learning.
Student-led	Transforms the learner's understanding of their world	
Seamless learning	Life-long process of growth and adaptation	
a-Curricular environment	All learning is acknowledged as valid	

Instead of lamenting what we have lost; we should be celebrating the inherent human spirit that maintains our cognitive strengths despite the deliberate psychological battering it gets during our formative years. Long live our attraction for feral learning. According to Mary Hall [15]:

> *"for the most part, it does not reside in formal education centres. It lives in early childhood, (the pre-school sector) and in the social interactions and interests of people outside of formal education. Most of all, it rules the internet. This is not, as some have suggested, a problem to be overcome. It is the energy that powers the new pedagogy. Rather than farmers taming the landscape, the educators of the new age must learn to be conservators of the natural world."*

For the most part we can say that ICT tools may promote feral learning if they are implemented to encourage: holistic, student-led, seamless learning in *"a-curricular"* environments. *Table 21* reveals how this would be possible.

The trick with all this will be to recognize how much of our own feral learning survived the schooling process, while retaining the requirements for the formal assessment of what we already know. Drawing analogies from different learning environments, today energized ICT tools can be implemented in such a manner to ignite the imagination, providing relative freedom from imposed teaching and learning strategies. Moreover, the adaptive approach towards learning systems design suits the notions of feral learning. We are already seeing these features emerging on the exciting side of the techno-educational landscape.

Ambient Computing

Perhaps the newest techno-kids on the block are the proponents who draw many of the more popular ICTs together as commercialized wireless solutions for pervasive HCI and networking environments. Often these new techno-environments comprise advanced hardware and software management tools, which in turn create smart robust technologies that enhance business computing operations. These cutting edge technologies have the potential to empower organizations through smart video conferencing facilities, desktop portability and centralized resource allocation. One way of explaining this exciting advancement towards an *information nirvana* for business is to refer to a scenario posed in a Technical Report, from the University of Kansas, Information and Telecommunication Technology Centre[17] page-5:

"Herman completes editing his presentation in his office environment. He picks up a small lightweight device, we call a Personal Interactive Device (PID), and heads down the hall toward the conference room. The conference room is equipped with tabletop display screens, video/computer display projectors, sound system, microphone system, controllable video camera, and controllable lighting. When he enters, the conference room senses his entry and turns on the ambient light. Herman sits at a tabletop station and presses his thumb against a reader, is identified and his working context is brought up on the nearby display. Herman directs, through gestures, voice commands, and conventional computer interaction, to put the presentation on the right screen, point "that video camera" at "that seat", "put the remote video feed on the left screen", and so forth. The conference room reacts to Herman's voice commands, gestures, and computer mediated commands."

While these systems may be at the high end of the machine-dimension of the techno-landscape; in some cases, they do reveal a concerted interest to define the *human-dimensions of HCI* that until now has been totally ignored. One group of enthusiastic researchers based in France, are interested in the design and development of spatial information systems. Their overall objectives are to combine three techno-phenomena that permit the emergence of environment-aware person-centric applications and services[18]. The first relates to the popularity of people's portable telecommunications devices, like mobile phones and Personal Digital Assistants known as PDAs. The second phenomenon is the large number of everyday devices that contain embedded systems, which include their own processor and memory to control physical objects. Yet a third phenomenon relates to the wireless techno-gadgets, like Bluetooth, Wi-Fi and GPS. As such they mirror the properties of the physical world in their *"Ambient Computing and Embedded Systems"* (ACES) project, mimicking the relative positioning of physical objects and their movements [18]. To design and implement these highly sophisticated systems they require efficient distributed mechanisms to spread and sense contextual information, as well as appropriate programming models to handle the physical context of the applications.

An important focus of this work is the importance that is placed by the researchers on the need for ambient computing to facilitate mobility. In doing this, they synthesize perfectly the aspirations of the *human-dimensions of HCI* with the technical aspects of the machine-dimension. In other words, they are progressing *effective HCI* by:

- first, developing the means to deliver functioning systems which require minimal device manipulation by the device handler. It is well understood amongst this visionary group of researchers that their devices must operate as an extension of the human, rather than operating as a mere tool
- second, that these new devices should model the physical environment exactly, to operate seamlessly – importing data from the environment, which in turn modifies the environment when appropriate
- third, their applications must be able to accommodate and adapt to the changeable nature of the limited storage and processing capabilities of mobile devices, as well as the variable and intermittent coverage of the wireless networks

Natural Learning Environments

Some may talk freely about feral learning as a person's natural propensity for learning in a de-institutionalised environment, where grazing occurs unlike the more traditional lesson-sized meal.   By contrast to this free-wheeling approach to knowledge acquisition, natural learning environments have been described as the tools that generate learner responsibility. In other words, they ask questions, seeking the answers and analyse information, which in turn leads to more questioning.   Due to the broadening nature of the spiraling enquiry, there is often no real answer. Those of us lucky enough to have grown up in this never ending knowledge seeking environment will recognize the premise that training such as this conditions the mind to keep searching: even when a perfectly reasonable answer has been found [19]. As learners tap into worldly knowledge with relatively little trouble for their efforts, one of the more attractive aspects of surfing the Internet is the seemingly unfettered access to all sorts of information.

Moreover the valuable networking that occurs along the information highway is enhanced by an individual's intuitive antenna. It would be good to see some solid research into the interactive effects of emotional fatigue and sensible decision making upon episodes of productive informational grazing. People report being caught in a type of techno-piggybacking that takes over their knowledge acquisition: one hot lead advancing a person into yet another enquiry line. The trouble with this unbridled enquiry is to know when to stop.

Situational Awareness

The issue of knowing when to stop as it relates to our travels along the information highway forms part of the debate on situation awareness within the scientific literature. To fighter-jet pilots, situational awareness is a more pragmatic skill. It refers to the degree of accuracy by which one's perception of their current environment mirrors reality. The basic understanding of situation awareness comprises 3-levels [20], they involve:

- level-1 perception of elements
- level-2 comprehending what those elements mean
- level-3 using that understanding to project future states

In other words, this means a total immersion within your environment. However, researchers cannot agree on how to articulate the perception of humanoid connectivity with their technological surroundings. Some believe it's about the way we eventually reduce all information into our working memories [21].   Others relate to expert performance, whether it is doing something relatively mundane like driving a car or steering a ship, or more complicated like flying a plane. Ordinary people can aspire to become expert enough to accomplish all these things. Consequently, a novice car driver has many things to learn before they become competent. For instance, they must know how to observe the road rules, as well as coordinate all the physical aspects that relate to concentration and safely managing a vehicle on the road. After much practice they eventually become very familiar with their driving surroundings, to such an extent that they can respond automatically. So doing, experts totally absorb themselves within the context of a given task, adjusting the use of information gained from their surrounding environment *(Table 22)*.

Table 22 : Factors that Reduce Situation Awareness

Factors that reduce situational awareness	Implications for the *human-dimensions of HCI*
Insufficient Communication	Expect the personal digital-awareness characteristics of the techno-humanoid landscape to cause stress for each of these factors to reduce the individual's situational awareness. For instance, take the position of a novice-learner/user. Unless they are given a thorough knowledge in navigation of the techno-situation they will become confused and not be capable of achieving the final outcome. While the more experienced person, accessing the information *(who may simply want to refresh rusty parts of their knowledge)* will need to access segmented parts of the knowledge-base to pick and choose between information options.
Fatigue / Stress	
Task Overload	
Task Underload	
Group Mindset	
"Press on Regardless" Philosophy	
Degraded Operating Conditions	

The behaviour of team collaboration has been investigated by researchers at Australia's *"Commonwealth Scientific and Industrial Research Organisation"* (CSIRO). Their research involves the HxI Initiative which is a three-way partnership among the CSIRO, *"Defense Science and Technology Organisation"* (DSTO) and *"National ICT Australia"* (NICTA). Together they have developed the HxI Reference Model *(Figure 38)* to provide the context and a common point of understanding for the HxI research thrusts, science challenges and research activities undertaken jointly between organisations and disciplines [22].

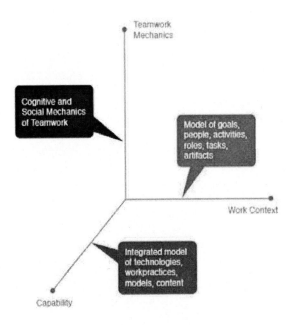

Figure 38 : HxI Reference Model

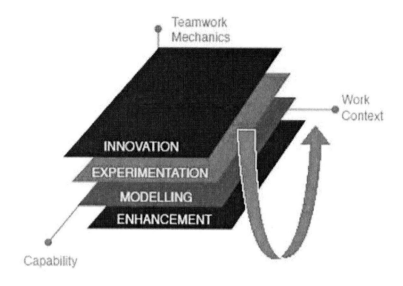

Figure 39 : HxI Reference Model – 4-Key Enabling Mechanisms

Their HxI Reference Model defines 4-key enabling mechanisms *(Figure 39)*: innovation, experimentation, modelling and enhancement. This model describes how people use their capabilities within particular work contexts and addresses the fundamental mechanisms of teamwork, such as communication, awareness, synthesis and decision making. A key challenge for the HxI Initiative is to define how these 4-research thrusts can be integrated *(Table 23)*.

Following the advent of high powered ICT tools and the consequential increased interest in interface-design, there is a concurrent dilemma for *effective HCI*, where the techno-solutions to problems that involve the higher socio-psychological context of human problems are becoming a limiting factor [23]. For instance, consider the difficulties that surround the real-time collaboration between co-workers who are positioned in different locations. For the sake of this discussion, perhaps we can say these people are part of a collaborative disaster recovery operation. In these rather special circumstances teams of decision makers are positioned across territorial boundaries. In order to get the job done, they will utilise telecommunications and groupware solutions to carry out their collaborative decision making. However dichotomous contextual problems will arise due to the need for improved understandings of the situational awareness cues that are critical to their complicated decision making [23].

Table 23 : Key Enablers for the HxI Model

HxI Reference Model Key enablers	Implications for the *human-dimensions of HCI*
Innovation	The process of adapting and enhancing capabilities required by the work context. Innovation can increase the effectiveness of team activities through the rapid adaptation of technologies, work environments, work practices and information sources.
Experimentation	This plays an important role in developing and evaluating capabilities within particular work contexts, especially the role of innovation in the context of teamwork. It covers a range of activities including evaluation, laboratory experiments and ethnography. Experimentation is undertaken in relation to teamwork mechanics. Experimentation poses some significant challenges for the types of work contexts and capabilities that are the focus of HxI research: intense collaboration involving creative teamwork of combinations of co-located and distributed teams.
Modelling	Developing solid theoretical foundations by consolidating knowledge and understanding, often derived through experimentation, into sets of underlying models. A range of models is required to support HxI, including: Models of teamwork activities Capability models that show the relationship between sets of technologies Work practices and information resources Ethnographic models that support the fusion of observational data collected by ICT sensors and human analysts Models of teamwork mechanics. Models that support reasoning and models that can be enacted using ICT approaches such as intelligent services are also centrally important for the HxI Initiative.
Enhancement	An enabler of team performance and improvement that uses the results of experimentation to augment capabilities in relation to specific work contexts and particular teamwork mechanics. For example, the project seeks to develop new types of intelligent services to support team thinking and interaction.

Mentoring

The development of high level skills across the workforce is expensive and requires major investment from individuals, governments and employers. Traditionally, employers view training as an expensive solution that is implemented to fix problems. A research project is currently underway to develop a theory of Web-mediated learning reinforcement as a better basis for investigating qualities of training in context. Currently, the usefulness of online mentoring is largely misunderstood. Online mentoring should not remain stationary. Instead it should respond to the context and progressive knowledge development between the mentor and the mentee. Employers need to know the impact of their continual investments in human capital development on institutional effectiveness. Furthermore, with people remaining in the workforce beyond the traditional retirement age, we need to know what the consequences of retraining that involves online facilitation, and what are the consequences for retaining a paper-based facilitator-led training program.

At this point, although the benefits of online mentoring systems that involve Web-mediated learning reinforcement strategies are just beginning to emerge through the literature; they do not exist in practice yet. For instance, new demands for knowledge within the academic environment sometimes results in new ways of working [24]. In recent times there has been an increase in the prevalence of university-industry co-operation [25]. Furthermore, the advancements in ICT tools for the Internet have opened up various implementation possibilities [26], especially with regard to cross-collaboration and inter-institutional online mentoring programs.

With the advent of work-place reform, virtual reality may yet prove to bring about optimal learning outcomes: not only for new workers entering the workforce (novice learners) but also for longer-term (experienced) workers who need to increase their knowledge and skill profile. It is important to differentiate what an individual knows from what they do not [27];[28]. However, obtaining accurate measurement of employees' knowledge and skill is adding to the training dilemmas facing employers, made worse through ICT. Often problems arise following training sessions, when employees are expected to translate what they have learned during their training sessions into their work-place. To dissipate these dilemmas, we suggest a custom designed Web-based knowledge navigation tool to enable employees to remain engaged with their training materials.

However, there is a discrepancy in the literature concerning mentoring [29]. The confusion is between the role of a mentor, and the changeable nature of the relationship between the mentor and mentee. This dilemma comes about through the intangibility of the knowledge constructs involved. This includes the information passed back and forth from mentor to mentee, the changes to the mentee's knowledge, the shared ideas, and the innovation and creativity [30]. This fluidity has been noticed. As the mentee learns from the mentor, the growth and learning potential inherent in the mentoring relationship decreases [31]. Instead, as the mentee's achievement potential rises, as they move through the mentoring/mentee interaction, a distinctly different knowledge exchange takes over in the form of a two-way process of influence and becomes a highly-developed collaborative working relationship [32]. A well-structured mentoring relationship should therefore empower the mentee to a point of interactive co-learning, in which the mentee also shares ideas. As such, the mentee benefits in terms of increased self-confidence and knowledge. Moreover, the organisation also benefits in terms of enhanced corporate knowledge assets. Beyond the academic institution, it has been shown that practitioners in organisations can become part of the process of engaging their employees in the professional development process.

It is very important to place the mentoring relationship within a context that is familiar for the student/trainee. The afforded benefits of this type of situated learning approach emerge as they begin to form concepts together about the practical aspects of their work. The awareness for the importance of this type of learning context can also be translated to a Web-based mentorship system [33].

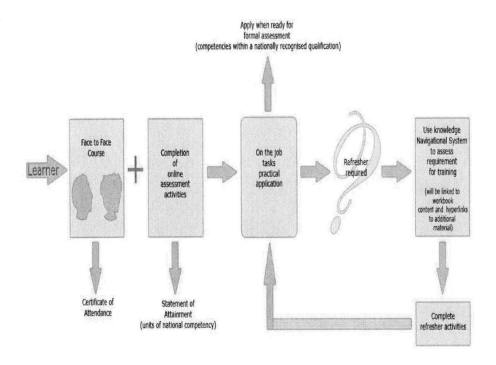

Figure 40 : Pilot Knowledge Navigation Tool

A *"Pilot Knowledge Navigation Tool"* currently under construction provides trainees with the opportunity to immediately transfer their newly acquired knowledge and skills with real applicability to their *"on the job tasks" (Figure 40)*. Moreover, to contextualize the Web-based mentoring component, the instructional system differentiates the novice (or beginner) from the more experienced (advanced) learner.

In other words, the novice will be guided through a standard knowledge development methodology that is designed to progress their training towards achieving the learning outcomes. The experienced learner on the other hand (who may only require a refresher will be able to select which instructional content they interact with.

Magical Metaphors

Some times when we want to describe the techno-landscape, our language seems utterly inadequate. It can be quite difficult to find the right words when we want to explain particular aspects of a very complex system. This is because we have millions of words from which to choose for what seem to be a very limited number of basic worldly principles [34]. When this happens some people are better than others at finding the right metaphor as a conduit to convey meaning. For instance in the following metaphorical system, watch as the words conjure up a mental picture of the relationship between a computer and the Internet:

"The CPU is the central hub of the computer. Its ports are the gateways through which it may communicate with the rest of the computer. Among these many ports, are ones that allow you to travel the many lanes of the information superhighway. One is wise to have their computer protected by a firewall, which is a protective shell that prevents unwanted bugs from being planted in your computer by hackers. This will give some computers less room to move around in, as much space is needed for the computer to pin up virtual "Wanted - Dead or Alive" posters. As you surf the net, you may run into a few boundaries where a password will be required. The password is your key to such things as e-mail or online banking. When you are finished surfing, it is wise to close your browser window and empty your cache. This will lighten the load on your CPU, so you can do other tasks - such as copying files - without the burden of your travels weighing down the processor." [34] para:2.

Language and metaphor form a tightly coupled linguistic unit. As such, people have been using the metaphor to illustrate ideas, control thoughts of others and induce certain types of behaviours in others. Using a metaphorical language becomes particularly troublesome within our (metaphorical) techno-landscape when people may not differentiate between the model and the real techno-instance. On the one hand the model can provide a make-believe picture; while the other is to believe that it is real [35].

However before devising a new techno-landscape metaphor, think of the trickery that the metaphor can invoke. Keep the visual language simple. Most people will respond intuitively when the metaphor is fairly literal: the Macintosh example of deleting a document by tossing it in the trash can, for example [2].

Human-Machine Interaction Network on Emotion (HUMAINE) Completes the Cycle

Getting to the grit of the *human-dimensions of HCI* isn't as easy as it sounds [1]. We have been seeking out ways to express human endeavour long before the first twinkles of the techno-landscape. However, ways to show the interactive effects of people and their techno-gadgetry on popular usage are only just emerging. It would seem therefore that we have gone the full circle. As with most partnerships, we need both sides of the human-machine dimensioned environment to initiate *effective HCI*.

Emotion-oriented computing is a broad research area involving many disciplines. The EU-funded network of excellence, HUMAINE, is currently making a coordinated effort to come to a shared understanding of the issues involved, and to propose exemplary research methods in various areas. This overview presents a proposed *map* of the research area, distinguishing core technologies from application-oriented and psychologically oriented work (see http://emotion-research.net/). Current research issues in the various areas are briefly outlined, and references for further reading are given. Figure 41 represents their proposed map of the thematic areas involved in emotion-oriented computing.

The central column represents the areas where purely technological challenges loom largest. Detection and synthesis are distinguished because the background technologies used are very different. *"Planning action"* involves modelling action patterns that might be expected in a particular emotional state, either for driving an artificial agent or for anticipating a human's action tendencies in a given state.

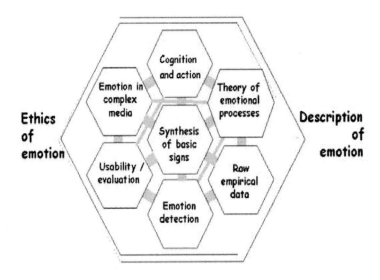

Figure 41 : Human-Machine Interaction Network on Emotion (HUMAINE)

The left hand column deals with issues where application is most obviously of concern. Emotion-related usability issues are more difficult to address than task-oriented ones, because emotional responses are subtle and easily disrupted by interventions that are meant to measure them. Iterative user-centred design methods are used for tuning a system to non-rational preferences and dispositions in the user. Work on emotion in complex media is treated separately because the perspective towards applications in the relatively near future requires a different approach from the core technologies in the central column.

The right hand column contains the sub-areas with the strongest roots in psychology. HUMAINE distinguish theory and empirical data because existing theory is informed by different kinds of data from what seems relevant for emotion-oriented computing. As a result, there are creative tensions between that kind of data collection and existing psychological theory. Similarly, psychological theory can use technology to test its accuracy and completeness, because the actions of artificial agents can be controlled with a precision that is impossible with humans.

The task of synthesising agents that can interact emotionally is at the centre because it summarises the state of the art. It cannot be done well without satisfactory progress in all the others. At either edge of the diagram are issues with a strong philosophical element. These affect the whole enterprise: finding appropriate ways to describe emotions and emotion-related states, and the ethics of emotion-oriented systems. Recommended further reading: Roddy Cowie's 2005 white paper [36].

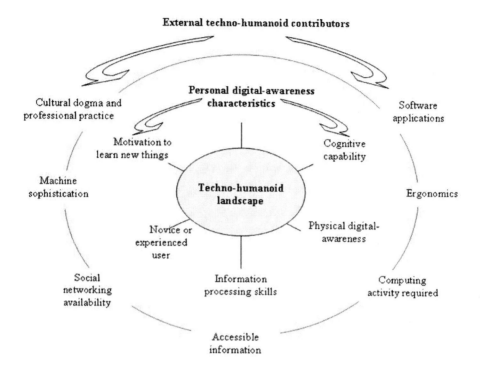

Figure 42 : Techno-Humanoid Landscape

Techno-Humanoid Landscape

The *human-dimensions of HCI* are complex with many environmental factors influencing how things turn out. The purpose of this model is to suggest that there may be two layers of pressure that form the techno-humanoid landscape. Let us firstly take up the notion that the techno-humanoid landscape is the focal point for explaining the *human-dimensions of HCI*. The more personal digital-awareness characteristics are shown here forming the closest layer, while the more distant external techno-humanoid contributors simmer away to complete the techno-scenario. At any given moment the pressures from these layers can cause an interactive effect that ripples through to cause positive or negative outcomes for the comfort zone of the techno-landscape *(Figure 42)*. We could of course extend the number of layers to include infrastructure elements like political and economic climate. For the moment however, this discussion will concentrate on the aspects of the techno-humanoid landscape that are closest to home.

External Techno-Humanoid Contributors

At the outer edge of this metaphorical universe there is a never ending supply of contributors that impact on our personal computing space. When they are perfectly meshed together they combine to form a powerful comfort zone that affords the user relative control over their computing environment. Mostly they will tick away unnoticed until something goes wrong.

Cultural Dogma and Professional Practice

The terms cultural dogma and professional practice are used here in the sense that a given culture (or professional practice) provides parameters for individual members to live and interact with others. By contrast, in the past we have thought about culture in a more closed environment bounded by traditional elements that dictate values and norms: religious belief and geographic location, for example. These days we also acknowledge that cultural groupings can conform to a number of interesting sub-groups. Still it would be fair to say there are a number of contributing factors that combine to form cultural specific parameters that may include:

- Administrative systems – to establish the rules of the overall social environment
- Economic systems – things which determine our survival and personal fulfillment
- Technology – ability to survive and prosper
- Physical assets - education systems in place for handing on generational values
- Creative pursuit – an endless list of activities that will vary upon circumstances

Machine Sophistication

There can be no doubt that ever since the techno-generations commenced their march through the passage of time, with their beefed up microprocessor brain power, access to everyday computing has become almost commonplace; including all the general whiz-bangery of the Internet. Strange as it may be to any of the techno-Luddites left in the land, as the computing power increases the machinery and costs are downsizing. All this digi-freedom however does come at a cost to the quality of our travels around the information highway. Unless one's machine has the ability to deal with the connectivity issues that surround hauling the huge bits per second of broadcasting channels, one can forget about using applications that involve image and sound.

Social Networking Availability

Various ICT tools support our cyberspace wanderings. Prowling the Internet for opportunities to find and share information is a thing of the (recent) past. While it is very useful knowing how to push an Internet search engine around, it affords more of a solitary peek into the knowledge pool. It is no longer sufficient to rely upon these devices to do this type of information seeking hack-work. Instead these days, there is a whole new approach to sharing information that involves so-called social networking sites. These sites are where ordinary people can and do let themselves go, revealing all sorts of personal information to anybody out there in cyberspace. Some of the more interesting and successful places that involve this type of social networking include (Table 24):

Table 24 : Successful Social Networking Web-Sites

Online social networking sites	Purpose	Implications for the *human-dimensions of HCI*
http://www.myspace.com/ http://orkut.com http://www.flickr.com/	finding friends	Exploits the more traditional Web searching techniques that involve hyperlink navigation. At the same time relies upon information from implicit and explicit user feedback. Enables the leveraging costs of conventional Web searches, while ranking results that are relative to the interests of the social grouping.
http://www.flickr.com/	sharing photos	
http://www.youtube.com/ http://video.google.com.au/	sharing videos	
http://www.blogger.com/start http://www.livejournal.com/	writing blogs	

Another way people go about their social networking online effectively is to simply pass URLs to interested people you know. This method is typical of a hidden mass of private knowledge navigation, where the original author of the content found in Web pages has no control over their material spreading through cyberspace. One of the drawbacks of this type of social networking relates to the timeliness of the postings. There is no guarantee that URLs remain constant over time.

Accessible Information

The ability to access and use information through the various ICT tools has become a major daily activity for ordinary folk around the world. It has become an essential ingredient for the full participation of students in academic and other school-related activities. Sadly for most of the educational institutions, accessibility is commonly addressed as an afterthought and on an individual basis, often making it difficult, time-consuming, and costly to provide adequate access. A better approach is to consider the needs of all possible users in the planning phase, when considering the role that technologies will play in an educational entity's future. This type of approach is known as universal design, which should result in a technology-enhanced learning environment that benefits all users, including those with and without disabilities.

For more on universal design see the AccessIT Knowledge Base article entitled - What is Universal Design? from http://www.washington.edu/accessit/articles?108 .

If an educational entity's technology environment has been established with a universal design process, all students and staff can participate in and benefit equally from the activities of that entity. Below are a few examples:

Accessible web pages allow students with disabilities to access information; share their work; communicate with peers, teachers, and mentors; and take advantage of distance learning options.

Accessible instructional software (on disks, CDs, or other media) allows students with disabilities to participate side by side with their peers in computer labs and classrooms as they complete assignments; collaborate with peers; create and view presentations, documents, and spreadsheets; and actively participate in simulations and all other academic activities.

Accessible *multi-media*, including captions and audio descriptions, is accessible to all students, including those with visual or hearing impairments, and is more easily understood by students for whom the video is not in their first language or who learn best or otherwise benefit from multi-sensory input.

Accessible telecommunications and office equipment make communication and educational administrative functions accessible to everyone, including those with mobility, visual, and hearing impairments.

Computing Activity Required

Before we do something it is usual for us to seek out how we will know when we have achieved a successful outcome. This is the leading WYSIWYG principle of What You See Is What You Get. People deciding to undertake any sort of task on the Internet especially will expect feedback along the way. For instance, in a Web-mediated environment there should be some type of correct performance indicator that typically has a form of knowledge of results or outcome feedback available. This is the most common type of feedback that lets someone know whether their performance is heading towards the desired goals (van Merrienboer, 1997). Due to the speed at which we cognitively move around in cyberspace, these knowledge results should be crisp and to the point, carrying no additional information about the performed task other than its direct outcomes.

Consequently timely knowledge results are an inherent aspect of performing a recurrent constituent skill. Like when people are learning how to perform a word processing task. Performing particular procedures will typically yield information indicating when the particular goals have been reached.

Ergonomics

Safety, comfort and reliability are central to making tasks easier to perform. Interest in human factors relating to physical comfort, or ergonomics, was activated through a combination of a number of otherwise disparate disciplines during World War II. These days, ergonomics as it refers to HCI is about ensuring safe workstation design and readability of screen-based information [37], and how long individuals spend at a computer without taking adequate breaks. Similarly, much has been printed about the perils of long haul flights, where passengers sit for hours in cramped conditions, placing them at risk of developing deep vein thrombosis. Of particular interest in recent years is the likelihood of radiation levels [38] emitted from visual display units causing harmful effects on unwary computer users. Other types of health threats from non-CRT technology include: "repetitive stress injuries" known as carpal tunnel syndrome.

Software Applications

In defining what a software application is, we must first mention that most often a computer program or group of programs are designed to make life easier for ordinary computer users (or end users). Software can be divided into two general classes: systems software and applications software (Figure 43). Systems software consists of low-level programs that interact with the computer at a very basic level. This includes machine-related things like the computer's operating systems, compilers, and utilities for managing computer resources.

In contrast to the systems software, applications software (also called end-user programs) includes database programs, word processors, and spreadsheets. Figuratively speaking, applications software sits on top of systems software because it is unable to run without the operating system and system utilities.

We will leave this discussion on the outer edge of our metaphorical techno-universe where there are many hidden contributors that affect personal computing. In the main, unless the user has technical expertise it is best, when asked by a software application, to simply accept the system defaults. This is one time when blissful ignorance should maintain your techno-status quo. Now moving to the inner circle of the techno-humanoid landscape, let's examine some of the more personal aspects of HCI.

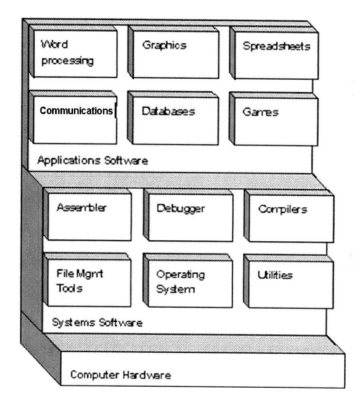

Figure 43 : Classes of Systems' Software

Personal Digital-Awareness Characteristics

Closer to the core of the techno-humanoid landscape is one's personal orientation or slice of the HCI action. For the purposes of explaining the more personalized contextual factors, one needs to note that it is usually easier for lay people to alter their HCI environment than to do anything else.

Motivation to Learn New Things

Humans have an innate drive to master their environment that remains a life-long trait, both at a personal and at a worldly level. Some people report huge satisfaction in completing a somewhat tricky task such as mastering how to download software from the Internet and install the application on their home pc. Competence motivation has a broadly based biological origin that explains human behaviour through our persistence of activities that constitute effective interaction with the environment [39]. These include: exploration, activity and manipulation.

In business circles the widely acclaimed Maslow's *"hierarchy of needs"* [40] is still held in high distinction today. These relatively common sense steps to self-actualization include:
1. Basic needs – play
2. Security needs – seniority plans, unions and severance payments
3. Belonging needs – formal and informal work-groups
4. Esteem needs – titles, status symbols, promotions, banquets
5. Self-Actualization – leading to a person's motivation to transform perception of self to reality

However it was Herzberg who extended Maslow's work to develop a specific content theory of work motivation. Herzberg identified *"satisfiers"* as (motivators) and *"dissatisfiers"* (hygiene factors). Taken together, these became known as Herzberg's 2-factor theory of motivation [40]:201).

Table 25 : Herzberg's 2-Factor Theory

Hygiene factors	Motivators
Company policy & administration	Achievement
Supervision, technical	Recognition
Salary	Work itself
Interpersonal relations, supervisor	Responsibility
Working conditions	Advancement

Novice/Experienced Dichotomy

Knowing how to learn new skills is something that we get better at as we grow older. For the most part, as we journey down the life-long learning path, it becomes easier to differentiate which instructional strategies are likely to suit us best. The trouble we run into, especially when using Web-mediated instructional environments, is likely to be whether there are any fast-tracking options for the learning tasks. It is well known that novice-learners require the full range of rules and information relating to learning something new, where an experienced person may only require a quick brush up. Novice learners will therefore respond best to measured amounts of guidance through progressively more complex instructional/learning content with strategic opportunities for interactive practice examples along the way. Alternatively, a person possessing a more experienced grasp of the particular task will want to experiment first, only dipping into the rules and basic information when they get into trouble. Unfortunately there are many Web-mediated instructional strategies that do not cater for this dichotomy. When the instructional systems cannot adapt to this important requirement, they run the risk of de-motivating both groups of learners. The result will produce confusion for novices when the primary rules and examples are not explicit enough. The same will cause utter boredom and frustration for the experienced when forced into involvement with the complete instructional strategy.

Information Processing Skills

While there are many well known theories that explain how our information processing per se (or thinking skills) work ([41]; [42]; [43]), researchers today remain keen to extend this earlier work as it would apply to Web-mediated learning. For a mere sample of research in this domain, interested readers are referred to [44] and [45]. However, while there are many high quality research investigations into various aspects of a user's psychological and physiological differences, they have not produced results that can be generalized to a wider Web-mediated learning community.

Physical Digital-Awareness

Perhaps an effective way to clarify the notion of a physical digital awareness as it pertains to the *human-dimensions of HCI* is to firstly rule out what it is not. Often digital awareness is published in the popular press (including the Internet) as being associated with new business practices that involve interactive ICT tools. Instead the definition should be one of a personalized awareness for the holistic nature of where a person cognitively fits within cyberspace, if at all. Accordingly this type of digi-cognitive presence means different things to different people. Furthermore, the notion of physical digital-awareness is predominantly a fluid environment that is constantly changing as the individual alters their position. As an example, let us consider the context of an individual's digital-awareness within wireless technologies.

Cognitive Capability

In keeping with the notion that people have an inherent learning capability that lasts for a life-time, we are able to extend this vision to qualify capability in terms of intellectual skills. To do this it is useful to return to Robert Gagne's five major categories of learned capabilities *(Table 26)*. They are known as: (1) Intellectual skills, (2) Verbal information, (3) Cognitive strategies, (4) Motor skills, and (5) Attitudes [39]. At some point, while engaged in any learning event facilitated by some sort of the many ICT tools that are used these days, it is likely that an individual will eventually need to operate using purely symbolic representations of physical objects. Therefore it can be said that an ability that requires transfer of symbolic operations within one's head (using imagination to operate a piece of machinery), or by writing (or typing at a keyboard about using the machine) and/or drawing. How a person uses the machine is very different from the actual physical actions that are required, where the learner is physically involved with an object. These capabilities are what Gagne means by *intellectual skill*.

Table 26 : Gagne's Major Categories of Learned Capabilities

Capability (learning outcome)	Examples of possible performance	Implications for *human-dimensions of HCI*
INTELLECTUAL SKILL	Demonstrating symbol use for:	In order to bring forward sufficient examples/non-examples; best practice in instructional systems design requires the need to consolidate a repository of reusable objects.
Discrimination	Like: distinguishing printed m's and n's.	
Concrete concept	Like: identifying the spatial relation "underneath"; identifying a "side" of an object.	
Defined concept rule	Like: classifying a *family*, using a definition.	
Rule	Like: demonstrating the agreement in number of subject and verb sentences.	
Higher-order rule	Like: generating a rule for predicting the size of an image, given the distance of a light source and the curvature of a lens.	
COGNITIVE STRATEGY	Like: using an efficient method for recalling names, like originating a solution for the problem of conserving gasoline.	The instructional architecture should cater for adaptable interactivity that provides timely and sufficient feedback to the user – responding to input from the keyboard, voice activation or touch screen tools.
VERBAL INFORMATION	Like: stating the provisions of a nation's political agenda.	
MOTOR SKILL	Like: printing the letter R; or skating a figure-8 on ice.	
ATTITUDE	Like: choosing to listen to classical music.	

Chapter-6 has further defined the practical aspects of *effective HCI* using the framework of the techno-humanoid landscape. Whilst many people access information through their computers, often isolated in a physical sense from other human-beings, this chapter has explained how to capitalize on the collaborative techno-humanoid possibilities that arise when plugging into the Internet. Having passed the mid-point of this book, the remaining chapters again present the dichotomy of the *human-machine dimensions of HCI*. This time, however, we do not differentiate between the two dimensions. Instead, it is assumed that the reader can differentiate when each causes an impact that will cause harm towards the *effectiveness of HCI*.

In the light of this discussion, the way one determines whether '*they know when they have reached their personal information nirvana*' will depend upon how they deal with the techno-humanoid landscape that includes:

- cyberspace etiquette – notions of managing the travels on the Information Highways of the Internet
- one's capacity for sharing mental models – coordinating one's situation awareness factors
- dealing with the online collaborative group forming processes
- the sophistication (or otherwise) of one's eye-mind-imagination pathways
- natural learning environments

Chapter-7 therefore commences with a commentary that leads the reader to further understand the turbulence of cyberspace.

Chapter Reference List

[1] Feldman, J.A., *From Molecule to Metaphor: A Neural Theory of Language*. 2006, Cambridge, MN: MIT Press, USA ISBN 0-262-06253-4.

[2] Rohrer, T., Conceptual blending on the information highway: How metaphorical inferences work, 1997, *Paper presented at the International Cognitive Linguistics Conference '95 Proceedings*, V.2. Retrieved 20/01/08 from http://philosophy.uoregon.edu/metaphor/iclacnf4.htm

[3] Bradley, G., *Social and Community Informatics: Humans on the Net*, 2006. NY: Routledge. 265

[4] Toffler, A. and Toffler, H., *Creating a New Civilization*. 1994, Atlanta: Turner Publishing.

[5] Hopp, P., Smith, C.A.P., and Hayne, S.C., *Literature Review of Shared Cognition*. 2002, Office of Naval Research, Grant #66001-00-1-8967: Dr Mike Letsky.

[6] Richards, D., Coordination and shared mental models. *American Journal of Political Science*, 2000. 45:2(April 2001): 259-276.

[7] Tuckman, B., *Bruce Tuckman's 1965 Forming Storming Norming Performing team-development model*, Retrieved 20/01/08 from http://www.businessballs.com/tuckmanformingstormingnormingperforming.htm.

[8] Alleman, G.B., *Forming, Storming, Norming, Performing and Adjourning*, 2004, Retrieved 20/01/08 from http://www.niwotridge.com/PDFs/FormStormNormPerform.pdf.

[9] Wallace, P., *The Psychology of the Internet*. 1999, UK: Cambidge University Press. 264.

[10] Magee, J.J., Dream analysis as an aid to older adults' life review. *Journal of Gerontological Social Work*, 1991. 18(1-2): 163-173.

[11] Dharma, S.K. and Stauth, C., *Brain Longevity: The Breakthrough Medical Program that Improves Your Mind and Memory, Regenerate Your Concentration, Energy, and Learning Ability for a Lifetime of Pea*. 2000: Warner Books ISBN: 0-446-67373-0.

[12] Shneiderman, S. and Plaisant, C., *Designing the user interface: Strategies for effective human-computer interaction (4th ed.)*. 2005, Reading, MA: Addison-Wesley.

[13] Horsnell, M., Sony takes 3-D cinema directly to the brain, in *TimesOnline*, 2005. Retrieved 20/01/08 from http://www.timesonline.co.uk/article/0,,2-1557733,00.html.

[14] Cline, M.S., *Power, Madness, and Immortality: The future of virtual reality*, 2005. University Village Press. Retrieved 20/01/08 from http://millimedia.com/textpattern/design/17/power-madness-book-design.

[15] Hall, M., *The New Pedagogy: Feral Learning*, 2004. Retrieved 25/01/07 from http://my_learning_log.blogspot.com/2004/10/new-pedagogy-feral-learning.html .

[16] Nunan, T., Flexible Delivery – What is it and Why is it a Part of Current Educational Debate? *1996. Conference paper in the HERDSA proceedings*.

[17] Becker, B., Frost, V., and Evans, J., Implementation of Ambient Computing Environments Concepts in Microsoft Windows. 2001, *Technical Report from The University of Kansas Centre for Research, Inc.* ITTC-FY2002-22731-01: KS, USA. p. ITTC-FY2002-22731-01.

[18] Banatre, M., *Ambient Computing and Embedded Systems - Activity Report*. 2006, Institut National de Recherche en Informatique et en Automatique.

[19] Webb, B., *Natural Learning Environments: Tools for student responsibility*, 2000. South Carolina, USA. Retrieved 20/01/08 from http://www.motivation-tools.com/youth/natural_learning.htm.

[20]   Endsley, M.R. Situation awareness global assessment technique (SAGAT). Paper in the proceedings of the *National Aerospace and Electronics Conference (NAECON)*. 1988. NY: 789-795 IEEE.

[21]   Bell, H.H. and Lyon, D.R., *Using Observer Ratings to Assess Situation Awareness*, in *Situation Awareness Analysis and Measurement*, M.R. Endsley, Editor. 2000, Lawrence Earlbaum Associates: Mahwah, NJ.

[22]   Vernik, R.J., et al., *HxI: A National Research Initiative in ICT-Augmented Human Interactivity. HxI Internal Report,* 2006. Retrieved 20/01/08 from http://www.hxi.org.au/ .

[23]   Schremmer, C., Epps, J., and Vernik, R. Supporting awareness in intense distributed collaboration. 2006. *Full day workshop at the OzCHI '06.* November 22-24, Sydney, Australia, paper available (20/01/08) through the ACM Digital Library http://portal.acm.org/dl.cfm .

[24]   Dutton, C., Mentoring: The contextualisation of learning - mentor, protege and organisationsl gain in higher education, 2003. *Education and Training.* 45(1): 22-29.

[25]   Hellstrom, T. and Hustead, K., Mapping knowledge and intellectual capital in academic environments: A focus group study. *Journal of Intellectual Capital*, 2004. 5(1): 165-180.

[26]   Phillips-Jones, L., *Mentorship and e-Learning.* 2003.

[27]   McKay, E., Measurement of cognitive performance in computer programming concept acquisition: Interactive effects of visual metaphors and the cognitive style construct. *Journal of Applied Measurement*, 2000. 1(3): 257-286.

[28]   Izard, J., Impediments to sound use of formative assessment (and actions we should take to improve assessment for learning), P.L. Jeffrey, Editor. 2004, *Paper presented at the Australian Association for Research Education (AARE 2004): Positioning education research*, held Nov 28 - Dec 2, in Melbourne.

[29]   Melander, E.R., Educating the practioner: Strategies for focusing on the student in the undergraduate business curriculum, 2001, in *Beyond Teaching to Mentoring*, A.G. Reinarz and E.R. White, Editors. Spring. 85-94.

[30]   Malholtra, Y., Measuring knowledge assets of a nation: Knowledge systems for development. State of Research 2002-2003, 2003. *Research paper United Nations Advisory Meeting of the Department of Economic and Social Affairs: Division for Public Administration and Development.* NY.

[31]   Scandura, R.A., et al., Perspectives on mentoring. *Leadership and Organization*, 1996. 17(3): 50-56.

[32]   Gibb, S., Evaluating mentoring, in *Education and Training*, 1994. 36: p. 323-339.

[33]   Axmann, M. and Synyman, M.M., Developing human capital in an online mentorship system, 2003(4) in *Journal for Intellectual Capital*. 605-617.

[34]   Casnig, J.D., *A Language of Metaphors,* 1997-2006. Kingston, Ontario, Canada: Knowgramming.com Retrieved 20/01/08 from http://knowgramming.com/metaphors/metaphor_in_language.htm .

[35]   Sewell, E.H., *Visual Symbols*, in *Visual Literacy: A spectrum of visual learning*, D.M. Moore and F.M. Dwyer, Editors. 1994, *Educational Technology*, NJ. 435.

[36]   Cowie, R., *Emotion-Oriented Computing: State of the Art and Key Challenges, UK, 2005.* Retrieved 20/01/08 from http://emotion-research.net/aboutHUMAINE/HUMAINE%20white%20paper.pdf.

[37]   Preece, J., et al., *Human-Computer Interaction.* 1994, Harlow - UK: Addison-Wesley. 775.

[38]   EPA, *Risk Communication in Action: Environmental Case Studies,* EMP A C T Environmental Monitoring for Public Access & Community Tracking United States Environmental Protection Agency1EPA, 2007. Retrieved 20/01/08 from http://www.epa.gov/nrmrl/pubs/625r02011/625r02011.pdf.

[39]   Gagne, R.M., *The Conditions of Learning: And the theory of instruction.* 4th ed. 1985, NY: Holt/Rinehart/Winston.

[40]   Luthan, F., *Organizational Behavior.* 1985, NY: McGraw-Hill.

[41]   Atkinson, R.C. and Shriffrin, R.M., *Human memory: A proposed system and its control processes*, in *The Psychology of Learning and Motivation: Advances in Research and Theory*, 1968. K.W.Spence and J.T.Spence, Academic Press: NY.

[42]   Lindsay, P.H. and Norman, D.A., *Human Information Processing: An Introduction to Psychology.* 2nd ed. 1977, NY: Academic Press.

[43]   Anderson, R.C. and Faust, G.W., *Educational Psychology: The science of instruction and learning.* 1973, NY: Dodd, Mead, & Co.

[44]   Chen, S.Y., Fan, J., and Macredie, R.D., Navigation in Hypermedia Learning Systems: Experts vs Novices. *Computers in Human Behavior*, 2006. 22(2): 251-266.

[45]   Baran, B. and Çağıltay, K., *Teachers' Experiences in Online Professional Development Environment,* 2006. TOJDE. 7(4): 110-122.

Chapter-7

Inter-Group Conflict and HCI: Managing Multi-Disciplinary Work-Teams

After our previous chapter's indulgence with an ethereal cyberspace metaphor, this chapter returns the reader to the more Earthly perspective of HCI. It's time in our journey into the *human-dimensions of HCI* to look at some of the systems design issues that may be affecting our online behaviour. Whenever people share ideas through the Internet, sooner or later the communication among the group members becomes a little tricky. However, collaborative environments online need to be built by people who understand human behaviour, often this is simply not the case. Designing for *effective HCI* takes the combined effort of a multi-disciplinary team. This chapter uncovers what happens when this collaborative design environment isn't managed well.

Information System Development

The purpose of this chapter is to introduce the concept of project management as a pivotal tool that underpins successful (educational) information system's design. Sadly, acknowledgement for the strength of the *human-dimensions of HCI* is often missed by designers of information systems. Perhaps a reason for this oversight may be concealed in the dichotomy of techno-human issues that spring up along the way to challenge the systems design process and remain, in many cases, unresolved for the life of the project. Some of these problematic issues relate to the inevitable conflicts that crop up whenever there are multi-disciplined project teams.

Combining expertise from disparate disciplines can be tricky in any project team, particularly with information systems design for Web-mediated learning environments. Therefore it is not unreasonable to find continual competing tensions between various project team members. For instance, on the one hand there may be people with vested interests in different aspects of the end-user (or online learner) requirements. On the other hand, there could be a well meaning educationalist in the team, wanting to enhance the pedagogy using the correct ICT tool. There could also be a technologist team-member, who wants to concentrate on the information system functioning well enough to support the ICT tools. If the actual building of the information system has been outsourced (as so often happens these days) another challenge for the project team may come from an over zealous developer with aspirations for widening their product brief. Then and quite understandably, is the pressure from the project manager to complete a successful project on time and within budget.

In cases where the requirements for the information system physically affect human behaviour, imperative ethical issues may arise which permeate every aspect of the system design. It may be difficult for an outsider to occupational psychology to understand why certain techno-elements (or safeguards for maintaining privacy of information) should be built into the ICT tool development. At times the whole project team may need to undergo familiarization with the ontological reach of the system. As an example of this, consider how far reaching the field of clinical psychology is. It integrates science, theory, and practice, so as to understand, predict, and alleviate maladjustment, disability, and discomfort. It is thus required to promote human adaptation, adjustment, and personal development. Moreover, clinical psychology focuses on the intellectual, emotional, biological, psychological, social, and behavioral aspects of human functioning across the life span, in varying cultures, and at all socioeconomic levels.

Often confusion arises over a particular team member's role and responsibility [1]. For instance, who gets to write the system specifications? In some cases when the information system is small, the temptation to describe everything in sight is a trap for the unwary novice developer. Be that as it may, initial specifications for the fledgling information system can be developed by anyone on the project familiar enough with the duality of the techno-human factors. There should be some delineation of the technical functionality of the system right from the beginning of the design process. Also, the specifications for the content (learning resources) are often annotated in a storyboard that is kept separate.

People should try very hard right from the start of the information systems design process, to keep the focus of capturing enough techno-human information within the (agreed) scope of the project. This means, describing the technical requirements of the system as well as the conceptual issues relating to navigating the content. To ensure there are no surprise packages delivered by the system developer, the design and delivery of visual metaphors and textual captions that conform to accessibility standards of the 'World Wide Consortium' (W3C) should all be implemented according to the agreed specifications.

It can be too late, once the techno-horse has bolted from the drawing board, so to speak.

Project Management

It is generally well accepted that the future of organizations depends upon their ability and readiness to take on the power of ICT (Schwalbe,2006). Having said that, let us look first at what constitutes the discipline of project management, and then discuss the impact on the *human-dimensions of HCI*. First of all, project management is generally recognized as the discipline of organizing and managing resources in such a way that they deliver all the work required to complete a project within the defined scope, time, and cost constraints. That's all fine and very much commonsense. This definition however, still needs to be extended to convey what is being managed. Therefore let us bring in a definition for what constitutes a project. A project is simply considered as being a temporary, one-time endeavour that is undertaken, often by a group of people, to create a unique product or service [2]. So saying, the temporary nature of this one-time undertaking contrasts with the multiple processes, or operations (that are considered to be permanent or semi-permanent), as ongoing project related functional work that is required to create the same product or service over and over again. The management duality of these two systems (the temporary/repetitiveness) is often very different and requires varying technical skills and philosophies, hence requiring the development of project management.

An initial project management challenge is to ensure that the project is delivered within the defined constraints. Secondly, and perhaps more ambitious, is the challenge for the most optimized allocation and integration of the inputs needed to meet those pre-defined objectives. While the project is therefore, by definition, a carefully selected set of activities chosen to use resources (time, money, people, materials, energy, space, provisions, communication, quality, risk, etc.) to meet those pre-defined objectives. The good news is that there are many respectable project management methodologies available on the market to assist you with this challenge.

For instance, PRINCE2, is used mostly by the IT industry, finance and banking sectors for IT project management. Whereas the *'IT infrastructure library'* (ITIL) is used for corporate sector IT operation's management. Other major users are the construction industry and several Government bodies, in particular the Defense and Health Departments of Australia, UK, Holland and South Africa. PRINCE2 also has an affiliation with the US based Project Management Institute, which brings this comprehensive tool forward as a world renowned ICT project management tool. PRINCE2 is a process-based method that emphasises control (the *"C"* in the acronym PRINCE). Consequently, it can be said that control in projects is about ensuring (within reason) that there are no unplanned, unexplained, unknown or unfortunate events. Control is about eliminating surprises and monitoring progress so that problems can be identified, scoped, analysed and solved so that the project plans are based on reality.

At times, the project may have problems and it may fail to deliver its outcomes. When this occurs, it may be terminated early without delivering its products, and hopefully before excessive resources have been expended. The establishment of sound and efficient controls ensures that everything that can be known and can be done to ensure that the project succeeds, is in place. However, whether or not the project delivers, controls are essential to ensure that the correct decisions are made concerning the project and its products. To achieve this, appropriate and suitable control measures are necessary [3]. Furthermore, change control ensures that there is a proper process in place for controlling changes to the scope of the project, and that a *'free range'* does not get out of hand, causing chaotic developments. The implementation of PRINCE2 implies that the establishment and management of each type and size of project will follow a standard, repeatable pattern (subject to the constraints of the tailoring process). However, if every project is archived in a knowledge repository, then it is reasonable to expect that the requirement to constantly invent new processes, templates and techniques will progressively decline over time. As new projects are initiated, it will be possible to go to the knowledge repository and select most (or all) of the requirements for the new project. Moreover, it goes without saying, that writing a project plan may simply be a case of editing and updating an existing plan. Repeatable processes and a knowledge database save time and effort as they promote the recreation of already learned skills. It also avoids repeating previous mistakes as the organization is now learning from past experiences. As the great historian Santayana stated: *"If we do not learn from the past then we are destined to repeat it."*

The nice thing about this type of comprehensive project management ICT tool is its capacity to institutionalize improvements with an inbuilt capacity to capture problems that help people learn from the past for the benefit of the future.

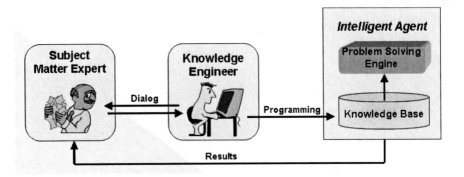

Figure 44 : Knowledge Engineers are Centre Stage for Information Systems Development

Unravelling the Expert Knowledge

As we have seen in earlier chapters of this book, if we were able to peek inside the computer science realm these days, sooner or later artificial intelligence (otherwise known as AI) would certainly surface as a popular research topic. Understandably we would also find a preoccupation within the AI community on how to capture certain aspects of the human endeavour for digital replication. The reason for this is because ICT tools offer the perfect environment for capturing information for reuse. As you can see in *Figure 44* (produced at the Learning Agents Centre [4]), knowledge engineers are central to unravelling the knowledge from other people. For the purposes of this discussion at this point, let us refer to them as the subject matter experts or *'subject matter expert'* (SME). Consequently the knowledge engineer studies how a SME reasons and solves problems. The resulting information gleaned from the SME is then encoded digitally by the knowledge engineer into a database, feeding into a problem solving application for use by others. Provided the problem solving logic engine has been designed with robust rules, the SME can examine the solutions generated by a type of intelligent agent (the information database and the problem solving application) to identify errors; passing them back to the knowledge engineer for correction.

The tricky part of this AI focused knowledge extraction scenario as depicted in the diagram above, is twofold. Firstly, the person taking the role of the knowledge engineer needs to immerse themselves in each new genre to become deeply involved within the SME's problem solving expertise. Typical methods people use to articulate their knowledge in a form that may be useful for others' use includes: natural language, visual schemas and common sense. However this leads to the second dilemma facing the knowledge engineer: experts may use very informal ways to express their knowledge, at times leaving out critical pieces of information considered too obvious to record. Moreover, the AI systems development process often causes a knowledge acquisition bottleneck [4]. The transferring and transformation of information captured from the domain expert, passing through the knowledge engineer to the digital agent is often a long, painful and inefficient pathway.

Let us leave the computer science domain to bring this discussion back to the educational technology community, where it is more usual to find people lacking the techno-skills to cope with the rigour of the AI discipline. Within the educational sector, SMEs are more often called upon to devise the online learning content as an appropriate resource for traditional lecture/classroom resources. Their role shifts from the AI context, where the SME expertise is gathered to form an informational database, to a person who is directly responsible for the instructional design and development of electronic media for student use. In this type of educational setting, the SME provides the instructional strategies to support the learning context. This means devising and implementing the exercises and activities, as well as implementing the assessment that is required to reinforce the instructional materials [5].

When people want to develop an online course, in ideal conditions they should have access to instructional media developers [6]. Sadly this is not the perfect world we all desire; it is rare to find someone with enough educational technology savvy to create suitable electronic resources[1]. Instead Caplan [6] suggests online course development can include para-academics who, as the metaphor suggests, are first on the educational technology scene. As such they liaise with the course owner or SME. This interactive relationship can therefore keep track of the knowledge extraction (or content authoring process), removing distracting barriers to the learning context as they crop up along the developmental pathway. Retrieving information from a SME is not the end of the story either, especially these days when interaction with the Internet is a daily event. Para-academics can also look after many of those tricky little jobs that bog down ordinary folk, such as obtaining copyright permissions for images and content that the SME wants to include.

Turbulence Along the Information Highway

At any one time there can be an upset in the design and development process of an information system. This will result in turbulence for the designers as they go about their development of an information system for the educational sector. Turbulence extends, too, to the learners as they go about their learning activities. To see some of the types of complex issues which surround both asynchronous (interaction that occurs randomly at any time that may be mediated by technology) and synchronous (instant interaction between student/facilitator) learning environments, it is useful to examine the diagram below. A conceptual model which shows the complexity of the educational technology online courseware development has been developed *(Figure 45) [7]*. In devising this model the researchers investigated a tool for the use of computer mediated communication and computer conferencing in supporting an educational experience. Central to their study is their model of community inquiry that constitutes 3-elements essential to an educational transaction–cognitive presence, social presence, and teaching presence. Indicators (key words/phrases) for each of the 3-elements emerged from the analysis of computer-conferencing transcripts. They describe indicators that represent a template or tool for researchers to analyze written transcripts, as well as a guide to educators for the optimal use of computer conferencing as a medium to facilitate an educational transaction. This research would suggest that computer conferencing has considerable potential to create a community of inquiry for educational purposes.

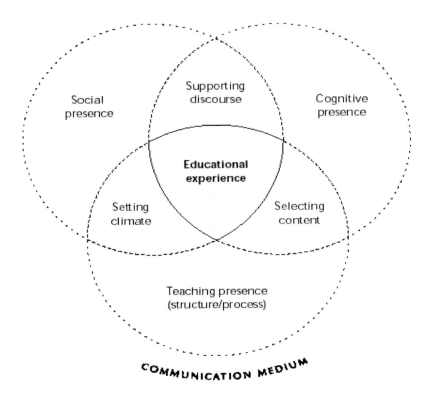

Figure 45 : Anderson et al's Communication Medium

This model draws on the notion of both a physical presence of face-to-face interaction as well as the more conceptual presence that is experienced through the Internet: cognitive, social and teaching. The first one relates to the serious nature of learning where the contextual environment should be designed to support the development of critical thinking skills relating to the particular learning content. The foundations of this learning platform include: the theory of knowledge, the cultural and social expression of the particular content to support the development of critical thinking skills. Clashes of belief or turbulence may occur in the cognitive presence of the online learning environment when the learner may not be ready, at that particular time, to absorb the propositional knowledge of the learning content due to the cultural positioning of their personal digital-awareness. (For more information on how these characteristics interact, see the techno-humanoid landscape model explained in previous chapter). This means that online courseware resources must be designed in such a way that a novice learner can access the basic rules. For example, in learning about mathematics, to know that $2 + 2 = 4$.

The second, online presence should afford students a comfortable environment where they feel safe expressing their fledgling ideas within a collaborative context.

Friction for the student will arise when this environment is not functioning well. This means conflicts among the students will arise when they cannot reach a shared view, possibly because they were not comfortable enough to express disagreement and explore their differences. One way to reduce the techno-turbulence of the social presence is to establish the behavioural protocols early. This is where the cognitive modelling in cyberspace will require special efforts to facilitate the collaborative coordination of the situational awareness. (For more information on the group development phases, see chapter-6). This means that online resources must have interactive facilitation that guides and protects the individual learners when the behaviour runs contra to the protocol. Perhaps the most dangerous environments are the synchronous chat room, where behaviour can get out of hand quickly. Patricia Wallace [8] explains how *"flame-wars"* develop quickly online when there are misperceptions of opinion that can turn nasty; unless managed well these clashes of opinion can over heat. Unfortunately, there is a dark side to the psychology of the Internet. It is loaded with fighting and flaming. Such aggressive behaviour is higher online than off [8].

The third online presence relates to when the professional practice of the teacher takes on the SME role to direct the various instructional strategies that are put in place to serve to assist the students reach positive learning outcomes. Some of the ways to achieve an effective online teaching presence, according to Anderson, Rourke, Archer & Garrison [9]; [7], begins before the course commences. By this they mean taking a proactive approach to instructional design, with the planning and preparation of course related studies that continue throughout the duration of the course. Taking this type of a proactive approach provides a teaching presence that is ready to facilitate direct instruction, should the need arise.

Pressures on Non-Conventional Environment

There can be no doubt there are expectations to the premise that the Internet can be used to solve the challenge of distributing learning resources to a wide audience. Overnight it seems that educational technologists have taken on the burden of providing techno-solutions for distance learning. The trouble with this egalitarian, one size fits all approach, is that it is not going to promote comfortable learning spaces for most people. There are palpable pressures when the techno-learning shoe doesn't fit. Perhaps it's nothing more than the evident power of online learning environments that conjure up the communicative techno-threads that connect learners with their facilitators/tutors.

In many instances of online learning programmes today, there appears to be an expectation on behalf of the courseware designer that the learning content will somehow leap out automatically towards the learner and their learning-peers. Moreover, these days we employ various ICT tools that provide the techno-channels, spilling out the visual stimuli to (hopefully) invoke the desire to learn. This is where it all gets complicated, because various presentation modes employ different types of responses in learners. As an example, think of the way that printed words on paper channel the text. There are of course, other types of techno-channels that have been used for many years in the transmission of distance learning environments to convey learning content.   According to Fahy [10] they include: computer and television screens, over-head projectors, films (moving or still).

To understand the online learning environment, let us look at the 3-types of interaction in any distance course delivery [11]. These examples remain valid planning tools today for implementing effective strategies for the human-dimension HCI. Moore proposed a triangulated model that highlights the meaning of the core learning concept within the context of different delivery media, including:

- Learner – content
- Learner – instructor
- Learner – learner

The parameters of the learner - content interaction as Michael G. Moore [11] describes is the type of interaction between the learner and the content. Depending upon the concepts to be learned, the online course can be content interactive, or it can provide for a one-way communication and information-giving learning environment. These days, we are witnessing a real metamorphosis of online learning (more commonly called eLearning), where learning that requires instruction belongs within the training domain, and informational requirements should adopt a knowledge management approach *(Figure 46)* [12].

Course designers should firstly examine the learning goals and expected performance outcomes. Secondly, they need to decide upon an instructional strategy to achieve the instructional objectives. The difference between aims and behavioural objectives is poorly understood. Aims are usually presented as overall objectives.

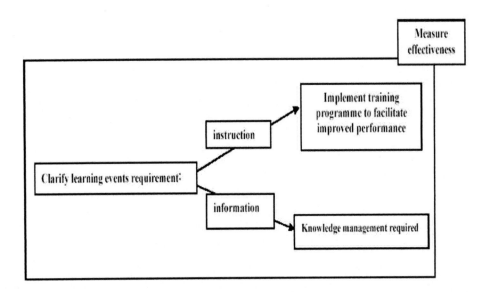

Figure 46 : The Metamorphosis of e-Learning

For instance: the primary aim of this book is to fill the gap in the literature that only sparely deals with the *human-dimensions* or social context of *effective HCI*. Whereas, behavioural objectives are usually expressed as a statement setting out what people will be expected to do when they have completed specified instruction. Objectives are stated in terms of observable performances [13]. For instance: on completion of this chapter-6 of this book the reader should be able to list the elements of personal digital-awareness characteristics.

The last but not the least important element of an effective eLearning event is the measurement strategy that must be installed to measure the effectiveness of the event. The challenge, however, is to identify and distinguish between the need for instruction (online training) and information (knowledge management), and to understand how they work in tandem [14].

The parameters for Moore's learner–instructor interaction can be thought of as the interaction that occurs between the learner and the SME and the learner and the teacher/tutor or learning facilitator. This learner–instructor interaction is a key factor in motivating people to take on the learning as well as enhancing the learner's ongoing interest in the subject matter. As we have seen in the earlier section of this chapter, the SMEs' agenda is to try to organize the application of the learner's knowledge into practice. It is the teacher/tutor or learning facilitator on the other hand, who provides the necessary and timely feedback that is so critical to trigger the individual's learning/knowledge developmental pathways.

The learner-learner interaction signifies the third Moore interaction parameter, which identifies how one learner interacts with other learners, either in a unilateral sense (alone) or in groups, with or without a real-time instructor. It is this techno-dimension of online learning that brought about the newer initiatives for managing distance learning during the early 1990's.

Nobody's Listening

As we have seen in the beginning of this chapter, combining expertise from disparate disciplines can be rather tricky. Consequently, to achieve the necessary collaboration among the various team members working towards producing an effective information system for the education arena requires skilful communication between partners that transcends disciplinary boundaries [1]. At times it may feel as though nobody's listening, or that particular project team-members have completely lost sight of the project goals. Long before reaching this dilemma, when it may be too late to salvage crumpled egos, project managers should implement strategies for effective conflict prevention and resolution. This will mean adopting skilful communication to ensure that quality relationships with people take account of values and beliefs, and identify areas of possible conflict.

Assistive strategies can be communicated in verbal and non-verbal behaviours that are face-to-face as well as via eMail. Reliance on eMails, however, has its own set of dangers. As we have already seen in the previous chapter, there are very real possibilities for misperceptions if the different ways some people may react during stressful events are left unchecked. They can lead to giant flame-wars that take a great deal of understanding and forgiveness to wind back. The real trouble with relying upon eMail communications alone is that although they are a fast and efficient means of transmitting messages, they do not provide opportunities for people to observe and respond to the more usual behaviour cues they are accustomed to receiving. Non-verbal behaviour including posture, facial expression, movement and tone of voice are absent. Moreover, using techno-forums exclusively may in some cases remove the listening component whereby people usually reach an understanding of the other person's verbal messages, and the opportunity to check for congruency between verbal and non verbal communications. Popular Internet communication tools like Skype and Microsoft's Windows Live Messenger, allow some of these visual cuing activities to take place.

Effective multi-disciplinary communication requires an understanding of the different cultures within each discipline. The guiding principles include [1]:

- Preparing yourself
- Recognizing and facing fears and concerns
- Recognizing the differences between your own discipline and those from different disciplines
- Recognizing the differences among members of different disciplines – avoiding stereotyping
- Recognizing the various and different meanings in verbal, non-verbal and e-communications
- Following the cultural rules and customs according to each discipline [15]

When developing information systems with a multi-disciplinary team, it is well worth taking advantage of the preparation time to find out about each different discipline and the interests of the various discipline team members. Doing this is all about being open to new possibilities and admitting areas that are confusing or unclear due to all the various disciplinary differences. It is also about recognizing these stated differences and facing the (often unknown) fears stemming from an unfamiliar knowledge domain. Often in HCI projects these differences are in relation to up-skilling flagging experiential knowledge for using new technologies by those from different discipline areas.

At certain times, some people may feel put down when they feel they have to ask what may appear to the informed person to be very basic questions. The negativity caused by this apprehension may arise as a barrier for further clarification later on in the project, and when this occurs, miscommunications are likely to continue. The best option may be to simply place people working with familiar concepts, and so keep them within the comfort zone of their own particular disciplines.

Another conflict preventative strategy is to develop discipline project timelines that provide expertise at different times, depending upon the expertise required at a particular stage of the project. Whilst on the one hand this seems like a sensible way to proceed, it results in an inter-sectional approach where disciplines meet at the crossroads to hand over and exchange information. This is not multi-disciplinary collaboration in a true sense because each discipline is still predominantly working in isolation: albeit on different component parts of the same project. Effective multi-disciplinary communication moves beyond this approach to a model of active collaboration by members of different disciplines throughout the project. This provides continuity across all disciplines and provides opportunities for joint learning and teamwork. A free-flow exchange of information occurs across disciplines thereby enhancing communication and increasing the likelihood of creative solutions that integrate knowledge from a variety of disciplines. This is particularly important for complex problem-solving as answers generally do not sit within discreet disciplines [1].

Design-Personae

The new millennium has brought about a mixed bag of techno-goodies for teaching and learning [16]. While some of the treats add value to the student experience, there are many detractors. Having said that, often in the higher education sector the high-level management decisions for implementing ICT tools are made within the context of declining fiscal resources. To complicate matters, students these days are less likely to afford the time to remain on-campus due to their paid-work commitments; and these are usually necessary to cover their education costs. Today, students are primarily driven by different considerations in seeking their tertiary education. Accordingly, attracting students to enroll has become very competitive for most universities around the world. As a result, most university course designers try very hard to accommodate the demands that students make for more flexibility of their experiential learning without compromising the traditional values of the university community.

There are an increasing number of students wishing to complete their studies in a minimum amount of time with maximum learning and skill development. Typically, they need to clearly see how their learning outcomes are going to maximise employment and career opportunities. ICT tools can provide an effective learning experience. At this point, it is known by educational researchers that we are far enough down the information highway to achieve high-level animated pedagogical-agents to facilitate interactive learning environments [17].

While it is tempting to embrace these newer ICT tools to support undergraduate courses online, most Web-based courseware for undergraduate use at this point does offer students with a certain amount of flexibility. Lecture material is posted to most university Web-sites for downloading. However, recent feedback from undergraduate students reveals this is not exactly what they want. They say that education extends beyond reading copious amounts of materials online, chatting to lecturers and other students electronically, and meeting assessment requirements. In fact, many undergraduate students complain bitterly about the amount of online learning that is being used in university courses. Instead, they state a preference for face-to-face learning [18]. It is only a small minority who prefer this type of online learning [19]. Not surprisingly, students value quality learning experiences to meet their educational needs. This often includes a flexible delivery whereby learners retain the best combination of instructional strategies that include instructor-led classroom sessions and practical activities, which may be conducted elsewhere [20].

To assist the courseware design process to meet the requirements of students, the current use of a design-persona as a hypothetical user provides a reference point for the relevance of content as well as for designing the means and methods of delivery. In this sense, the design-persona is useful for getting started in the use of ICT tools–by providing a reference point for the design process [1].

Providing a reference point for all aspects of educational design may safeguard against design elements that are inappropriate or not suited to the intended student population. A design-persona assists in understanding user information needs, informing design and accessibility and ultimately suitability [21]. The design-persona represents the characteristics of a hypothetical student embodying the main features of the student cohort.

User profiles have been utilized for some time in marketing and project design, particularly since the late 1990s. Personae are seen to have replaced the so-called elastic user by replacing them with a caricature of a real person who becomes an integral part of the project design process. It was argued that designing a persona was better than designing for a vaguely defined group of users. The design-persona provides a conduit for transmitting a wide range of information about design and use. Representation of the user group is crucial and this is the main advantage of using a design-persona.

A design-persona provides a lens that includes the socio-political context. By focusing attention on a particular user group, personae assist in identifying different kinds of users as well as those who are not being designed for [22]. Designing the right persona or set of personae can be challenging. A common mistake to avoid, is choosing flashy technology over accessibility. Hourihan [23] warns against the project team designing for themselves and losing sight of the intended user group.

A design-persona is developed through a number of quantitative and qualitative processes including interviews, observations, ethnographies, focus groups, brainstorming, market research and usability studies [21]. Members of the project team ultimately direct any changes and modifications required to the design-persona throughout a courseware development project to ensure relevance and responsiveness, so as to enact required changes [21]. It is essential that representative individuals from user groups are included in all aspects of project design including the development of the design-persona. It must not be seen as a replacement for active user involvement.

Slowly the design-persona comes to life as a real person when given a name. Empathic planning and decision-making can be made with this name and identity clarified. For instance, rather than thinking, how would a student use this? As such, questions can be personalised to reflect for example, how would Sally use this? In this example, Sally's name is chosen as the representative of the intended user group to embody all of the personal features of the intended user group. These features might include age, gender, educational background, class, health, ability/disability, race, ethnicity and culture, sexuality and spirituality [24]. A common vision and commitment to the design-persona is essential for successful educational design and implementation. Communication processes will influence how the persona is included within the design-team at all stages of project development. Communication is therefore an important aspect of project management, particularly for those who may be absent from meetings when the persona is being planned [1]. Creative strategies are required to keep the design-persona relevant and the focus of the project's design activities. Detailed documentation that succinctly describes the main features of each design-persona is essential. For instance, the level of detail suggested by Freydenson [25] includes at least a first and last name, age, goals, background story, a telling quote, e-mail address, job title and a photograph. Over time, the design-persona may change and develop along with the project. Occasionally more than one persona may be required, particularly in instances of extreme diversity amongst potential user groups. The development of multiple personae, where each is given a status according to some hierarchy [25]. These categorized personae can therefore extend beyond a primary-persona defined for students. They may include others in a secondary-persona status, such as administration and management, professional associations and employer groups. In the end, the primary-persona must be satisfied with the system you deliver [23].

Applied to an educational institution, this type of design-persona becomes a hypothetical student on a journey through a higher-degree or similar course of study. In this context, the challenge for an educational course design-team is to identify the routine tasks and procedures to create a personal and user friendly instructional environment. The use of such a design-persona in an educational environment may bring a student's profile to life as a reference point. In an educational setting the design-persona involves many contextual decisions.

Therefore conducting a thorough learning-task analysis [13] is useful in identifying the cognitive processes involved in gaining a university education. Often there are clear developmental stages that may include: pre-entry, entry, engagement and exit. Pre-entry includes consideration of marketing and promotion, study pre-requisites, and processes for applying, student selection and enrolment. The pre-entry stage may also include consideration of credit transfers and pathways from other educational institutions, particularly in the *"technical and further education"* (TAFE) distance education network in Australia. At times, there may be additional issues that impact upon a student's learning environment around access and equity, and special learning requirements for particular students. Entry into the TAFE sector includes orientation, preparation for success at (Australian) tertiary-level study, and a sense of focus and belonging. Engagement extends to maintaining and developing this focus in a student-centred environment that is responsive to student learning needs. Exit from TAFE requires adequate preparation for transition from university to the workplace, including professional socialisation and ongoing links and relationships with the university. Alongside the identification of learning processes and associated tasks at a university level, the expected learning outcomes should be aligned with the students' expectations [13], thereby identifying the personal and social features of the design-persona.

Instructional Architecture

After much investigation into the possible learning effects of hypermedia delivered through the Internet, educational researchers now realize that media per se do not promote learning [26]. Rather than concentrating on the whiz-bangery of the ICT tools, they suggest, it is more important to concentrate on the way the media are implemented to promote learning: that makes all the difference [27]. As we have seen in an earlier chapter of this book, it is the instructional strategies that make all the difference when implementing techno-educational programmes. Recall that the discussion on setting up a learning house (the instructional architecture) for computer-aided learning commenced in chapter-4. *Table 27* shows Clark's [27] 4-common instructional architectures:

Table 27 : 4-Common Instructional Architectures

Instructional Architecture	Environment Encouraged	Implications for *effective HCI*
Receptive	Passive absorption of information.	Custom designed textual documents as well as including power-point presentations, video vignettes
Directive	Gradual building of knowledge chains through frequent learner responses and timely feedback.	Programmed instruction works perfectly well here – like most software development training.
Guided Discovery	Knowledge and skills constructed by engaging in solving authentic job problems with support. Mistakes made are considered to be learning opportunities.	Problem-centered training courseware will flourish with this architecture. Educational researchers have to identify the cognitive apprenticeship models.
Exploratory	Learners take responsibility for their learning.	Opportunities for hyperlinks that must be refreshed (maintained) to reflect possible changes.

In keeping with the focus of this chapter we now look more closely at why there may be some confusion and possibility for conflict developing among the members of an educational courseware design-team. Differentiating between instructional methods and architectures can be complex for the novice courseware designer. Therefore and particularly in a multi-disciplined project-team, conflicts may arise through a misunderstanding of the differences between instructional methods and architectures.

On the one hand instructional methods are the techniques or professional practice (tools-of-the-trade) that teachers/tutors and other learning facilitators bring into a classroom or online learning environment. These tools cover a wide ranging bag-of-tricks, when applied in an appropriate manner for each learning audience encountered. Such tools clearly should capture the imagination of the learners. After all, the main purpose of a carefully planned instructional method is to reinforce the learner's psychological processes that will be necessary for them to translate the learning content into meaningful internal knowledge, and thereby enhancing their overall skill development. Effective instructional strategies are the ones that avoid methods that disrupt an individual's learning processes. Good examples of common instructional methods include: learning content overviews that include well defined learning outcomes, examples (and non-examples), kinds-of lessons, parts-of lessons, analogies, and practice exercises with appropriate feedback [28]. These instructional methods can be delivered to the learners in a wide range of media, including: textual listings, graphics and video vignettes. There are of course a wide variety of instructional methods that can be implemented to bring about quality learning outcomes using appropriate ICT tools. In her book on Building Expertise, Ruth Clark [27] examines in detail the complementary instructional methods that should build mental models in a learner's memory. She also differentiates those methods from other ones that promote and augment limited working memory capacity through specially designed cognitive load management strategies.

On the other hand instructional architecture is the metaphorical dwelling, which houses the instructional methods or professional practice of the teacher/tutor or online learning facilitator. In other words, the methods could be the building blocks with the architecture providing the overall framework upon which the building blocks are assembled [27]. Designing for the instructional architecture usually occurs during the instructional design phase of the educational systems development. Instructional methods should be developed separately during instructional (learning content) development [27]. Some types of architectures will omit particular instructional methods. For instance, a receptive architecture generally does not include practice strategies, as they are designed to involve the learner in the reception of information only. Some instructional methods on the other hand, such as the example metaphors will be inclined to make an appearance in most architectures.

Knowledge Navigation

Investigating a new knowledge domain can be tricky. Quite understandably some people become confused about where to start. A good reference point is to go to a library and to seek the help of a librarian with the necessary navigation expertise. The professional practice of librarians involves knowledge management. They are usually trained to guide an individual through their thinking processes in order to reach relevant information that will support their quest for knowledge development in unfamiliar domains. At this point in time it is common knowledge that we are drowning in information; that is, suffering an information overload.

In a book entitled *A Library for All Times* that has been published by the Swedish National council for Cultural Affairs [29]; there is a wonderful description of how people typically behave when they visit a library. Some background is given by the author of this story according to which, learners when faced by a teacher with group project work, instead of collaborating to find the best way to investigate a knowledge domain, would run around independently almost as soon as they were given the assignment specifications. The story continues. Many years later the same teacher made the following observations about why people are running around the library.

"Now I am standing here, looking down at the large book hall in Malmö's old central library. I see people sitting, absorbed in books at two large tables. Over by the computers the scene changes quickly. The librarians are printing out new queue numbers at the desk.

But mostly it seems like mass confusion. People are running here and there. Even those who sit are only still for a little while, before they get up to do something else. People at the various tables get up and are replaced fairly quickly, and even those who stay a while usually shift between sitting, searching the stacks or using the terminals.

Why are people running around the library? Why aren't they sitting down and analyzing, structuring and formulating strategies for their searches?"

Maybe a comparison can be drawn with this little story with what happens to people when they are facing an online learning programme, especially for the first time. While it may be very useful to investigate a new knowledge domain to uncover the distinct ontology (hierarchy of knowledge) this may not be appropriate for a novice learner as they approach their online learning resources.

Table 28 : The Knowledge-Navigation Development Model

Knowledge Navigation / Development Model			
Knowledge Development Methodology	**Learning Methods / Activities**		
	How to lessons		
Rules	Text – specifying information necessary to complete the learning objectives		
Learning Outcome			
Values & Principles			
Examples		Parts of lessons	Kinds of lessons
Non-examples and their consequences for not following the correct path		Try me activity & feedback	
Show me – assessment or evaluation of learning outcome	Transfer to a new environment		

To alleviate this dilemma a *'Knowledge Navigation/Development Methodology'* is proposed as an adaptable instructional method to lead learners through a learning environment *(Table 28)*. This tool has been devised to operate in two separate ways according to whether the learner is a novice (new to the learning domain) or experienced (knows the ropes, but simply needs a refresher). The novice-navigation path leads the activities through a series of seven instructional method activities or events, while the experienced learner is given the option to choose their learning events independently.

Consequently, the sequence of events for the novice-learner follows the Merrill ID^2 instructional strategy [30]. The following comprise this strategy:

1. Rules
2. Learning outcomes
3. Values and principles
4. Examples
5. Non-examples and the consequences of not taking the correct approach
6. Try me - providing the opportunity to practice – receiving timely feedback
7. Show me - assessment of learning outcome

As a result, the *'How To'* lesson is the opening activity of the *'Knowledge Navigation/Development Model'*; providing the novice learner with the expected *'Learning Outcome'*. Here is where the novice-learner can expect to receive all the *'Rules'* or information about a specific topic. This could include requiring the novice-learner to know about things like:

- using devices
- facts about people
- places and creatures
- certain basic activities
- task processes, etc, etc

The *'Values and Principles'* will offer domain specific cultural values that underpin this particular activity. At times these activities will take a generic format such as the social acceptability (or otherwise) of using a mobile phone while using public transport. It is interesting to note that in some countries (such as Japan) the use of a mobile phone is forbidden while travelling on their trains. In the UK, merely touching a cell phone while driving a car is an infringement, punishable by a £2,000 fine for a first offence.

The *'Examples'* activities of the *'Knowledge Navigation/Development Model'* will be to engage the novice-learner with material that is directly applicable to the learning content. Activities relating to the *'Non-Examples'*, on the other hand, are designed to show the novice-learner a clear example of something that does not represent the expected learning outcome: and what can go wrong if the correct path is not followed. Within this instructional strategy there are *'Parts Of'* lessons, which are most appropriate for learning about:

- new terminology
- places
- the control of a device
- the parts of a form (including a diagram, chart, text format, etc).

Next, the novice-learner will be taken through a series of activities that will involve them in a series of *'Kinds Of'* lessons. These *'Kinds Of'* lessons involve:

- identifying a new object
- an activity
- or how to do something that may already be known

Merrill says that *'Kinds Of'* lessons are appropriate for comparing similar devices, activities, processes, or jobs. *'Kinds Of'* lessons are appropriate for recognizing the variety that can occur within a given class of things. Moreover, *'Kinds Of'* lessons are perhaps one of the most important types of instructional strategy. However, as Merrill confirms, they are often neglected. The ability to transfer or use the knowledge and skill in a new situation requires *'Kinds Of'* lessons in order for the novice-learner to know how to generalize. Simultaneously, the ability to recognize when a given activity or procedure *may not be appropriate* in a new situation needs to be learnt. This too requires a *'Kinds Of'* lesson in order for the novice-learner to learn to discriminate.

It is therefore fitting to end this chapter here, leaving the reader with notions from the abovementioned *'knowledge navigation model'* to reflect on ways to pass experiential learning from one domain to another. In this chapter we covered the issues that surround managing the multi-disciplinary Web-design team to include:

- conflict management to ward off our super-ego's
- the impact of project management strategies for ICT tool development
- a conceptual communication model to captures online experiences
- pressures on non-conventional learning/training environments
- to include an (electronic) design-persona in an information systems project
- the relationship between instructional architecture and knowledge navigation

Chapter Reference List

[1]   McKay, E. and Martin, J., Multi-disciplinary collaboration to unravel expert knowledge: Designing for effective human-computer interaction, in *Instructional Design: Case Studies in Communities of Practice*, 2007. M. Keppell, Editor. IGI. ISBN: 978-1-59904-322-7: UK. 309-329.

[2]   Schwalbe, K., *Information Technology Project Management*.(4th ed). 2006, Canada: Thomson - Course Technology.

[3]   Conscium-International, 2007. Retrieved 20/01/08 from http://www.mit.com.au/pm_prince2_161_foundation.htm.

[4]   Tecuci, G., Research Reports, *Learning Agents Centre - Mason*, 2007. Retrieved 20/01/08 from http://lac.gmu.edu/.

[5]   Sanders, G., *Theory and Practice of Online Learning*. 2004, Anderson, T. and Elloumi, F., Editors. Athabasca University. ISBN: 0-919737-59-5.

[6]   Caplan, D., The development of online courses, in *Theory and Practice of Online Learning*, T. Anderson and F. Elloumi, Editors. 2004, Athabasca University: ISBN: 0-919737-59-5: Canada.

[7]   Anderson, T., et al., Assessing teaching presence in computer conferencing transcripts. *Journal of the Asynchronous Learning Network*, 2001. 5(2): Retrieved 20/01/08 from http://www.aln.org/publications/jaln/v5n2/v5n2_anderson.asp.

[8]   Wallace, P., The Psychology of the Internet. 1999, UK: Cambidge University Press. 264.

[9]   Garrison, D.R., Anderson, T., and Archer, W., Critical inquiry in a text-based environment: Computer conferencing in higher education. *The Internet and Higher Education*, 2000. 2(2-3): 87-105.

[10] Fahy, J.F., Media characteristics and online learning technology, in *Theory and Practice of Online Learning*, T.A.F. Elloumi, Editor. 2004, Athabasca University. Retrieved 20/01/08 from http://cde.athabascau.ca/online_book/copyright.html ISBN: 0-919737-59-5: Canada.

[11] Moore, M.G., Three types of interaction, in *The American Journal of Distance Education*, 1989. 3(2): 1-6.

[12] McKay, E. and Merrill, M.D. Cognitive skill and Web-based educational systems. *Conference paper in the proceedings of the eLearning Conference on Design and Development: Instructional Design - Applying first principles of instruction,* 2003. Informit Library: Australasian Publications On-Line: [Online] 20/01/08 http://www.informit.com.au/library/ .

[13] Dick, W.O., Carey, L., and O'Carey, J., *The Systematic Design of Instruction*. (6th ed). 2004, ISBN: 0205412742: Allyn & Bacon.

[14] Rosenberg, M.J., *e-Learning: Strategies for delivering knowledge in the digital age*. 2001, NY: McGraw-Hill. 343.

[15] Martin, J. and Hess, L. Chinese culture and recovery from mental illness. *Paper in the proceedings of The Mental Health Services Conference of Australia and New Zealand*. 2004. Gold Coast Convention Centre, Broadbeach, Queensland, Australia.

[16] McKay, E., et al., Design-personae: Matching students' learning profiles in Web-based education, in *Enhancing Learning Through Human-Computer Interaction*, 2007. E.McKay, Editor. IGI: London. 266.

[17] Lester, J.C., et al. The persona affect: Affective impact of animated pedagogical agents. *Paper in the conference proceeding of CHI 97: Looking to the Future*. 1997. Atlanta, Georgia, USA: ACM. Retrieved 20/01/08 from http://www.sigchi.org/chi97/proceedings/paper/jl.htm and from http://research.csc.ncsu.edu/intellimedia/papers/dap-chi-97.pdf: ACM.

[18] Dennen, V.P., *Designing Peer Feedback Opportunities into Online Learning Experiences*. 2003, The Board of Regents of the University of Wisconsin System.

[19] Hammond, M. and Wiriyapinit, M., Learning through online discussion: A case of triangulation in research. *Australasian Journal of Educational Technology*, 2005. 21(3): 283-302.

[20] Collis, B. Putting theories into practice: Technologies for flexible learning in universities and corporate settings, 2004. Paper in the proceedings of the *International Conference on Computers in Education - Acquiring and Constructing Knowledge Through Human-Computer Interaction: Creating new visions for the future of learning*. Melbourne Exhibition Centre, Australia: Nov 30th to Dec 3rd: Common Ground Publishing.

[21] Sinha, R., *Creating Personas for Information-Rich Sites*. 2002.

[22] Pruitt, J. and Grudin, J., *Personas: Practice and Theory*. 2003, ACM.

[23] Hourihan, M., *Taking the 'You' Out of User: My Experience Using personas*. 2002.

[24] Giroux, H. and Shannon, P., (Editors). *Education and Cultural Studies: Toward a Performative Practice*. 1997, Routledge: NY.

[25] Freydenson, E., Bringing your personas to life in real life. 2002, *Boxes and Arrows*.

[26] Dillon and Gabbard, (Editors). Hypermedia as an educational technology: A review of the empirical literature on learner comprehension, control and style: Review of educational research (1998 - 68(3) 322-349). Reprinted in *The Psychology of Education: Major Themes*, London, P. Smith and A. Pellegrinni (Editors). Vol: 3. 2000, Routledge, 496-531: London.

[27] Clark, R.C., Chapter 1. Expertise, learning, and instruction, in *Building Expertise*, (2nd Edition). 2003, International Society for Performance Improvement: ISBN 1-890289-13-2; ISPI No.5103: MN. 256.

[28] Merrill, M.D. Keynote Address: Does your instruction rate 5 stars? *Conference Keynote address in eLearning Conference on Design and Development: Instructional Design - Applying first principles of instruction.* 2003. Melbourne: Informit Library: Australasian Publications On-Line: Available 20/01/08 from http://www.informit.com.au/library/.

[29] Anon, Swedish National Council for cultural Affairs (1997), *A Library for All Times*, Retrieved 20/01/08 from http://www.futurum.polyvalent.se/libpres.htm .

[30] Merrill, M.D., Li, Z., and Jones, M.K., Second generation instructional design (ID$_2$). *Educational Technology*, 1990(February): 7-14.

Chapter-8

Web-Mediated HCI: Realizing the Richness of the Internet

This chapter shifts the discussion back towards the *machine-side of HCI* to rethink our connectivity to improve the effectiveness of our HCI. This is where the proponents for a more social context [1] for the *human-dimensions of HCI* are showing signs of progress.

Balancing the HCI Scales

So far in this book we have travelled through the techno-landscape on a journey seeking out ways to understand how the *human-dimensions of HCI* fit within today's techno-landscape. In the beginning of this techno-saga we saw that the early adopters were inclined to use a computer for complex calculations and serious record keeping. This, of course, makes good use of the machine's capability to gobble up just about anything into a database for safekeeping. However, while the techno-scales were tilting towards the physical sciences for taking care of massive amounts of data, some people were becoming greedy: the more visionary were inventing technologies to make the machinery go faster, and faster. In this regard, the HCI balance was always tipping towards increasing the power and capacity and to do more for less (human effort that is). Unless one was actively involved with computers for doing one's work, many people were oblivious to the techno-revolution that was taking place around them.

Apart from delving into the literature for a more formal confirmation, it is relatively easy to identify a gradual recognition by the general community to innovate computer usage for everyday tasks. For a while the software giants waged war on us all. Clever marketing strategies fired smart GUIs to hook ordinary folk into buying more and more techno-products.

Flicking the Historical-Dimension

Perhaps we should be asking ourselves whether there could be a cross generational misunderstanding of the *human-dimensions of HCI?* It is entirely possible that there are two distinct varieties of computer users travelling along the information highway. Due to their extreme differences, one of Rudyard Kipling's 1892 back-room ballads "never the twain shall meet" is entirely relevant for our cyberspace scenario. On the one side are the people who take the longer way, worrying about the consequences of everything they do. By contrast, others dive straight into the techno-pond with blissful ignorance for what lies ahead. Some computer users strongly cling to their techno-comfort zones. They appear to be more comfortable using a computer like an electronic typewriter. For instance, instead of using a word-processing style template to make life easier, they happily tap away at the space bar to position text. The consequence of this blissful ignorance means they miss out on the feast of ICT tools that make such tedious tasks easier. It is almost impossible to break through their long-suffering ignorance. Perhaps the explanation for their resistance towards learning new techno-techniques comes from earlier exposure to those hefty and thoroughly boring software manuals. Also, possibly, the fear of having to learn something new which they believe that they cannot master [1]. Being shown up as inadequate before others, etc.

Thankfully we no longer need to clog up our book-shelves with out-dated computer manuals. Instead procedural texts are conveniently offered on CDs or online through the Internet. Moreover it is no longer necessary to learn everything there is to know about a new software application. Instead, to enjoy the full techno-landscape there is one basic set of eSkills that people need. This means developing enough self confidence to throw away the manual mentality, and to investigate new ways of doing things. Perhaps it is not such a bad thing that computer users these days are coerced into problem solving activities they would not necessarily do. When something comes up that is beyond their eSkills-set, the answer may unfold during a collaborative venture with other people.

Rethinking our Connectivity

The tipping of the techno-scales is gradually bringing about more ways that people can improve the effectiveness of their HCI. We can see this occurring when people make connections with others to share knowledge and expertise. Web-mediated communication is taking us into new techno-places. Think of all the ways we can transfer information these days. We don't rely anymore upon sending and receiving electronic files through eMail and facsimile transmission. At our finger-tips we have the ability to communicate with others; to talk while watching and listening to them through our Internet Web-cams.

However it is through these innovative types of HCI that we continue to challenge the debate between the cognitive scientists (who say that knowledge is represented in memory as picture-like images), language-like statements, or distributed representations. Multi-media provides a rich pool of picture-like resources that is relatively easy to access through the Internet, providing budding Web developers with endless visual metaphors to underpin their content. While most people developing course content are familiar with the need to develop appropriate language-like statements to assist knowledge acquisition, it is the distributed representations that are perhaps the most troublesome to comprehend. This apprehension is likely because of the free flowing nature of the distributed symbolic and rule-based characteristics. One of the contentious issues of this long-standing debate is the non-agreement on the part that propositions, images and distributed representations play in our cognitive processing [2].

Consider how we exercise our creativity on the techno-trot. During our live Internet chats, we look, listen, and may reflect on what we've heard: then speak and share files practically all at the same time. Earlier in this book we demonstrated that our knowledge/concept learning is highly organized. In chapter-6 there was a discussion on concept learning from an information processing perspective. Let us extend that story to reveal how talking with others via Web-mediated devices has the potential to enhance our cognitive awareness for newly encountered information. Given the immediacy of the ICT tools, we can conjure up vivid memories of similar instances, or recognize where we cannot.

Take for instance the famous Schank and Abelson's [3] script. This visual schema is an excellent example of how people organize their thoughts relating to dining out at a popular restaurant. The various steps in this event would perhaps fall into the following conceptual categories: entering, ordering, eating and then leaving. Most people would be able to quickly answer questions that relate to what happens when they visit their favourite restaurant *(Figure 47)*.

You could for instance close your eyes for one moment to consider how you can share what happens before you enter the restaurant. There are a number of issues that relate to the transportation to get you there, whether you were able to park your car easily, and what happens when the weather prevents you from walking any great distance to get there. All this information can be conveyed directly through regular conversation on a Web-cam.

Figure 47 : Visual Metaphor

However you also have the luxury of perhaps showing a map to convey the location, parking, transportation, etc. While the impact of these ICT tools may be pretty obvious, there are a number of usability problems that have crept into the design of the GUIs that drive those Internet communication tools. For instance, how frustrating it is when the voice activation equipment stops working and people have to revert to using the text-chat facility. People then have to cognitively switch quickly between aural to a more tactile communication and find the text chat option.

Internet Influences Social Context of Computing

Much has already been said about using computers for everyday activities. However the emerging knowledge that adds value to the techno-landscape is coming from people who promote a new type of personal digital awareness. It's not so much that we need more gadgets. Heaven knows there is always going to be plenty of room to cram them in whenever they appear on the techno-horizon. Nicolai, Yoneki, Bhrens and Kenn [4] explore the social context of the wireless ICT tools. They are studying the effectiveness of the Bluetooth proximity with consumer devices and its effects on group dynamics. We need to know much more about what happens when people interact freely through GUI environments with members of an existing group or forming new groups. This is where it would be useful to know how to balance our personal digital awareness within a techno-socializing event. Moreover, Fröhlich and Kraut [5] say it is not so much a functionality of available software and services. It's more about the techno-logistics of who can get on the Internet, in which room, at what time, and for how long. It would seem these issues are very important for most families, taking precedence over what family members can do once they are online. Here again we see market driven implications for home-computing ICT tool development.

eBusiness

The term eBusiness was coined by Louis V. Gerstner, CEO of IBM. Broadly speaking the notion of eBusiness has been brought forward in recent times to convey any type of business operation that is automated by most types of business information systems. These days there is an expectation that people are referring to Web-mediated ICT tools that promote most business practice. eBusiness links a corporation's internal and external data processing systems, providing efficiencies through the practice of *effective HCI*. As such ICT tools enhance business partnerships to work more directly with all their stakeholders. The entire business operations can bask in the techno-glory. For instance there is an endless list of the business operations that have derived benefit from computerization. These include: electronic purchasing, supply chain management, order processing, and improved customer service to name but a few. Moreover special technical standards promote integration of intra-inter corporate processing. These days eBusiness is most referred to business that is conducted through the Web. In other words eBusiness reaps the benefit of the plethora of Web-servers that store and disseminate Web-pages to anyone with access to the Internet. At the heart of the Web technology is the hyperlink, commonly referred to as the URL, which connects each Web-page or eDocument to each other. This eBusiness connectivity can relate to local or around the world by simply clicking a link. The click here mentality caused the Web to explode in the mid 1990s. The Web turned the Internet into the largest online shopping mall and information source in the world: and the eMarketers are still laughing all the way to the bank.

eTraining

A highly skilled workforce is widely viewed as essential for prosperity in economies characterised by rapid technological change. Consequently, the implication is that high and growing incomes can only be sustained by high and growing levels of worker productivity. These in turn demand ever-increasing levels of worker skills [1];[6]. However, the development of high level skills across the workforce is expensive and requires major investment from individuals, governments and employers. In confirmation for Australia, over a decade ago, nevertheless still relevant in 2007, the cost to employers of vocational education and structured training was estimated by the Australian National Training Authority in 1996 as $6.186 billion, which is 57% of the total cost of all corporate sponsored education and training (of $10.845 billion) [6]. Traditionally, employers view training as an expensive solution that is implemented to fix problems. In a climate of changing work practices, every time a new technology enters the work-environment employers seem to pour endless amounts of money into upgrading their employees' skill base. What then is the impact on institutional effectiveness of this continual investment on work-place learning? Furthermore, with people remaining in the workforce beyond the traditional retirement age, what are the consequences of their need for retraining?

Important new Web-based learning management tools have emerged recently such as the *"Learning Activity Management System"* (LAMS). The LAMS foundation, based at Macquarie University, in Sydney, Australia, offers open source eLearning software reflecting the dedication of a well known non-profit organisation researching the concepts of learning design. However, while this type of learning management tool may engage an active participation in learning activities per se, it cannot take account of individual skill development.

In another Australian research project, a collaborative academic/industry research venture is underway to investigate the effectiveness of a learning strategy model which may accommodate changing information requirements through dynamic change management [7]. This research project implements research design and assessment methodologies to evaluate applications of ePedagogies within a corporate training context for government employees. These researchers are investigating the effectiveness of the eLearning strategies to inform the business community of changes that are likely to lead to more efficient training practice by direct contrast with conventional training methodologies. An expected outcome of the project will be a model of best practice for corporate eTraining, building upon the existing eLearning strategies for training government employees.

There is little doubt that this type of learning reinforcement is set to innovate the field of computer-based training. Large investment of funds, employee time, and resources have been made in various modes of training but there is little quality evidence about which strategies are effective and the conditions that support effective training in diverse contexts. The rationale for learning reinforcement is based on the need to ensure government staff are skilled to achieve organizational goals in a changing work environment, with possibilities of certification of key achievements [8].

However, no research has been undertaken to measure qualities of training that employs learning reinforcement in the government sector as directly compared with traditional training environments.   Innovations in Web-based training and skill acquisition processes are being driven by demands on the human workforce to maintain their competency, knowledge and competitiveness [9].

Moreover, the McKay research team propose that learning reinforcement strategies offer a conduit for skill development in a government training environment to maximize the organizational technology potential [10]. It is interesting to note that the McKay use of the term learning reinforcement is special [7]. These researchers do not propose to argue, however, that conventional training does not use reinforcement to facilitate learning as described by the well known psychological learning theories [11].

Balancing the Techno-Sea Saw

It is entirely possible to reach our much sought after state of information nirvana or techno-equilibrium that will enable *effective HCI*. However, people will have to remain ever vigilant to ensure the human-dimension is truly represented in the techno-landscape.   It's as much about making sure that the personal digital awareness characteristics do not collide with the external techno-humanoid contributors, as anything else.

On the one side, in previous chapters of this book, we have seen how the human-dimension relates to all the intuitive things that can make a computer easy and indeed fun for everyone to use: not isolating those people who currently have difficulty gaining access. On the other, we have also seen that the human-dimension of the techno-landscape should inform the machine-dimension to encourage Web-richness strategies that will draw out *effective HCI*.

Dynamic Server-Side Functionality

Typically many Web-pages that you access through the Internet can be customised or used by people to complete an interactive task online. When this happens, one is probably involved with either a client-side or server-side scripting. Scripting simply means programming. Fortunately most people won't need to know anything about these highly technical environments. Basically, client-side scripting enables interaction within a Web-page. The programming-code required to process the user-input is sent or downloaded from your computer and compiled (translated into machine language) by the browser (Internet Explorer, Firefox etc), or a plug-in. Plug-ins can be hardware or software modules that add a specific feature or service to a larger system. The idea behind the concept of a plug-in is for the new component to simply plug into an existing system. For example, there are many plug-ins designed for the popular Internet browsers that enable them to display different types of audio or video messages.

Server-side scripting therefore is required to complete an activity that involves sending information to another computer (often called a server) across the Internet. The server then runs a program that processes the information and returns the results, which often is a Web-page. Search engines use server-side processing. When a keyword is typed by a person into a computer accessing the Internet, a program on a server matches the word or phrase entered against an index of Web-site content. If the same search were to take place on the client-side, the process would require the browser to download the entire search engine and its index.

Popular server-side scripting languages include *'active-server-pages'* (ASP) and *'personal home page'* (PHP) tools. ASP is an authoring environment that is commonly used for developing databases for the Web. PHP can mean *'hypertext pre-processor'*; it is known as open-source software; that is, programming-code that is freely available to the general public. Over time, the networking of computers capabilities afforded by the Internet has caused concern. However, since open source code is available for inspection by anyone, this transparency has reduced this problem (so long as the inspector understands the open source code). Moreover, an additional benefit is the collaborative contribution by programmers to the continued development of a shared programming-code library.

The PHP programming-language can be used to write new routines that develop new programming-code. PHP is also popular for connecting to a Web-based database, which retrieves, adds or updates Web-page content. As a result PHP is an ideal programming-language for creating large Web-sites. A single PHP template can be written to retrieve and display all database records, for example product listings for a marketing company. A nice feature of PHP is that each product Web-page that is generated can use the same programming-routines to reflect a wide range of retail operations. These include: availability, price, shipping costs, etc.

To complicate matters if you are trying to get your head around all this terminology, there are stateless interactions that enable a third type of scripting or interaction. The popular Flash application architecture can store and process information on both the client-side and the server-side. An example of this type of stateless interaction is a Flash-based checkout process. Information that the user enters, such as credit card details, delivery instructions, and billing address, can be stored and validated on the client-side. Once the required information has been completed a connection is established to the server and the order is sent for processing.

There are certain differences between the functionality of client-side and server-side interactions. On the client-side for instance, once the programming-code is downloaded, the response to interaction may be more immediate. Services are secure, as no information is sent anywhere from the user's browser. Moreover, the client-side is reliant on the user utilising a specific browser and/or plug-in on their computer, which in turn is affected by the processing speed of the user's computer. The server-side interaction, on the other hand, involves complex processes that are often more efficient, as the program and the associated resources remain on the server. There are security considerations when sending sensitive information. Server-side logic does not rely on the user having a specific browser or plug-in to be affected by the processing speed of the host server. The user's Internet connection will affect both forms of interaction. On the client-side it is the scripting time for downloading, while the server-side it is the processing that affects the time taken for information to be sent to the server and the response downloaded.

What is Web 2.0?

In earlier times the semantic Web was brought forward to describe a common theoretical yet realistic framework that allows computerized data to be shared and reused across application, enterprise, and community boundaries. As such it is a collaborative effort that was led by the W3C (http://www.w3.org/2001/sw/). The term Web 2.0 is a newer phrase that was coined in 2004 by O'Reilly Media, an American media company established by Tim O'Reilly that publishes book and Web-sites, as well as hosting IT conferences. It thus comes as no surprise that the Web 2.0 is a conceptualized Web-based publishing environment. At the time of the Web 2.0 conception it was perceived as a second generation of Web-based services, consisting of newly developed sites for social networking in which the notions of digital ethnography has been gaining recognition. Other Web-publishing forums include for instance: blogs, Wikis, tag-based folksonomies, RSS feeds, and podcasting. The Web 2.0 environment has emerged through a series of conferences where developers and marketers adopted the catch-phase. The exact meaning of Web 2.0 remains open to debate according to the inventor of the *"World Wide Web"* (Sir Timothy Berners-Lee). However, this whole debate on finding ways to describe the growth of the Web has been on the rise for quite some time. In the 1980's Tim O'Reilly proposed a project based on the concept of hypertext to facilitate the sharing and updating of information among researchers [12]. As the *Figure 48* confirms, our use of the terminology for Web-based publishing has been changing over time [1].

Looking at the suggested time bar of Web 2.0 of *Figure 48*, one notes the age of some of the terms which are often used and misused in a Web 2.0 context.

- The transition of Web-site from isolated information silos to sources of content and functionality, thus becoming computing platforms serving up Web-applications to users. See how the proliferation of YouTube (http://www.youtube.com/) where people are encouraged to broadcast (publish) anything they like, and do.
- A social phenomenon embracing an approach to generating and distributing Web content itself, characterised by open communication, decentralization of authority, freedom to share and re-use, and the market-place as a conversation in its own right.
- Enhanced organization and categorization of content, emphasizing deeply embedded hyper-linking
- A rise or fall in the economic value of the Web, possibly surpassing the impact of the dot-com boom of the late 1990's

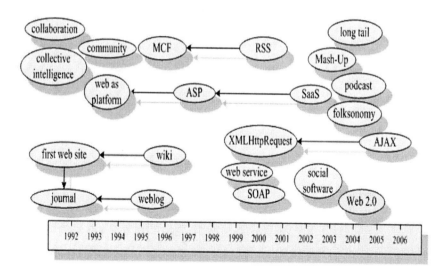

Figure 48 : Hypertext History

Tim O'Reilly's focus is to encourage the *human-dimensions of HCI* wherever possible. This emphasis can be seen in the examples he uses to demonstrate the concept of Web 2.0 to embody four plus one levels of hierarchy, which include:

- *Level-3 applications:* can only exist on the Internet, deriving their power from the human connections and network. Growing in effectiveness the more people use them. For example you may have notice the following: eBay, craigslist, Wikipedia, del.icio.us, Skype, dodgeball, and Adsense.

- *Level-2 applications:* can operate offline; however, gain advantages from going online. For example: Flickr (which benefits from its shared photo-database and from its community-generated tag database facility)

- *Level-1 applications:* also can be available offline; however, can gain extra features online. O'Reilly points to Writely (since 10 October 2006: Google Docs and Spreadsheets, offering group-editing capability online) and iTunes (because of its music-store portion).

- *Level-0 applications:* can work as well offline. For example: MapQuest, Yahoo! Local, and Google Maps. Note there that O'Reilly also says that mapping applications using contributions from users to advantage can rank as Level-2.

- non-Web applications like eMail, instant-messaging clients and the telephone.

In summary, whether they refer to the notions of a semantic Web or the Web 2.0 environment, we are describing the Web as a platform. Data in never ending forms are the driving force, with an overarching information architecture derived from the users' participation and collaborative effort. At last we are witnessing innovation in the assembly of information systems and Web-sites that are drawn together from distributed and independent Web-developers through their shared open-source coding. Emerging out of this fanciful Web 2.0 platform are tangible, lightweight business applications that signify the end of the software adoption cycle, at last to rid us of those never ending beta development scenarios [12].

Plain HTML

As we have seen in the previous section of this chapter, the extra functionality provided by Web 2.0 is determined by the willingness of users to collaborate with data stored on servers. The best way to achieve this is to employ forms that are mounted as *'hypertext markup language'* (HTML)-pages through a common scripting language such as Javascript, or Flash tools. Some have said that the Web is the Gutenberg press of our time. Almost anyone can create their own Web-site, presenting or publishing it to the Internet public at large. These Web-pages are published in many different guises. Some belong to corporate businesses as they try to use all kinds of marketing tricks to sell you something, while others belong to individuals with information to share with anyone. The good thing about all this is that ordinary people can get to choose what their Web-page will look like. However, this is possibly where the good news ends.

One sticking point for the would-be novice-developer is that all Web-pages are written in a programming language called hypertext markup language commonly known as HTML. HTML lets you format text, add graphics, sound, and video, saving it all in a *"text only"* or *'American Standard Code for Information Interchange'* (ASCII) file that can be read by any computer. It goes without saying perhaps that to display video or play audio files, the computer must have the necessary hardware. Central to the HTML language are the tags, which are keywords encased in *"<"* and *">"* signs. This coding indicates to the machine the kind of content to expect. If you are freaking out while you read this, it is because you don't feel that you know anything about programming: you can relax. In fact, there are quite a number of Web-page development applications that create the HTML code for you (even MSWord purports to)! Called HTML Editors they range in sophistication from high-end and very expensive to shareware with minimal cost.

Table 29 demonstrates an example of some HTML where there is a centred heading and a following paragraph. It is quite easy to see the syntax rules where there are distinct tag-sets; the opening command of the set is encased within the symbols < and > (eg: <html >) while the closing tag must have a "/" inserted (</html>).

Table 29 : HTML Code Centre Heading

```
<html>
<body>
<h1 align="center">This is heading 1</h1>
<p>Programmer inputs lines of text here to display beneath the heading. </p>
</body>
</html>
```

At the high-end people can buy Adobe products like Flash and Dreamweaver. The middle-to-low-end has FileMaker, Microsoft FrontPage and the Netscape Composer. Text-based offerings include such applications as, HotDog Professional, and Bare Bones Software. The shareware offers World Wide Web Weaver and Ant_HTML. In fact, any text editor can be used to write the HTML. For example people use SimpleText (Macintosh), WordPad for Windows, or *'vi'* for the Unix operating environment. The HTML code that is generated with these simpler programs is no different from the HTML produced by the more high-end complex HTML editors. A simple text editor works like a basic SLR 35 mm camera. Only with a camera, you have to set up your f-stop and aperture manually, then focus before shooting. "For those unfamiliar with this techno-camera term this is a measure of the size of a camera's aperture. The higher the f-stop, the smaller the aperture." The more dedicated HTML editors are more like the point-and-shoot variety of camera. Generally they are more expensive and less flexible [13]. The type of assistance an HTML editor provides includes:

- inserting opening and closing tags with a single click
- check and verify syntax in the HTML as well as for the typo's in your text
- adding attributes by clicking buttons instead of typing words in correct order
- varying degrees of WYSIWYG display of your Web-page
- often correct mistakes in existing HTML pages
- permit easy use special characters

The beauty of HTML is found in its universality. HTML documents are saved as ASCII or *'text only files'* that can be read by any computer. This means that visitors can access your Web-page using a Macintosh and/or Windows-based machines. It also does not matter whether they are using a Unix powered system, or even a Palm-held device. This is the up-side of HTML. The down-side means that whilst HTML is available for all kinds of devices, they will not have the same view of the resulting screen display (or output format). There will be differences according to the computer, the monitor, and the speed of the Internet connection. In addition, the browser you use to access the information will produce different results.

Table 30 : HTML Code Setting CSS Background Colour

```
<html>
<head>
<style type="text/css">
body
h1 {background-color: #00ff00}
h2 {background-color: transparent}
p {background-color: rgb(250,0,255)}
</style>
</head>
<body>
<h1>This is header 1</h1>
<h2>This is header 2</h2>
<p>This is a paragraph</p>
</body>
</html>
```

However there has been a concerted effort to end the ongoing browser war with a push to standardize practice by the *"World Wide Web Consortium"* (www.w3.org – led by Tim Berners-Lee). Unfortunately, thus far software development houses still expend 25% of their time and energy circumventing the W3C standards to produce proprietary tags. Also, they direct different versions towards each browser, with attendant marketing to alert their clients [13]. *"Cascading style sheets"*, more commonly known as CSS, have been put forward by the W3C as a peace offering. The term cascading was selected for the potential affordance for multiple re-use in the same

Web-page. These system (design) devices are intended to separate the content of a Web-page (that is written in HTML), from the format (that is written in CSS, which is a new feature that has been added the HTML). For instance, the CSS can be implemented to retain the parameters for things like the Web-header and any appropriate links. In the following example of a CSS you can see that the background for the Web-page is set for yellow, with directions for heading highlight to be colour from green (00ff00), to transparent to pink (RGB(250,0,255)).

The intention is to allow more control over the design of a Web-page while keeping the page universal. In addition using the CSS can save the Web-developer by storing all the formatting in one file. Moreover, within word processing and desktop publishing, a style sheet is a file or form that defines the layout of a document. When you fill in a style sheet, you specify such parameters as the page size, margins, and fonts. Style sheets are useful because you can use the same style sheet for many documents. For example, you could define one style sheet for personal letters, another for official letters, and a third for reports.

Effectiveness of Rich Internet Applications

In chapter-3 we were introduced to the emerging field of RIAs *(Rich Internet Applications)* that offer the benefits of distributed, server-side Internet applications. While in the previous section above we discussed the dynamics of Web-based server-side / client-side to increase functionality of one's Internet experiences. Consequently, these rich interface environments provide enhanced interaction capabilities on your desktop applications.

However, there is a key difference between a typical Flash Web-site and an RIA [14]. The RIA functionality should interact with and manipulate data, rather than simply visualize or present it. Moreover, while RIAs do hold significant promise, many in the Flash community don't have the opportunity to work with interaction designers, information architects, or other user experienced professionals. Instead, Flash or other rich technologies employ all the bells and whistles that detract from user comfort. To this end McMullin & Skinner [14] list a number of usability issues that were also presented in chapter-3. In a recent *"Special Edition on the Effectiveness of RIAs for Education and Training in the International Journal of Continuing Engineering Education and Life-Long Learning"* [15], there were 10-contributions from educational technology practitioners. All of these showed how RIA platforms are utilised to implement their instructional strategies.

Effectiveness of RIA for Education and Training

In their paper entitled Meeting Accessibility Guidelines: Lessons from Australia, Marsha Berry, Laurie Armstrong and Reece Lamshed, provide an insightful view of why it is so difficult to break down the barriers that remain as techno-turbulence for people with disabilities. Their research study found there were conformance difficulties with differing government policies that underpin the *"Web Accessibility Initiative"* (WAI) guidelines. Meeting accessibility guidelines should be upper most for all involved in the educational sector [16]. As such Berry et al. [16] have proposed Figure 49 shows their 6-parts model for the implementation process for meeting accessibility. Although universal access was expressed as an idea in some of the policies, all subscribed to access and equity. The Disability Discrimination Act 1992 is a key motivating driver of policy, and that risk assessments are a strategy used to determine the necessity for levels of conformance. Impediments to policy implementation exist, while professional development is conducted on an ad hoc basis.

Figure 49 : Towards Meeting WAI Guidelines

In his paper entitled: Evaluating Cultural Learning in an Online Virtual Environment, Erik Champion [17] shows how to evaluate cultural understanding using virtual environments. Erik has attempted to answer this question by designing, building and evaluating a virtual heritage environment to assess which modes of interactivity most helped understanding. His case study attempts to evaluate the effect on cultural understanding of three different interaction modes. Each of these is teamed with a specific slice of the digitally reconstructed environment. The three interaction modes were derived from a descriptive theory of cultural learning as instruction, observation and action (trial and error). Results for all three groups were collected through questionnaires, automatic PHP scripts, and observation by a single tester. His statistical formulae were applied. In summary his results showed the importance of recording demographics (for his research this meant age, group and gender), the strong effect of context on the choice of interaction, the strong effect of navigation, and a significant relation between gaming experience, task performance, and understanding. He also uncovered a potential new factor for consideration by researchers. Further, he proposed there was a type of cognitive overloading, which included too many interactive processes for the participant to cope with effectively whilst interacting with a virtual environment.

While not strictly an RIA application, Candace Chou and Carole Bagley's paper entitled: eFolio: A Rich Internet Application K-12 In-Service Teachers' Attitudes Toward Electronic Portfolios [18], is taking the term rich to convey a richness of learning content within the framework of an RIA. As such they can show that an ePortfolio serves not only as a depository of a student's works for future employers or certification but also a powerful tool for technology integration for K-12 teachers. The use of an ePortfolio to demonstrate competency in subject areas has become a common practice in most pre-service teacher programs. It is of equal importance to use an ePortfolio for in-service teacher training [18]. Moreover, ePortfolio serves many purposes: to demonstrate competency in technology and curriculum design, national board certification, and evidence of life-long learning. Since an ePortfolio is generally considered a tool for job searching, in-service teachers who are licensed classroom teachers tend to downplay the relative advantages of an ePortfolio. This study examines in-service teachers' attitudes toward eFolio, a free Web-based authoring system for all Minnesota educators and residents. Chou & Bagley also review the pros and cons of using an ePortfolio and the interface design that facilitates the process. They conclude that the effective use of an ePortfolio cannot be isolated from the building of a learning community. To encourage the use of ePortfolio for life-long learning, peer-review and support play an important role.

Then Brian Ferry, Lisa Kervin and Karl Rudd [19] in their paper entitled: Use of Rich Internet Applications to Develop an Online Classroom-Based Simulation, produced an interesting commentary of how ICTs provide a range of powerful tools. Tools that allow: easier access, updating capability, scheduling of tasks, and flexible learning environments. Their paper reports on the design of an online simulation developed to enhance the pre-service teacher practicum experience in the important area of literacy teaching at one university. Their simulation was designed to store user data in PHP scripts in a temporary session management system as text files. Their research was conducted with more than 200 users showing that the simulation gave pre-service teachers the opportunity to slow down or accelerate classroom events, revisit and reflect critical decision points and replay events in the light of new understandings. Their pre-service teachers reported that their experience with the simulation helped to make their practicum experience more focused. They claimed that it gave them the knowledge and experience to more fully appreciate the impact of subtle changes that experienced teachers made during lessons.

Wolfgang Hurst, Rainer Mueller, and Thomas Ottmann's [20] paper entitled: The AOF Method for Automatic Production of Educational Content and RIA Generation, demonstrate that an automatic recording of live lectures and presentations has been explored and evaluated by various research projects since the mid 90s and has meanwhile been adapted by a number of commercial systems. These researchers are able to show that with these types of ICT tools, teachers can automatically capture their live lectures and presentations in classrooms and lecture halls. They can make them available as 'eLectures' in a variety of output formats for access over the internet, and use them as the kernels of Web-based learning modules. Hurst et al, suggest that one special incarnation of this idea is the process of *"Authoring on the Fly"* (AOF). They give an overview of the whole concept of lecture recording utilizing the AOF technique, describing all necessary steps involved in the production process. They summarize their basic approach, highlighting its relevance for RIA generation, and report on evaluations and field studies describing the usage of the produced e-lectures and their influence on teaching and learning.

Sau-Yin Lam, Sui-Cheung Kong and Lam-For Kwok [21] in their paper entitled: Extending a Rich Web-Based Cognitive Tool to a Mobile Computer-supported Collaborative Learning Environment, described Web-based cognitive tool previously built for learners, which help them to comprehend the procedural knowledge of fraction addition and subtraction, with unlike denominators. A series of experiments were conducted to validate the effectiveness of the Web-based cognitive tool in assisting learners to acquire the concept of fractions. In this study, they attempt to extend this rich Web-based cognitive tool to a collaborative environment that allows learners to interact with each other and co-construct a procedural knowledge of fraction addition with unlike denominators. They introduce the Web-based cognitive tool, describe its features on the mobile platform, illustrate how it can support collaborative interaction in a designed learning activity, and describe a scenario of using the mobile computer-supported cognitive tool to attain new procedural knowledge of fraction addition.

Gunnar Liestol [22] presents his paper entitled: Conducting Genre Convergence for Learning, to reveal that his perspective on RIAs is derived from the humanities. As a consequence, he promotes a synthetic—analytic approach to inventing new and improved communication forms. The construction and updating of document types, which he calls digital genres, are successfully learnt when the learner combines the procedures of both construction and interpretation. To this end Gunnar asks a central question: *"How are we to fully develop the potential of RIAs, and to exploit both multimedia and multimodal functionality when applying ICT tools for learning?"* Within his framework of the divergence—convergence dichotomy, this paper attempts to answer the question by re-applying the topical operation of rhetoric as a method for making presentations. He demonstrates how this methodology could be used to find, select and combine features and qualities from relevant existing genres to form new (potential) digital genres within the context of learning. Gunnar's paper is based on research funded by the Norwegian Network for IT-Research and Competence in Education (ITU).

Joerd de Vries and Italo De Diana's [23] paper entitled: Towards Personal Portals for Professional Development, discuss that general online learning platforms are institution-based and mainly meant for the management of course-based education. These authors say that from the perspective of a lifelong learner, such platforms are only temporarily useful for specific courses and have no significance for further professional development. These researchers are however interested in the realisation of personal portals for lifelong learning. They say that these types of professionalisation portals are personalised and give access to a wide range of local and networked personal study. Also that the professionalisation services, which are formal as well as informal, may be derived from a variety of institutions. Moreover, they focus their paper on the concept of a personal professionalisation portal as a RIA. In their paper they pose this question: *"What is this portal and what factors contribute to the effectiveness of these portals?"* They conclude with a discussion on future trends in the development and application of these portals and related research issues.

Wang-Chan Wong, Myron Sheu and Eric Moy's [24] paper entitled: A Rich Internet Application Edutainment Training System, incorporates entertaining elements within the learning process. The authors of this stimulating paper hope that edutainment can attract and retain learners and motivate them to become more active in learning. Wong et al., propose that edutainment comes in many forms, such as TV programs and computer games. Because lots of college students and young adults consider gaming an everyday part of life, educators and researchers have been working on developing computer games for educational and training purposes. Online edutainment will be even more desirable because it can reach a wider audience with better user management and monitoring. In this paper, they present a new edutainment training platform that is based on a *'role playing game'* (RPG) and is built within the context of an RIA environment. These researchers claim that their platform is different from other edutainment systems in the following aspects: (1) it provides a unique game engine and a training administration module. Their game engine manages the storyline and dialogue scripts of the RPG and is decoupled from the training and testing materials that are managed by the training administration module, (2) it has a flexible reward system that the training administration can easily configure, and (3) it provides extensive management and monitoring functions for the management.

While the final paper in this Special Edition on The Effectiveness of RIAs for Education and Training is presented by Slavi Stoyanov and Piet Kommers [25] entitled: WWW-Intensive Concept Mapping for Meta-Cognition in Solving Ill-Structured Problems. These researchers propose that concept mapping is one of the most intimate and most dynamic learning support activities, but that it needs still a drastic further evolution of methods and tools. Through this paper they show how the idea of WWW-based concept mapping is gaining momentum and how the need for a solid reviewing of the various approaches and the empirical effects is required. Their discussion bridges the technological advancement of WWW-based concept mapping tools with the more recent effects on learning by problem solving. Their results show there is added value manifesting in the phases of idea generation and selection. They claim that their mapping approach brings forward a broader perception and a greater diversity of ideas. They conclude that further investments are needed to make WWW-based mapping more accessible and integrated in WWW-based learning management systems.

To summarize this chapter does its best to convey the most striking feature of our connectivity through the implementation of rich internet applications, as described above. This approach is to widen the interpretation of 'interaction'. In the era of early technologies: like interactive video, clickable hypertext, questioning-and-answers. Then it was a de facto merit, if the learner could react in diverse ways and received an answer that essentially rested upon the correction of an earlier reply. Instead 'interaction' has become more complex. In its new context it means relational learning: based upon some-one's personality and even someone's attraction for identification. 'Interaction' is a much broader process than instruction, questioning or sharing information [15].

For the reader wishing to enter this emerging field will be well advised to take notice of the *human-dimensions of HCI*. Find ways to build in the 'interaction' you wish for. If you don't think you have the techno-savvy – network until you find a sole-mate. At all costs, don't be put off by the techno-jargon. With the right multi-media development support; just about anything is possible these days.

Chapter Reference List

[1] Bradley, G., *Social and Community Informatics: Humans on the Net*, 2006. NY: Routledge.265

[2] Preece, J., et al., *Human-Computer Interaction*. 1994, Harlow - UK: Addison-Wesley. 775.

[3] Schank, R. & Abelson, R., *Scripts, Plans, Goals and Understanding*. 1977, Hillsdale: Erlbaum.

[4] Nicolai, T., et al., *Exploring the Social Context with the Wireless Rope*, 2006. Retrieved 20/01/08 from http://www.tzi.de/fileadmin/user_upload/wearlab/downloads/wearlab-Publication/nicolai06_exploring.pdf.

[5] Fröhlich, D. & Kraut, R., *The Social Context of Home Computing, Submission to Harper in Home Design*, 2002. Retrieved 20/01/08 from http://www.cs.cmu.edu/~kraut/RKraut.site.files/articles/frochlich02-FamComputing-2.pdf .

[6] Richardson, S., Employers' Contribution to Training. 2004, *Formal Report: National Centre for Vocational Education Research (NCVER)*. ISBN 1 92086 00 7.

[7] McKay, E., et al. Towards Web-mediated learning reinforcement: Rewards for online mentoring through effective human-computer interaction. *Paper in the proceedings of the 6th IASTED International Conference on Web-Based Education. Held March 14-16*. 2007. Chamonix, France, 210-215, ISBN:978-0-88986-650-8.

[8] AQF, *The AQF and Quality Assurance Processes in Australian Education and Training*, 2005. Retrieved 20/01/08 from http://www.aqf.edu.au/quality.htm#theaqf.

[9] Rosenberg, M.J., *e-Learning: Strategies for delivering knowledge in the digital age*. 2001, NY: McGraw-Hill. 343.

[10] Corbitt, B., Holt, D., & Seagrave, S. From product centricism to systems-wide education design: Making corporate technology systems work for the learning organisation. Paper in the proceedings of the *2004 Information Systems Adoption and Business Productivity, the Eighth Pacific Asia Conference on Information Systems*, 2004. Shanghai, China: PACIS.

[11] Hilgard, E.R. & Bower, G.H., *Theories of Learning*, (4th edition). 1975, Englewood Cliffs, NJ: Prentice-Hal.

[12] Wikipedia-contributors, Bibliographic details for Web 2.0, 2007, in *Wikipedia, The Free Encyclopedia: Permanent link. Retrieved 20/01/08 from* http://en.wikipedia.org/w/index.php?title=Web_2.0&oldid=151173387

[13] Castro, E., *HTML for the World Wide Web*. (4th edition). 2000, CA: Peachpit Press - Addison Wesley Longman. 384.

[14] McMullin, J. & Skinner, G., *Usability Heuristics for Rich Internet Applications*. 2007.

[15] McKay, E. & Kommers, P., *(Editorial). International Journal for Continuing Engineering Education and Life-Long Learning: Special Edition - The Effectiveness of Rich Internet Application for Education and Training*, 2006. Viewed on 20/01/08 at http://www.inderscience.com/editorials/f105621479128311.pdf, 16(3/4): 151-155.

[16] Berry, M., Armstrong, L., & Lanshed, R., Meeting accessibility guidelines: Lessons from Australia, in the *International Journal for Continuing Engineering Education and Life-Long Learning: Special Edition - The Effectiveness of Rich Internet Application for Education and Training*, 2006. Viewed on 20/01/08 at http://www.inderscience.com/editorials/f105621479128311.pdf, 16(3/4): 156-172.

[17] Champion, E., Evaluating cultural learning in an online virtual environment, in the *International Journal for Continuing Engineering Education and Life-Long Learning: Special Edition - The Effectiveness of Rich Internet Application for Education and Training*, 2006. Viewed on 20/01/08 at http://www.inderscience.com/editorials/f105621479128311.pdf, 16(3/4): 173-182.

[18] Chou, C.C. & Bagley, C., eFolio: A Rich Internet application K-12 In-Service Teachers' attitudes Toward Electronic Portfolios, in the *International Journal for Continuing Engineering Education and Life-Long Learning: Special Edition - The Effectiveness of Rich Internet Application for Education and Training*, 2006. Viewed on 20/01/08 at http://www.inderscience.com/editorials/f105621479128311.pdf, 16(3/4): 183-199.

[19] Ferry, B., Kervin, L., & Rudd, K., Use of rich Internet applications to develop an online classroom-based simulation, in the *International Journal for Continuing Engineering Education and Life-Long Learning: Special Edition - The Effectiveness of Rich Internet Application for Education and Training*,

2006. Viewed on 20/01/08 at http://www.inderscience.com/editorials/f105621479128311.pdf, 16(3/4): 200-214.

[20] Hurst, W., Mueller, R., & Ottman, T., The AOF method for automatic production of educational content and RIA generation, in the *International Journal for Continuing Engineering Education and Life-Long Learning: Special Edition - The Effectiveness of Rich Internet Application for Education and Training*, 2006. Viewed on 20/01/08 at http://www.inderscience.com/editorials/f105621479128311.pdf, 16(3/4): 215-237.

[21] Lam, S.-Y., Kong, S.-C., & Kwok, L.-F., Extending a rich Web-based cognitive tool to a learning environment, in the *International Journal for Continuing Engineering Education and Life-Long Learning: Special Edition - The Effectiveness of Rich Internet Application for Education and Training*, 2006. Viewed on 20/01/08 at http://www.inderscience.com/editorials/f105621479128311.pdf, 16(3/4): 238-254.

[22] Liestol, G., Conducting genre convergence for learning, in the *International Journal for Continuing Engineering Education and Life-Long Learning: Special Edition - The Effectiveness of Rich Internet Application for Education and Training*, 2006. Viewed on 20/01/08 at http://www.inderscience.com/editorials/f105621479128311.pdf, 16(3/4): 255-270.

[23] de Vries, S. & De Diana, I., Towards personal portals for professional development, in the *International Journal for Continuing Engineering Education and Life-Long Learning: Special Edition - The Effectiveness of Rich Internet Application for Education and Training*, 2006. Viewed on 20/01/08 at http://www.inderscience.com/editorials/f105621479128311.pdf, 16(3/4): 271-298.

[24] Wong, W.-C., Sheu, M., & Moy, E., A rich Internet application edutainment training system, in the *International Journal for Continuing Engineering Education and Life-Long Learning: Special Edition - The Effectiveness of Rich Internet Application for Education and Training*, 2006. Viewed on 20/01/08 at http://www.inderscience.com/editorials/f105621479128311.pdf, 16(3/4): 280-296.

[25] Stoyanov, S. & Kommers, P., WWW-intensive concept mapping for meta cognition in solving ill-structured problems, in the *International Journal for Continuing Engineering Education and Life-Long Learning: Special Edition - The Effectiveness of Rich Internet Application for Education and Training*, 2006. Viewed on 20/01/08 at http://www.inderscience.com/editorials/f105621479128311.pdf, 16(3/4): 297-316.

Chapter-9

Gender Issues of HCI:
Nurturing Effective HCI

In nearing the end of our techno-journey, as it was said at the commencement, one of the primary reasons for writing this book is to fill a gap in the literature that relates to the human-dimension or social context of *effective HCI*. Therefore in getting the message across to the general community; that is, appealing to a wider cross section of the general public, the book uses a narrative writing style. In bringing forward many of the hidden complexities of the *human-dimensions of HCI*, and due to the educative nature of the techno-saga this book was launched within The Future of Learning series with IOS Press. As previously noted, the target audience for this book is: IT professionals, postgraduate information systems' students, corporate trainers, general computer users, educational technology researchers, academics at universities and other types of community-based learning Institutions. Our commentary on the *human-dimensions of HCI* would not be complete without a section for dealing with gender and how it relates [1], if at all, to HCI.

Techno-Gender

In her recently published book entitled *"The Female Brain"*, Louann Brizendine, a medical Doctor [2], describes the stark reality between the genders' brain physiology. She suggests that we should all take a good look at this for applicability to the techno-landscape.

It has been felt for a long time that differences in gender attributes affect the way we respond to each other. Much has already been said using comical metaphors about how to improve relationships by understanding gender differences. For instance, in 1992 John Gray, also a medical Doctor, gave us his views on improving husband-wife relationships in his book *Men Are from Mars, Women are from Venus* [3]. Although Gray's book may be enlightening for some, he draws on an entertaining astrological model to articulate his message. He quickly asserts that his stereotypes (Martians and Venusians) cannot be applied to individuals, which in itself is slightly confusing. According to Gray some women relieve their stress by talking about it. Some men may interpret this chatty style of free-ranging talk as either an accusation or a request for finding a solution to a problem. Gray's book is thought provoking and has been very popular. Nevertheless it has drawn critical reviews from clinical psychologists who take John's use of the astrological metaphor seriously.

Other accounts for gender differences impacting on professional practice in IT, can be found in the ways some senior company executive women in the corporate sector speak to their IT audiences: particularly when there are more men than women present.

Cheryl Hannah, the Chief Information Officer for the Australian *"Department of Immigration and Multicultural Affairs"* (DIMA), knows to pitch her voice low and keep the buzz factor high. This is because, as Cheryl suggests, some men think that a woman's naturally higher tone and more rhythmical manner, with its tendency to reduce in pitch at the end of sentences, lacks authority. Hannah further points out that many men will tune out unless the talk is utterly compelling. Because of this, she crafts her words carefully as it is important to get the message across to these mostly male audiences. Her public speaking manner therefore employs a slower rate and deeper tone than she would otherwise use. For instance, she uses simpler and shorter words to avoid showing off her otherwise scholarly terminology.

Whether we like it or not, since its inception the realm of information technology has been peppered with the achievements of our male counterparts. While there are many men that have been acknowledged earlier in this book, we can see there are distinctly fewer women. Now this should not to be taken as an excuse to strike out anew for the feminist cause. Rather, it's just the way women's achievements in IT continue to be portrayed that presents particular problems for all.

High Time to be Upfront on Gender Differences

According to Dr Brizendine, the female brain processes thoughts very differently compared with the way a male's does. Let's not say here that one is better than another. Instead let us say they are just uniquely different. Louann comments for instance, that a woman may comfortably use approximately 20,000 words in her daily communications (heck that's two chapters of this book) while a man may only use about 7,000 each day [2].

"No wonder", you may say, *"that it is common to hear a woman report she gets tired as the day wears on."* Of course, men also report their energy levels wane by the afternoon. The reason for this discrepancy is the way we are wired, says Louann. Scientists now concur, as they have proved that until 8-weeks after conception, the human brain is female [2].

In showing how little girls differ from little boys, Brizendine talks about an observation of a small child flitting around a children's playground, connecting with other children whether she knows them or not. Picture if you will that this little person is on the verge of using language in two or three word phrases. Instead, however she chooses to make connections with other children with her contagious smile, together with other head movements (mostly empathic nods). The other little girls respond in the same manner. When words are spoken they would be for things like *"Dolly"* and *"shopping"*. As Brizedine suggests, soon a pint-sized community forms, complete with verbal chattering, games and imaginary families. When the same little girl is joined by her cousin, a boy, she is happy to see him, but the joy does not last long. The little boy grabs the blocks the little girls are using to build a house. Instead of joining the others, he wants to build a rocket by himself. Moreover the little boys in this playground are set on wrecking anything the girls create. The boys push the girls around, refuse to take turns, and ignore requests from a girl to give a particular toy back to her. By the end of the morning the little girl can be seen retreating to the other end of the play area with the other little girls, who were interested in playing house quietly together.

It's not rocket science. Watch them. Boys and girls behave differently. What we have not really registered is that the brain dictates these divergent behaviours. Brizedine explains that the impulses of children are so innate that they kick in even if the adults try to change the behaviour. She cites one of her own patients giving her three and a half year old daughter a bright red fire truck amongst other unisex toys. One afternoon this parent found the little girl cuddling the fire-truck in a blanket, rocking it back and forth saying,

"Don't worry, little truckle, everything will be alright"[4]:2. This behaviour is not socialization. It's because the little girl's brain is wired to do such things. By the time we are born our brains shape the way we use all our senses (sight, hearing, smell and taste). Apparently, nerves run from our sense organs directly to the brain, and then the brain does the interpreting [2]. With a good enough knock on the head in a specific area, one won't be able to smell or taste. Yet the brain can discriminate further. Consider the ways we think a person is good or bad, whether we like the weather today or not, and if we feel like doing our work. Moreover, for some people, stimulants such as tea/coffee/wine or even a lovely piece of chocolate may help us to change our mind at any particular point. Watch how some people just hate cloudy days (that turn brighter). For others, irritations caused by some upset lessen or seem to evaporate easily, due to the way the chemical substances of the aforementioned stimulants affect the brain.

In taking consideration of the affect of these chemical compounds on our brains' functionality, just imagine the different realities when two brains have different structures (male/female) as described by "[2];[3]. She explains that:

"if you were to watch a female and a male brain developing via time-lapse photography, you would see their circuit diagrams being laid down according to the blueprint drafted by both genes and sex hormones. A huge testosterone surge at the beginning in the eighth week will turn this unisex brain male by killing off some cells in the communication centres and growing more cells in the sex and aggression centres. If the testosterone surge doesn't happen, the female brain continues to grow unperturbed. The fetal girl's brain cells sprout more connections in the communication centers and areas that process emotion. How does fetal fork in the road affect us? For one thing, because of her larger communication center, this girl will grow up to be more talkative than her brother."

Gender in the Techno-Landscape

It has been reported that the average earnings of IT professionals may be twice the national average [5]. Women, however, remain the minority among IT students and employees in IT companies. There is an even darker side to the issue of this disparity. Nations the world over are recognizing they need to substantially increase their technological skill base. This realization is not new [6]. IT skill shortages are commonly reported by business leaders and government ministers. For instance they continually say that recruiting more women into the IT industry could go a long way to lessen, even reverse the current skills shortage [7]. However, the skills shortage is not just related to IT, we need to bring more people in general into science, engineering and technology to sustain economic growth. Many know that keeping women out of certain jobs can halve the available work force.

According to Miller & Perie [8]

"Gender segregation is seen in entries both to undergraduate and postgraduate courses in the technology sector. National Audit Office analyses of data from the Higher Education Council for England indicate that women constitute around 15% of engineering and

technology students and 19% of students in mathematical and computer sciences (National Audit Commission, 2002). The Institute for Employment Studies found that women constitute just 22% of employees in Information and Communication Technologies (ICT) occupations across sectors, and this proportion has, if anything, fallen since 1995 (Connor et al, 2001). More women are employed in ICT jobs in the non-ICT dedicated sector than in the ICT sector itself. Most of these are employed in lower level, computer operator jobs (54%); just 3% are employed in the fast growing software engineer group (Connor et al, ibid. ").

Australian educational researchers have also been watching this international trend for a lowering of participation rates by females relative to males in ICT related courses and professional practice. A recent collaborative academic/industry government funded partnership investigated the factors associated with low female participation rates in professional level ICT occupations and education pathways. The researchers confirm the dismal picture for the UK as well. Moreover, while acknowledging that the ICT sector is a vital part of the Australian economy, Senator Coonan, the Australian Minister for Communications, Information Technology and the Arts and Deputy Leader of the Government in the Senate, claimed that women comprise only about one fifth of the ICT workforce [9]. It may be interesting to note the Government commitment to convene a summit involving leaders in the ICT industry and education to identify and address the barriers that may be keeping women out of the ICT sector. The resulting Advisory Group comprised 10-prominent Australian women from the ICT and education sectors to identify the key issues for discussion at the summit.

Although enrolments in computing subjects continue to attract students in the belief that an IT qualification will set them up to choose an ICT career [10], the number of females enrolling is falling [11]. They gathered perceptions from years 11 and 12 school girls of the 2-advanced computing subjects that were available through Education Queensland, Australia. All the participants were taking subjects in Information Processing Technology and Information Technology Systems. The researchers found that they were facing similar trends that were evident in other western countries; that is, the female enrolments in these two subjects are declining to a level causing concern. In response to the research questions *"the subjects are interesting"* and *"I am interested in computers"*, the responses indicate these subjects were generally perceived by girls in high school as boring, dull and uninteresting [11].

Trends in Gender and IT

If we can accept that our use of ICT tools is widespread within Western society, then computer literacy emerges as an important survival skill for people as they carry out their every day tasks. These days, as we have witness in earlier chapters of this book, people in developed countries are generally required to use computers to negotiate many types of basic transactions: health care, banking or booking an airline ticket, for example. For instance, many major airports offer customers a fast-track checking-in facility where travelers can submit their eTickets to automate seat allocation. Software developers and the supporting ICT industry are in fact cultural architects [11]. While the literature says much about the importance of the ICT sector, it would appear that ICT is below the radar of many young people when considering possible future careers, particularly in the case of young women.

In their 2001 book entitled Unlocking the Clubhouse [12], Jane Margolis (a social scientist) and Allen Fisher (computer scientist and educator) described how girls and women are left out of the information technology revolution that is transforming society [12]. Margolis and Fisher claim that while women do surf the Web in equal numbers to men, females make the majority of online purchases. Few women however are actually involved in helping to innovate new technologies.

It would seem that the lion's share of the financial benefits that are derived from new inventions go towards men: and it is largely men's perspectives and priorities that inform the development of any new ICT artefact. Because only a fraction of high school and college computer science students are female, the field is likely to remain a boys only club(house) [12]. Unlocking the Clubhouse, is based on interviews with more than 100 computer science students of both sexes from Carnegie Mellon University in the USA. These authors conducted their survey over a period of 4-years. Additionally, they made classroom observations and had unstructured conversations with hundreds of college and high school faculty members. The interviews captured the dynamic details of the female computing experience, which relate to the family computer kept in a brother's bedroom. These interviews also identified women's feelings of alienation in college computing classes. They investigate the familial, educational, and institutional origins of the computing gender gap. They also describe educational reforms that have made a dramatic difference at Carnegie Mellon. Here the percentage of women entering the School of Computer Science rose from 7% in 1995 to 42% in 2000. Similar demographic trends were noted at high schools around the country.

Even though it has been shown that women comprise over 50% of the users of technology in the USA, and despite the increasing numbers shown by Margolis & Jagger in 2001, the numbers of females who get involved in creating software applications development are decreasing [13]. This is despite some universities taking extraordinary measures to change the way people perceive the field of computer science. For example, at Carnegie Mellon, they are actively diversifying the image that surrounds IT and those who work in it. The campaign involves changing the perception that computer science is wider than the mere coding software programs. Frieze shows how this enterprising university offers an innovative and useful model for people who wish to launch an outreach program to encourage more girls and women (as well as boys and men) into computer science.

Stemming the Tide

The literature is loaded with research which identifies effective school practices as the way to overcome many of the (conceptual) barriers to science, mathematics, engineering, and dare we say, ICT. Consequently many learning institutions around the world are now reviewing their professional practices to stem the tide that is drawing people away from science and technology. Particularly in the last couple of years there has been a concerted shift by school and universities to adopt early intervention and mentoring programmes that cultivate student participation in IT related subjects; that is, subjects which lead to a career in ICT.

Some of the vexing issues on how to facilitate more confidence in students of computer science was described in a study by Carole Bagley and Candace Chou [14] at the University of St Thomas in the USA. These two researchers propose that a correlation exists between collaboration and success by novices when learning computer programming. Bagley and Chou are engaged in instruction and research that focuses on answering the following questions:

- At what time in their learning Java programming and algorithmic problem solving, would a student benefit best by collaboration?
- At what time during the problem solving process would the learner benefit greatest by collaboration?
- Would the student benefit greater by collaborating with 1-student in the class, a group, or an expert mentor/coach?
- What cognitive and affective strategies are used during various types of collaboration?
- Does collaboration significantly increase the problem solving performance by females?

The findings show that although there is no significant difference, the female means indicate that females rate the importance of collaboration higher. Although only 20-25% of the students in this research experiment were female, the course mean grades for females were higher. Those students working in pairs or with a mentor received higher overall course grades regardless of gender. Moreover females appear to spend a significantly greater amount of time when working in a group or alone [14].

Collaboration is an important pedagogy to use in teaching computer science and in performing java programming. This study indicates that the more complex a problem, the greater the importance of collaboration. The most important time for collaboration in the problem solving/programming process is: *'brainstorming and formulating the problem'*, and *'designing individual components/modules'*. Their groups tended to try out multiple algorithms and frequently reflected on a variety of strategies. Overall, course grades were significantly higher for those working in pairs or with a mentor regardless of gender.

"Therefore", they asked, *"can the extra time spent by groups be justified?"* Conceptual knowledge was higher for groups in understanding the importance of coming to the group with the concepts prior to discussion and experimentation of multiple strategies. Groups were more confident in presenting orally.

Procedural learning was significantly higher for groups, particularly in performing frequent checks, as they tried out different strategies, hypothesized and watched the effects. Females exhibited a significantly higher level of these procedural strategies.

Meta-cognitive strategies of brainstorming and devising strategies, especially in pairs, were significantly high. Females showed a significant difference in creating a better solution after performing full scale testing.

The affective characteristics of motivation to learn and the belief that learning increases with collaboration were stronger in groups. There was no significant gender difference.

Additional research by Bagley and Chou will compare group and paired learning and will determine the student characteristics that make up a successful pair or group; while more quantitative and qualitative data will deliver a higher degree of confidence with additional trials over time.

Jobs For The Girls

If we are to accept that females' brains are wired differently from males, we might as well seek out ways to accentuate the best attributes of each gender to harmonize the techno-landscape. Of course, breaking the discussion into techno-gender streams could be seen by some people as a controversial demarcation. This is not the intention. Instead it should be seen as an attempt to convey the complementary strengths of each gender in the hope to stimulate new ways of participatory collaboration amongst people.

Communication

To understand one of the more powerful female attributes, it is useful to recall that a testosterone surge at the beginning of the 8th week of gestation sets a human being's brain developmental pathway along with hereditary genes [2]. Recall that research has shown that females are comfortable using far more words each day than their male counterparts. Consider then, how important it is for the corporate sector to utilize this propensity for language skills in ways that promote increased communication. Jobs in IT that relate to transmission of conceptual notions into a linguistic framework would be perfect for a female.

For an example of professional practice in need of the female touch see http://www.access-board.gov/links/communication.htm. This is just one Web-site of many that can serve this discussion well. So doing, it emphasizes a broad range of interesting jobs relating to ICT tool development, and that match the female tendency for elevated communication skills. For instance, let us take the first category of jobs on the Web-page that are located within the Adaptive Technology Resource Centre at the University of Toronto, Canada. Here we see many opportunities where the female would excel; for example, in work that advances the development of accessible interoperability specifications and standards. Imagine the rewards for all stakeholders of an information systems' development team to gather a female's natural capacity to translate users' special needs. Moreover the SNOW Web-site (Special Needs Ontario Window) is a fine example where communication is encouraged among Internet users through ICT tool development. It is easy to see that SNOW's primary aim is to cultivate an inclusive education community. It provides anyone who can access the Internet with an opportunity to contribute and share information.

However, the caption taken from the SNOW-site http://snow.utoronto.ca/ serves as a warning of how miscommunication can result in software products suffering when females are not included in the design, development and usability testing:

Vista's user interface suffers from more 'friction' than its predecessor XP, a French analyst said today, and is actually a step back for Microsoft Corp. in its pursuit of Apple Inc.'s Mac OS X. In a reprise of research published last year, French analyst Andreas Pfeiffer oversaw testing of what he calls 'User Interface Friction', the fluidity and/or reactivity of an operating system to commands. He likens UIF to the reaction -- fast or not -- when stepping on a car's accelerator."

Connection

On the one hand medical schools taught their students in the 1970's and 80's that male and female animal brains developed differently in utero [2]. Impulses that relate to mating and bearing and rearing their young would be hardwired into an animal's brain. Yet on the other hand, medical students were also taught that human's gender differences were a reflection of our parental environment. The implication was, that our gender-based behaviour depended upon whether we were raised as a boy or a girl.

Research now reveals this explanation is not correct. Instead, according to Brizendine the human beings' male and female brains are different. Brizendine claims that this difference can be seen in the increased connection sprouts in the female's communications centre of their brain, which is larger relative to that of a male.

There has been much argument in the literature over time about gender differences and their similarities when using the Internet. This discourse is vast, ranging from the misconceptions and facts on women-focused content to factual offerings from psychology and child development. It is perhaps interesting to note that in a 2000 paper entitled *"Cyberjanes and Cyberjitters: Myths and Realities of Gender Differences and the Net"* by Phillis Weisbard, there is a quote from a piece by Herring [15] that is useful for this discussion to highlight the need for females to remain connected. Only, we can see here that this is an adult version of the earlier tale from the children's playgroup, ending with a similarly divergent if not hostile outcome:

> *"Men championed individual freedom as the highest good, women, "harmonious interpersonal interaction." Men like debate - "constructive denunciation" one male SWIP {Society for Women in Philosophy} member called it, but not open hostility or flaming. In contrast, many women did not distinguish between hostile angry adversarial comments and "rational adversariality." She also found that the differences in values permeated the netiquette guidelines exercised on the lists. Members of predominantly female lists tended to look with disfavor on people who posted long, frequent messages - bandwidth hogs - whereas the predominantly male lists saw this as an issue of individual rights. To the extent that CMC (computer-mediated-communication) was evolving following the male model, it would not ever be equally hospitable to both men and women."*

According to a recent *"PEW Internet Report"*, women have almost caught up in overall Internet use. Not surprisingly in the light of our previous discussion, they are framing their online experience around deepening connections with people. They are more likely than men to use eMail for contacting friends and family to share the latest news, worries, plan forthcoming events, jokes and funny stories [16]. To concur with this Patricia Wallace's observation in her book, *"The Psychology of the Internet"*, uncovers the gender differences in interaction style. She gives an interesting account of women placing greater emphasis on the socio-emotional role that words play to maintain cohesion and cooperation within a group [17].

Reading Reality

Another female gender strength is their ability to read another's emotional sensitivity. Once again as Brizendine explains [2]:

> *"Just about the first thing the female brain compels a baby to do is study faces. Cara, a former student of mine, brought her baby Leila in to see us for regular visits. We loved watching how Leila changed as she grew up, and we saw her pretty much from birth through kindergarten. At a few weeks old, Leila was studying every face that appeared in front of her. My staff and I made plenty of eye contact, and soon she was smiling back at us. We mirrored each other's faces and sounds, and it was fun bonding with her. I wanted to take her home with me, particularly because I hadn't had the same experience with my son.*

> *I loved that this baby girl wanted to look at me, and I wished my son had been so interested in my face. He was just the opposite. He wanted to look at everything else - mobiles, lights, and doorknobs - but not me. Making eye contact was at the bottom of his list of interesting things to do. I was taught in medical school that all babies are born with the need for mutual gazing because it is the key to developing the mother-infant bond, and for months I*

thought something was terribly wrong with my son. They didn't know back then about the many sex-specific differences in the brain. All babies were thought to be hardwired to gaze at faces, but it turns out that theories of the earliest stages of child development were female-biased. Girls, not boys, come out wired for mutual gazing. Girls do not experience the testosterone surge in utero that shrinks the centers for communication, observation, and processing of emotion, so their potential to develop skills in these areas are better at birth than boys'. Over the first three months of life, a baby girl's skills in eye contact and mutual facial gazing will increase by over 400 percent, whereas facial gazing skills in a boy during this time will not increase at all.

Baby girls are born interested in emotional expression. They take meaning about themselves from a look, a touch, every reaction from the people they come into contact with. From these cues they discover whether they are worthy, lovable, or annoying. But take away the signposts that an expressive face provides and you've taken away the female brain's main touchstone for reality. Watch a little girl as she approaches a mime. She'll try with everything she has to elicit an expression. Little girls do not tolerate at faces. They interpret an emotionless face that's turned toward them as a signal they are not doing something right. Like dogs chasing Frisbees, little girls will go after the face until they get a response. The girls will think that if they do it just right, they'll get the reaction they expect. It's the same kind of instinct that keeps a grown woman going after a narcissistic or otherwise emotionally unavailable man - "if I just do it right, he'll love me." You can imagine, then, the negative impact on a little girl's developing sense of self of the unresponsive, flat face of a depressed mother - or even one that's had too many Botox injections. The lack of facial expression is very confusing to a girl, and she may come to believe, because she can't get the expected reaction to a plea for attention or a gesture of affection, that her mother doesn't really like her. She will eventually turn her efforts to faces that are more responsive."

Responsiveness

To demonstrate how a young female child's responsiveness to cues from other people operates, Brizendine draws on a study conducted at the University of Texas, USA. This work involved 12-month old girls and boys to try and show the difference in desire and ability to observe. Each child and mother were brought into a room and left alone. They were instructed not to touch an object that was left in the room with them. While each mother stood to the side of the room, every move, glance, and utterance was captured on video. Very few of the little girls touched the forbidden object, even though their mothers didn't explicitly tell them not to touch. The girls looked back at their mothers' faces checking for approval/disapproval. This was more than 10 to 20 times more than the little boys' response with their mothers. By contrast, the little boys in this experiment, moved freely around the room, rarely glancing at their mothers' faces. Moreover, the little boys frequently touched the forbidden object, even though mothers' shouted, *"No!"* So much for the Adam and Eve myth! It would appear says Brizendine, that these one-year-old boys were driven by their testosterone-formed male brains, compelling them to investigate their environment, even when the objects were forbidden to touch. Is this the point where we can surely rejoice in our difference between the genders? This because the female brains do no undergo the testosterone marination in utero, which ensures their communication and emotion centres remain intact. Girls do arrive in the world much more able to read faces and hearing human vocal tones [2]. This innate ability is likened to the manner in which bats can hear sounds that even cats and dogs cannot. Apparently young females can hear a broader range of sound frequency and tones in the human voice than boys can [2].

Jobs For The Boys

Skimming the literature, it is not so easy to draw out the same amount of work on male's brain development per se relative to that which describes females' brains. Perhaps this is indicative of the differences [18];[2]. One might ask, is it that males generally are not motivated in enough numbers to explore why they are the way they are? Brizendine tells us that the male brain is wired in utero at roughly 8-weeks gestation by a testosterone surge. This kills off some cells in the communication centres, while more cells grow in the sex and aggression centres. As a result the males' communication cortex is much smaller than a females, explaining why men are less talkative than women. Although not all studies agree with this. Moreover Brizendine points out that the females' inclination for better observational skills comes with a brain that is more mature at birth than a boy's brain: girls' brains developing faster by one or two years. Legato on the other hand confirms why it is that blokes solve spatial problems differently.

In a study using a virtual reality maze, not only did the males and females use different parts of their brains to negotiate the space, they also used different strategies to find the exit. The women relied on the landmarks to guide them, while the men used Euclidian information to orient themselves within the structure, so as to navigate their way clear [18]. Men therefore have superior awareness for Euclidian space. This is the kind of space into which the axioms and definitions of Euclidian geometry fit. These are relative to straight lines and parallel lines; also called flat space, or homaloidal space, real or imagined. In a sense all Euclidean geometry is imagined, since none of the concepts can exactly be found in the real world. A point has position, but no size, for example.

This commentary is not meant to start an emotive verbal flame-war on the merits of males' vs females' abilities. Rather it is meant to identify strategies that bring out the best characteristics of each. If women ever wish to reach their information nirvana, they do need to understand why it is that males appear to dominate the IT industry.

Jobs for the boys, is a common term in use these days. It mostly gets used in a derogatory manner. We even swap the boys for girls as the context requires. According to a Web-site (http://www.phrases.org.uk/meanings/212000.html) *'jobs for boys'* simply means any group of men who share a common interest or background. These days it usually means favouritism where jobs or other patronage is given to friends and acquaintances. It has been suggested by others that the phrase comes from, and was inherent in the English class system. Many would confirm that this English class system survives in some form to the present, as does the term. As it did then, and to some extent it remains today, the concept of the old boys' network is still alive and well. For many onlookers, the notion of a boys-club per se, confines power and patronage within a closed upper class group. Moreover, another term "old boys" originated in the English public schools system. There's no record of the term *"jobs for the boys"* being used in a UK context until well into the 20th century. It had however been previously used widely in the USA. For example, this news-item from a New York newspaper The Syracuse Herald, October 1913 reads:

"Party government isn't organized for efficiency, nor to serve the people. It is organized to provide jobs for the boys."

However the term *"jobs for the boys"* had a different meaning when it was used as a slogan following both World Wars. This term was used to express public gratitude for the soldiers when they returned home. In a 1918 advertisement for the *"American United Illuminating Co" (AUI)*, they promised to:

> *"Dispel pessimism - create trade, confidence and brightness in the period of reconstruction. We will aid in creating new jobs for the boys in the Service when they return without crowding out those who have taken their place."*

As a quaint footnote to this, AUI were not shy of missing a good marketing opportunity. They had added to the above that it was in the readers' *"New Patriotic Duty to Use Electric Signs."*

Commanding Communication

Let's now return to Brizendine's [2] example of the entrenched characteristics that drive the way we react to our environment. While boys certainly know how to employ affiliative speech style, research shows that they typically don't use it. Brizendine suggests that they prefer instead to use language in a commanding manner to others: so as to get things done. Let us leave aside their propensity to brag, threaten, and ignore a partner's suggestion, for they also constantly override each other's attempts to speak. Not only will little boys wreck things that little girls make – boys will do this to each other. Moreover, they are not averse to the conflict – as competition is part of their makeup. The testosterone-formed male brain simply does not look for social connection in the same manner that the female brain does.

For instance, in her book entitled *"Why Men Never Remember and Women Never Forget"*, Marianne J. Legato, also a medical Doctor advises that listening is harder for men than it is for women [18]. It is therefore better to let a man know that you are about to say something that you really want him to hear. This type of attention seeking cue can be delivered in a gentle and uncritical manner, according to Legato. One can ask for eye-contact to ensure the message has really been understood.

Why Males are Better at Mathematics

It is understood that teen-age boys tend to be better at mathematics than their girl counterparts [19]. Males therefore are more prepared to tackle advanced mathematics courses like calculus. Moreover virtually all the great mathematicians have been men. This may well be true, but that is probably because most well-known mathematical theory was invented centuries ago, when women were not given much education anyway [20]. The explanation for this may well be the distinctive way that both animals and human beings access their right brain. Scientists tell us that the right brain houses the material that we need to navigate our way through both familiar and new environments. It is interesting to note that while both males and females activate part of the right brain, men use part of the left brain as well to do spatial tasks, which women don't [18]. Men for instance can imagine how a figure may appear if rotated in a 2 or 3-dimensional space *(Figure 50)*.

Achieving successful problem solving that involves advanced mathematics correlates with our ability to understand and manipulate 3-dimensional relationships [18]. According to two neurobiology researchers at the University of Hamburg in Germany higher testosterone levels in men correlated with their enhanced spatial ability [21]. The same study also revealed these levels corresponded with their diminished ability for verbal expression, an area in which we know women excel.

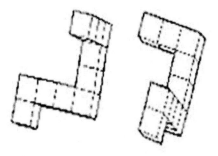

Figure 50 : Imagine Rotation of 2-D or 3-Dimensional Object

More on Gender and Computer Science

There are many reports on the numbers of males and their involvement in IT related fields. For a long time now men have reported more interest in computing than females [22]. For two decades, almost 70% of all employed computer specialists were men, despite the growth in the ICT industry. Although there was a sharp increase of males entering computer science between 1994 and 1999 relative to the numbers of females, there has been a significant and steady reduction from 2000 to 2004. In 2004, a 70% lower peak for men was observed, by comparison with figures for the early 1980's [23].

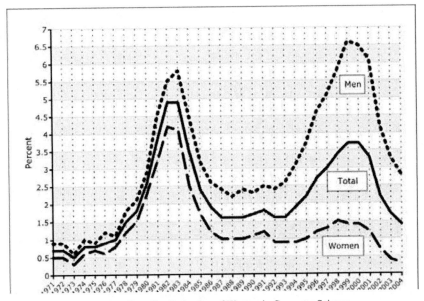

Figure 51 : Trending Reduction of Women in Computer Science

Techno-Caving

The stressed male has a propensity to retreat into the cave of his mind to focus on solving whatever he perceives as the problem at hand. Generally the most urgent issue or the most difficult will grasp his attention first, causing a temporary lack of awareness for other issues. Recall that John Gray uses a number of comical metaphors to articulate the differences between males and females. In this case we can benefit by looking at Gray's hypothesis, that while absorbed in his mind's cave, a male becomes increasingly distant, forgetful, unresponsive and preoccupied in his relationships. Gray suggests that this is why in having a conversation with a man at home, you may expect only a 5% of his mind is available for his relationship. The other 95% remains working on work-related issues. Gray goes on to show how women do not understand this concentrated and seemingly selective forgetfulness.

Towards a Genderless Digital-Awareness

Would it be unreasonable to propose here that we really are talking about finding our space within the realm of techno-humanoid landscape some people call cyberspace as genderless? Over time the generations are learning to deal with the differences between males and females. Perhaps this is the easy part. The more difficult could be the way we learn to deal with the differences among the members of each gender that is more important. In any event we don't really have all that much say in what happens. Or do we?

We commenced our techno-saga through this book with Linda Hogan's words. Let us now ponder whether the story has evolved to now be really about (a genderless) us. Maybe the ultimate *human-dimensions of HCI* is already taking place within the notions of the Web 2.0 environment. As Steven Johnson puts it:

"the fact is that most user-created content on the Web is not challenging the authority of a traditional expert. It's working in a zone where there are no experts or where the users themselves are the experts." [24]:55

In closing this chapter entitled *techno-gender* to convey a new approach to discussing gender differences and IT – to promote a vision for *'genderless digital-awareness'*. Whether we like to admit this or not, at some point in time, many of us type-cast our fellow techno-travellers. In the light of this discussion this chapter showed us that:

- it's high time to be upfront on gender differences
- there are worrying trends on gender and IT
- there are jobs for the girls in IT
- there are jobs for the boys in IT
- There's plenty of space for everyone. There's so much to do – why waste it?

Chapter Reference List

[1] Bradley, G., *Social and Community Informatics: Humans on the Net*, 2006. NY: Routledge.265
[2] Brizendine, L., *The Female Brain*. 1st ed. 2006, NY: Morgan Road Books. 279.
[3] Gray, J., *Men Are From Mars, Women Are From Venus*. 1992, London: Element - HarperCollins.

[4]   News, A., *Excerpt: The Female Brain' Learn What Women Really Think*, 2007. Retrieved 20/01/08 from http://abcnews.go.com/GMA/Books/story?id=2274147&page=3.

[5]   Wicks, M. The learning society: The challenging agenda, 2000. Paper presented at the *Research and Policy on Lifelong Conference*. Held 6th November in London.

[6]   Bushell, S., It takes a woman. CIO: Business Technology Leadership, 2006. Retrieved 20/01/08 from http://www.cio.com.au/index.php/id;858760820 .

[7]   Coonan, J., ICT is driving productivity growth in Australia, 2006. *Minister for Communications - Information Technology and the Arts in The Senate*, Media Release 22 March.

[8]   Miller, L. & Petrie, H. Gender segregation in IT: What influences choice of course and career? Paper in the *Gender Research Forum: The Gender Pay and Productivity Gap DTI*, 2002. UK.

[9]   Coonan, J., Women in ICT summit advisory group established, 2005. *Minister for Communications - Information Technology and the Arts in The Senate*, Media Release 8 March.

[10] Anderson, N., Klein, & Lankshear, C., Redressing the general imbalance in ICT professions: Toward state-level strategic approaches, 2005. Australian Educational Computing Journal of the Australian Council for Computers in Education. 20(2): 3-10.

[11] Timms, C., Courtney, L., & Anderson, N. Dimensions of 'boring": Secondary girls' perceptions of advanced ICT subjects. Paper presented at the *Australian Computers in Education Conference*, 2006. Cairns, Queensland, 2-4 October, KLA.

[12] Margolis, J. & Fisher, A., *Unlocking the Clubhouse: Women in Computing*. 2003, USA: MIT.

[13] Frieze, C., *Diversifying the Images of Computer Science: Undergraduate Women Take on the Challenge!* 2006, Carnegie Mellon University, 412-268-9071: School of Computer Science.

[14] Bagley, C.A. & Chou, C.C. Collaboration as a pedagogy and its impact on cognitive and affective strategies and problem solving by novices learning java computer programming, 2007. Paper in the proceedings of the *ITiCSE Conference '07*. 2007. Dundee, Scotland.

[15] Herring, S., Posting in a different voice, 1996, in Philosophical Perspectives on Computer-Mediated-Communication, C. Ess, Editor, State University of NY Press: NY.

[16] Bushell, S., Strangers in a strange land, 2006, in *CIO: Business Technology Leadership*, Retrieved 20/01/08 from http://www.cio.com.au/index.php/id;518696283.

[17] Wallace, P., *The Psychology of the Internet*. 1999, UK: Cambidge University Press. 264.

[18] Legato, M.J., *Why Men Never Remember & Women Never Forget*. 2005, London: Rodale.

[19] Anon, *Who is Really Better at Math, 1980*. Retrieved 20/01/08 from http://www.time.com/time/magazine/article/0,9171,953389,00.html, Times CNN.

[20] McLarnan, T., *Mathematics: Brain Cells and Mathematics* in *Women in Mathematics*, 2006. Retrieved 20/01/08 from http://www.math.earlham.edu/WomensBrains.html.

[21] Kimura, D., *Sex, Sexual Orientation and Sex Hormones Influence Human Cognitive Function*. 1996.

[22] Giacquinta, J.B., Bauer, J.A., & Levin, J.E., *Beyond Technology's Promise Cambridge*. 1993, UK: Cambridge University.

[23] Vegso, J., Interest in CS as a major drops among incoming freshmen. 2005, in Computing Research Association (CRA) - Computing Research News.

[24] Johnson, S., *It's all about us*. Time, 2007. December 25(2006 – January1, 2007).

Chapter-10

Closure

Upon reaching the end of this book, let's find some thinking space to reflect on where we've been. How many previously hidden complexities of the *human-dimensions of HCI* were uncovered along the way? Because the target audience for this book is diverse, parts of some chapters would have been more interesting than others for you.

The first 3-chapters were meant to ease the reader into dealing with the separation of the *human-dimensions HCI* from the machine-dimension. Chapter-1 introduced the notion of staying more attuned to Nature's way of speaking to us about the techno-landscape. Instead of converting almost anything related to our daily lives into a magical 'eNess' artefact. Because of this, can we now metaphorically give up our techno-reliance to reconsider our digital-awareness?

Chapter-2 peeled back the techno-veneer to uncover some of the more irritating issues that relate to computer use. Some of the many *human-dimensions of HCI* were identified here to first set the context for the journey ahead. Using computers isn't as easy for some as it may be for a large section of the community. Many of us have lost sight of this because of our propensity to press a button to satisfy our thirst for instant techno-gratification. Some people are quite besotted by the plethora of ICT devices on offer, blurring the techno-lines for ever. There are many who interact with their multi-media devices 24/7. This worrisome techno-trait means that the Dreyfus & Dreyfus [1] prediction has come true? Many of us forget to take a delayed approach to maintain comfortable communications with one another. Instead people demonstrate they want quick informational snap shots. As a consequence of this, our imaginations seem to have become completely captured by eMovement, eSound and eColour.

We know perfectly well that one size does not fit all. Yet Web-based information is still beyond the reach of many people in our community. This techno-friction causes tension between the usability of some ICT tools and their lack of accessibility to *effective HCI*. Even though there are standards, compliance is patchy. Only *'lip-service'* is paid to the regulations around the globe. Web-developers press on regardless, realizing they may also be breaking the law! It possibly is not surprising to know that while the Internet opens many extra opportunities for collaborative interaction – it also provides a virtual platform for abuse [2].

On a brighter side of the many *human-dimensions of HCI*, we are witnessing an iPod revolution that has empowered a whole new set of techno-advocates – any age, anywhere. This group of neuvo-technos are moving from their comfortable domesticity into the corporate sector. Demands are growing for groovy ICT tools to replace stuffy in-house training programmes. Once the workforce gets a taste of how multi-media enhances their corporate knowledge navigation; there will be no stopping them. The resulting surge in visual communication promotes shared eLearning/training spaces. Moreover along with the rush to embrace anything multi-media, desktop publishing has emerged as an exciting and successful *'do it yourself'* (DIY) industry.

Told through a social-contextual lens, chapter-3 discussed the *'machine-side'* of the HCI equation. We read that our clever computers didn't invent themselves after all. Even though modern computers are becoming relatively easy to use, they still require special techno-people to maintain them. This chapter gave us a potted history of where computers came from. It is important in a book such as this to balance the rather open-ended human-dimensions of HCI with the more pragmatic or business end of HCI. The techno-geeks and back-room boffins are hard at work trying to replicate human behaviours. Their dedication to things binary is commendable. Moreover, as long as the communications engineers and computer scientists keep playing with their techno-toys; eBusiness, eCommerce, eLearning and e-everything else is kept alive. A necessary part of keeping the techno-ship afloat, are the IEEE standards that do try to keep everyone on track. The smart way to sustain the many and varied *human-dimensions of HCI* is to employ the emerging implementations of *'Rich Internet Applications'*. This is the techno-nexus of the *human/machine dimensions of HCI* that reflects the maturing machine-side of the IT industry.

Having set the techno-scene for separating out some of the more prominent *human-dimensions of HCI*, the next three chapters discussed computer usage in general. Chapter-4 discussed ways people relate to their digital artefacts to enhance their problem solving abilities. We saw that an important aspect of *effective HCI* as it relates to the learning/education/training domain, is to differentiate between the type of learning and the instructional architecture. Due to the interactivity of effectiveness, efficiency and satisfaction in an online learning environment, complex usability issues arise whenever people engage with digital artefacts. Chapter-4 provided comment on the need to differentiate the type of learning people set out to do – and provide appropriate instructional architectures as robust information systems specifications for Web-development teams. In the light of the discussion on ways people use computers, to ensure *efficient and effective HCI*, the following three points are important:

- systems designers need to provide the online environments and tools that promote collaborative problem solving
- gender issues are alive and well – expecting ubiquitous interaction should be a thing of the past, we need proactive and adaptive information systems that encompass the principles of universal design
- GUIs often assume most people are visually literate – when the reverse is true for many

Chapter-5 proposed the notion of a *'techno-humanoid landscape'* as a theoretical model to identify the interactive components that bring about *effective HCI*. This chapter outlined the many facets of the *human-dimensions of HCI*. It synthesized the richness of the existing body of knowledge found in disparate professional practices (cognitive psychology, concept learning and instructional design). As such, it is perhaps the most theoretical chapter of this book, presenting the complexity of the interrelating aspects of Web-mediated learning in terms of how to promote *effective HCI*.

Chaper-6 left the Earthly comfort of the book's previous dialogue to resemble a make believe fiction book. This was to mark the mid-way point of our techno-saga. Finding the right linguistics for discussing information systems and HCI in a social-context is always difficult. At times, it seems that so much of what we need to deal with remains within the esoteric techno-community. This chapter further defined the practical aspects of *effective HCI* using the framework of the *'techno-humanoid landscape'*. We read that whilst many people access information through their computers, often isolated in a physical sense from other human-beings, this chapter explained how to capitalize on the collaborative techno-humanoid possibilities that arise when accessing the Internet.

Having passed the mid-point of this book, the remaining chapters presented the dichotomy of the *human-machine dimensions of HCI*. Only this time, however, they do not differentiate between the 2-dimensions. Instead, it is assumed that the reader can differentiate when each causes a negative impact likely to cause harm towards the *effectiveness of HCI*. Therefore, in the light of this, the way one determines whether *'they know when they have reached their personal information nirvana'* will depend upon how they deal with the techno-humanoid landscape, that includes:

- cyberspace etiquette
- coordinating one's situation awareness factors
- dealing with the online collaborative group forming processes
- the sophistication (or otherwise) of one's eye-mind-imagination pathways
- natural learning environments

The remaining three chapters reiterate the *human/machine side of HCI* again. Only in a more focused domain. Chapter-7 concentrated on the *human-dimensions of HCI* by returning the reader to the more Earthly perspective of HCI. It looked at some of the systems design issues that may affect our online behaviour. Whenever people share ideas through the Internet, sooner or later the communication among the group members becomes a little tricky. However, collaborative environments online need to be built by people who understand human behaviour; often this is simply not the case. Designing for *effective HCI* takes the combined effort of a multi-disciplinary team. This chapter uncovers what happens when this collaborative design environment isn't managed well. A *'knowledge navigation model'* was proposed to pass experiential learning from one domain to another. In this chapter we also covered the issues that surround managing the multi-disciplinary Web-design team such as:

- conflict management to ward off those times when our super-ego's may get in the way
- the impact of using good project management strategies for ICT tool development
- a conceptual communication model to capture the educational online experience
- pressures on non-conventional learning/training environments
- how to include an (electronic) design-persona in an information systems project
- the relationship between instructional architecture and knowledge navigation

Chapter-8 shifted the discussion back towards the *machine-side of HCI* to rethink our connectivity to improve the effectiveness of our HCI. This is where the proponents for a more social-context on the *machine-side of HCI* are showing signs of progress. This chapter conveyed the most striking feature of our connectivity through the implementation of Rich Internet Applications. This approach is set to widen the interpretation of *'interaction'*, which has become more complex. In this context it means relational learning: based upon some-one's personality and even someone's attraction for identification. *'Interaction'* is a much broader process than instruction, questioning or sharing information [3]. For the reader wishing to enter this emerging field they will be well advised to take notice of the *human-dimensions of HCI*. Find ways to build in the *'interaction'* you wish for. If you don't think you have the techno-savvy – network until you find a sole-mate. At all costs, don't be put off by the techno-jargon. With the right multi-media development support; just about anything is possible these days.

Our commentary on the *human-dimensions of HCI* would not be complete without a section for dealing with gender and how it relates, if at all, to HCI. Chapter-9 closed the book to discuss whether there is a *techno-gender* approach to HCI in general and more specifically to IT. Whether we like to admit this or not, at some point in time, many of us type-cast our fellow techno-travellers. In the light of this discussion this chapter showed us that:

- it's high time to be upfront on the gender differences
- there are worrying trends on gender and IT
- there are jobs for the girls in IT
- there are jobs for the boys in IT

In closing, I would like to thank you for travelling the HCI roller coaster with me. My sole purpose of this guided conceptual-journey was to bring together the techno-geeks and the Luddite-users into a collaborative partnership. Only then will we ensure the future of *effective HCI* and reach a shared techno-nirvana, and remember:

There's plenty of space for everyone. There's so much to do – why waste it?

"We don't accomplish anything in this world alone ... and whatever happens is the result of the whole tapestry of one's life and all the weavings of individual threads from one to another that creates something."
Sandra Day O'Connor: http://www.wisdomquotes.com/cat_teamwork.html

Chapter Reference List

[1]   Dreyfus, H.L. & Dreyfus, S.E., *Mind Over Machine: The power of human intuition and expertise in the era of the computer*. 1986, NY: Free Press. 231.
[2]   Wallace, P., *The Psychology of the Internet*. 1999, UK: Cambridge University Press. 264.
[3]   McKay, E. & Kommers, P., (Editorial). *International Journal for Continuing Engineering Education and Life-Long Learning: Special Edition - The Effectiveness of Rich Internet Application for Education and Training*, viewed on 20/01/08 at http://www.inderscience.com/editorials/f105621479128311.pdf, 2006. 16(3/4): 151-155.

Index

220

240

kerning, 37, 38

keyboards: 8, 9, 89, 118, 126, 141, 160
   (Figure 3), 9
   capacitative, 10
   dome-switch, 9
   DVORK, 9
   membrane, 9, 10
   QWERTY, 9

key enablers for the HxI model (Table 23), 147, 148
key-strokes (*menu selection*), 82
keyword indicators, 167
Khalsa, 139
Kirton, 45, 46, 110, 128
Klausmeier *(concept learning devmt.)*, 115, 127

knowledge:
   acquisition, 74, 103, 106, 110, 112, 114, 120,
     122, 126, 130, 145, 166, 184
   acquisition bottleneck, 166
   acquisition of abstract concepts, 106
   and cognitive style differences, 113
   base, 23, 51, 52, 95, 104, 120, 123, 126, 129, 155
   -based expert systems, 52
   -based instructional system design (see also
     KISD), 120
   base, 23, 51, 52, 95, 104, 120, 123, 126, 129, 155
   -channels, 95
   /concept learning (see also learning), 185
   consolidation, 148
   constructed from experience, 104
   construction of, 21, 67
   construction, basics of, 105
   constructs, intangibility of, 149
   database, 165
   deductive reasoning, 92
   development, 21, 148, 150, 171, 177
   development methodology, 150, 177
   discovery, 70, 92
   domain, 106, 133, 172, 177
   emerging, 183
   engineer, 45, 51, 95, 166
   -engineered text, 123
   engineering, 45, 51, 95
   engineers are centre stage for information, 166
   enhanced corporate, 149
   existing, 21, 23, 67
   exchange market, 95
   extraction, 166, 167
   experiential, 54, 71, 172
   expert system, 92
   exploration, 29
   gathering *(learning)* resources, 95
   -hoarding, 58, 64
   and increased self-confidence, 149
   inductive, 92
   information stored, 111
   and learning, 111, 127
   logical elements, 47
   levels of the learning task, 70

management *(librarians)*, 95, 170, 171, 177
management approach, 170
-mediated HCI, 75
-mediation strategies, 74
mega-knowledge repository (see database), 51
Knowledge-Navigation Devmnt. Model, 178
pool, 131, 154
procedural, 105, 114, 126, 191
progressive development, 148
relationships, 120
repository, 44, 51, 165
results, 156
schemas, 104, 133
sharing, 12, 19, 72, 74, 95, 134
and skill in a new situation, 111, 179
and skill profile, 20, 149
socially shared, 104
squirreling, 58
strategic engineering, 54
structures, 133
subsumption, 119
systems development (Figure 44), 166
team, 137
theory, 168
thinking/construction space, 21
thirst for, 4
through the Internet, 101
universal access, 5, 7, 18, 97, 195

knowledge navigation: 29, 45, 94, 120, 149, 150,
   155, 177, 178, 179, 215, 217
   development methodology, 120, 178, 179
   model, 178, 179, 217
   Swedish National Council for Cultural Affairs:
     Library for all times, 177
   unfamiliar domains, 172, 177

Kosslyn, 118, 130

labeling, 109
lack of awareness, 213
language difficulties, icons, 82
laptops (see also generational profiling), 5, 23, 57,
   58, 59
Laurillard, 104, 115, 127
law-breaking, 18
Gordon Lawrence, 80, 162
leadership *(jostling for)*, 137, 138, 162, 214

learner: 46, 65, 66, 67, 68, 69, 70, 71, 74, 101, 102,
   106, 108, 111, 112, 113, 115, 116, 117, 121, 122,
   123, 124, 125, 126, 127, 129, 145, 146, 150, 160,
   163, 168, 169, 170, 171, 176, 177, 178, 179, 197,
   198, 206
   5-steps from novice to expert, 112
   characteristics (see digital-awareness and
     cognitive style)
   conditions, 123, 124, 126, 127
   content, 70, 171
   control, 69, 115
   experienced, 102, 150, 178

Elspeth McKay

Senior Lecturer - Team Leader Industry Engagement
RMIT University - School of Business IT .. Building 108:17
GPO Box 2476V, Melbourne 3001 Australia
eMail: elspeth.mckay@rmit.edu.au
homepage: http://www.effective-HCI.com.au
http://www.rmit.edu.au

Dr McKay is a Senior Lecturer/Researcher in the School of Business IT at the RMIT University, Australia. Her PhD is in Computer Science and Information Systems, from Deakin University, Geelong, Australia. Elspeth also holds further qualifications in Instructional Design, Computer Education and Business Information Systems. She is passionate about designing effective eLearning resources for the education sector and industry training/reskilling programmes. Her research interests involve investigations of how individuals interpret text and graphics within Web-mediated learning environments. Her work involves developing specialist e-Learning tools implemented through rich internet applications; including: ARPS – an advanced repurposing pilot system, COGNIWARE – a multi-modal e-Learning framework, GEMS – a global eMuseum System, eWRAP – Electronic work readiness awareness programme, EASY – Educational/academic (skills) screening for the young, offering enhanced accessibility through touch screen technologies. Over the last decade Dr McKay has published extensively in the research fields of HCI and educational technology. In recognition of her contribution to the professional practice of information systems research, she was elected as a Fellow of the Australian Computer Society (FACS).

Gunilla Bradley

Professor Emerita Informatics, School of ICT, Royal Institute of Technology (KTH)
Department of Electronic, Computer and Software Systems (ECS)
Stockholm, Sweden
homepage: http://goto.glocalnet.net/gunillabradley/index.htm
eMail gbradley@kth.se   http://www.kth.se/ict?l=en
Best snail mail: Kullavägen 22, 19162 Lidingö, Sweden

Gunilla Bradley (GB) is Professor Emerita in Informatics at Royal Institute of Technology (KTH) – School of ICT, Department of Microelectronics and Information Technology (IMIT). 1997 – 2001 she was Professor of Informatics at Umeå University and Mid Sweden University with main task to build up research in Informatics at Mid Sweden University. She is educated as a psychologist and has a broad background in the social and behavioural sciences. Her research concerns the interplay between Information and Communication Technology (ICT), Human Beings, and Society – Social Informatics. Beginning in 1973, she initiated and led cross-disciplinary research programs on computerisation and working life at Stockholm University for twenty years. She has been a visiting scholar at Stanford University for two years and Professor of Technology and Social Change at the Royal Institute of Technology. GB has authored twelve books (mainly in Swedish) and numerous articles in international scientific journals, also contributed extensively to the popular science press. In 1997 GB received the prestigious Namur Award from the International Federation for Information Processing (IFIP) for her pioneering research to increase the social awareness of the impact of ICT. She is supporting the School of ICT at KTH in Stockholm, contributing in various research programs where the ICT disciplines collaborate closer with the behavioural sciences, as well as keeping advisory tasks at other Swedish and international universities. In 2003 she served as an advisor to the Swedish Government in a special committee on Electronic Communication. Her latest book Social and Community Informatics – Humans on the Net (Routledge 2006) is intended for educational purpose and has increased her international role.